Time weighs heavily on refugees from Nazi-dominated nations as they pass idle hours at a sidewalk café in Lisbon in 1941. The capital of neutral Portugal became an international center of transit — and a symbol of hope and frustration — for thousands of Europeans who were seeking visas and safe passage from their war-torn Continent.

THE NEUTRALS

This volume is one of a series that chronicles
in full the events of the Second World War.

WORLD WAR II · TIME-LIFE BOOKS · ALEXANDRIA, VIRGINIA

BY DENIS J. FODOR
AND THE EDITORS OF TIME-LIFE BOOKS

THE NEUTRALS

WORLD WAR II

Editor: Thomas H. Flaherty Jr.
Designer: Van W. Carney
Chief Researcher: Philip Brandt George

Editorial Staff for The Neutrals
Picture Editor: Jeremy Ross
Text Editors: Richard D. Kovar, Robert Menaker,
Richard Murphy
Writers: Donald Davison Cantlay, Paul N. Mathless
Researchers: Scarlet Cheng, Ann Dusel Corson,
Reginald H. Dickerson, Margaret Gray, Jane S.
Hanna, Marta Ann Sanchez, Paula York-Soderlund
Copy Coordinators: Ann Bartunek, Allan Fallow,
Elizabeth Graham, Barbara F. Quarmby
Art Assistant: Mikio Togashi
Picture Coordinator: Renée DeSandies
Editorial Assistants: Andrea E. Reynolds,
Myrna E. Traylor

Special Contributors:
Champ Clark (text), Christina Draper, Lettie Multhauf
(translations)

Editorial Operations
Design: Anne B. Landry (art coordinator);
James J. Cox (quality control)
Research: Jane Edwin (assistant director),
Louise D. Forstall
Copy Room: Diane Ullius (director), Celia Beattie
Production: Feliciano Madrid (director),
Gordon E. Buck, Peter Inchauteguiz

Correspondents: Elisabeth Kraemer (Bonn); Margot
Hapgood, Dorothy Bacon (London); Susan Jonas,
Miriam Hsia, Lucy T. Voulgaris (New York); Maria
Vincenza Aloisi, Josephine du Brusle (Paris); Ann
Natanson (Rome). Valuable assistance was also
provided by: Wibo van de Linde (Amsterdam);
Mehmet Ali Kislali (Ankara); Brigid Grauman
(Brussels); Nina Lindley (Buenos Aires); Sandy Jacobi,
Lois Lorimer (Copenhagen); Alex des Fontaines, Otto
Gobius, Robert Kroon (Geneva); Lance Keyworth
(Helsinki); Martha de la Cal, Lynn de Albuquerque
(Lisbon); Judy Aspinall, Lesley Coleman, Millicent
Trowbridge (London); Trini Bandres (Madrid); Edith
Nosow, Dee Pattee (Munich); Christina Lieberman,
Cornelis Verwaal (New York); Dag Christensen, Bent
Onsager (Oslo); Mimi Murphy, Ann Wise (Rome);
Mary Johnson (Stockholm).

The Author: DENIS J. FODOR is a writer and editor
based in Germany. He was a correspondent for Time
and Life in Central Europe and the Middle East. He
also served as a senior editor for the Reader's Digest
in Munich and Paris and was a reporter and editor for
the United Press and for the newspaper Neue Zeitung.

The Consultants: COLONEL JOHN R. ELTING, USA (Ret.),
is a military historian and author of The Battle of
Bunker's Hill, The Battles of Saratoga and Military
History and Atlas of the Napoleonic Wars. He
edited Military Uniforms in America: The Era of the American Revolution, 1755-1795 and Military Uniforms in
America: Years of Growth, 1796-1851, and was associate editor of The West Point Atlas of American Wars.

WILLARD ALLEN FLETCHER, Professor of History at the
University of Delaware, is an American who grew up
in Luxembourg and in 1942 was interned in Germany
as an enemy alien. Released in 1944, he joined the
U.S. Army and served in the 14th Armored Division.
Since the War, he has published numerous articles on
the German Occupation of Europe.

GERALD R. KLEINFELD, Professor of History at Arizona
State University, has lectured and written extensively
on European history and politics. He is the author of
German History to 1815 and co-author of Hitler's
Spanish Legion.

Library of Congress Cataloguing in Publication Data

Fodor, Denis J., 1927-
  The neutrals.

  (World War II)
  Bibliography: p.
  Includes index.
  1. World War, 1939-1945—Diplomatic history.
2. Neutrality—History—20th century.
I. Time-Life Books. II. Title. III. Series.
D749.F56   1982   940.53'35   82-10388
ISBN 0-8094-3431-8
ISBN 0-8094-3432-6 (lib. bdg.)
ISBN 0-8094-3433-4 (retail ed.)

For information about any Time-Life book, please write:

Reader Information
Time-Life Books
541 North Fairbanks Court
Chicago, Illinois 60611

CHAPTERS

1: A Vision Dimmed   8

2: The Perpetual Neutral   46

3: Dictators on a High Wire   76

4: Sweden: A Barometer of War   120

5: Two Stubborn Holdouts   166

PICTURE ESSAYS

Switzerland in Arms   28

Spain's Bitter Legacy   64

A Rush to Fight Communism   92

The Price of Neutrality   106

Haven in the North   140

Feisty Little Ireland   154

The Red Cross of Mercy   186

Bibliography   204

Picture Credits   205

Acknowledgments   205

Index   206

CONTENTS

ISLANDS OF PEACE IN A CONTINENT AT WAR

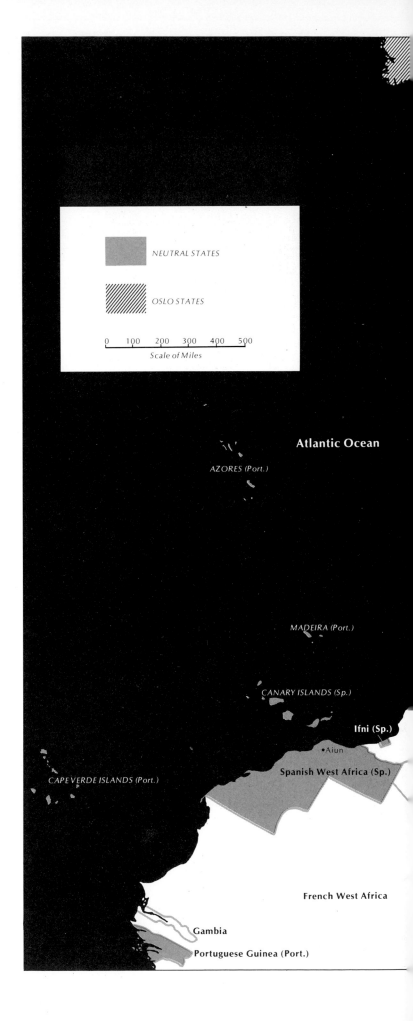

NEUTRAL STATES

OSLO STATES

0   100   200   300   400   500
Scale of Miles

Atlantic Ocean

AZORES (Port.)

MADEIRA (Port.)

CANARY ISLANDS (Sp.)

Ifni (Sp.)

•Aiun

Spanish West Africa (Sp.)

CAPE VERDE ISLANDS (Port.)

French West Africa

Gambia

Portuguese Guinea (Port.)

To declare for neutrality in World War II was to court the wrath of belligerents on all sides, and only a few countries managed to establish themselves as enclaves of peace on the map of wartime Europe. One group of nations, the seven so-called Oslo States (shaded diagonally) tried to chart a common course of neutrality. But their aspirations soon ran afoul of the combatants' designs. Denmark, Norway, the Netherlands, Belgium and Luxembourg were overrun by Nazi Germany. Finland twice was attacked by the Soviet Union. Of the seven countries, only Sweden—coveted for its mineral resources but respected for its military power—managed to remain neutral. Elsewhere in Europe, Switzerland, Spain, Portugal, Turkey and Ireland, shown in red, maneuvered to avoid the expanding conflict, each nervously balancing Allied and Axis demands with its own requirements for survival.

GREENLAND (Den.)

SPITSBERGEN (Nor.)   BEAR ISLAND (Nor.)

Barents Sea

JAN MAYEN (Nor.)

Reykjavik
Iceland

LOFOTEN ISLANDS
(Nor.)

Petsamo

Finland

White
Sea

FAEROE ISLANDS
(Den.)

Norwegian Sea

Sweden

LAKE
ONEGA

Norway

GULF OF BOTHNIA

Bergen

LAKE
LADOGA

Trondheim

Northern
Ireland

Viipuri

LOUGH
SWILLY

Edinburgh

Sola

Stockholm

GULF OF FINLAND

Tallinn

Union of Soviet Socialist Republics

Belfast

Kristiansand

Estonia

Ireland

North Sea

Baltic Sea

Riga

Cóbh

Dublin

Latvia

Moscow

Berehaven

Denmark

Copenhagen

Lithuania

SKAGERRAK

Malmo

East
Prussia

Vilna

KATTEGAT

Trelleborg

Danzig

Great Britain

Netherlands

London

Germany

Amsterdam

Berlin

Warsaw

Brussels

Poland

Paris

Belgium

Luxembourg

Prague

France

Czechoslovakia

Liechtenstein

Vienna

Zurich

Vichy

Geneva

Bern

Budapest

Rumania

Switzerland

Austria

Hungary

Vigo

Yugoslavia

Bucharest

Black Sea

Iran

Portugal

Spain

Andorra

Monaco

San
Marino

Belgrade

Bulgaria

BOSPORUS

Hendaye

Barcelona

Albania

Sofia

Turkey

Lisbon

Istanbul

Ankara

Madrid

BALEARIC
ISLANDS (Sp.)

CORSICA

Rome

Adriatic
Sea

DARDANELLES

Adana

Syria

Baghdad

Cádiz

Italy

STRAIT OF
GIBRALTAR

SARDINIA

Tyrrhenian
Sea

Tirana

Aegean
Sea

Iraq

Cartegena

Greece

Lebanon

Tetuán

Nicosia

Beirut

Tangier

Algiers

Ionian Sea

Athens

CYPRUS

Damascus

Casablanca

Tunis

SICILY

DODECANESE

Haifa

Spanish Morocco (Sp.)

Jerusalem

Amman

Morocco

MALTA

CRETE

Palestine

Trans-
Jordan

Tunisia

Mediterranean Sea

Alexandria

SUEZ
CANAL

Saudi Arabia

Tripoli

Benghazi

Cairo

Caspian
Sea

Red Sea

Algeria

Egypt

Libya

7

1

A King's message of hope and anxiety
A fraternity of nations held together by fear
The decline of "gentlemen's neutrality"
Norway's policy of "no foreign policy at all"
An excessive confidence in the British fleet
The Danish attitude of "What's the use?"
A draconian Dutch plan to open the dikes
The Nazis' "Nervenkrieg"
The last warning: "Tomorrow at dawn; hold tight"

In the late afternoon of August 22, 1939, six high-ranking diplomats and their entourages from as many nations disembarked from planes and trains in Brussels and stepped into waiting limousines to be driven to the fashionable Hotel Metropole. Their social and professional agenda in the Belgian capital was a crowded one. The diplomats met that evening at a reception given by Belgian Foreign Minister Hubert Pierlot in the mirrored *grand salon* of the Ministry of Foreign Affairs. The next day they held both morning and afternoon working sessions in the famous Foreign Office Red Room, adjourning only for a splendid luncheon in the ministry dining room. At the end of the afternoon, they hurried back to the Metropole to put on formal dress, with diplomatic cordons and decorations, for a state dinner at the Laeken Palace hosted by Leopold III, King of the Belgians.

The King received his guests not in white tie but in the uniform of Commander in Chief of the armed forces. He chatted a few minutes, then stepped to a microphone to deliver to the world a message of hope and anxiety prepared by his six honored guests and Foreign Minister Pierlot.

"Mistrust and suspicion are everywhere," declared Leopold in his slow, careful French. "Under our very eyes, encampments are forming, armies are grouping and horrible struggles are preparing." Europe, the King said, was about to "commit suicide," and "even small powers are afraid of being the victims," despite their "firm desire for neutrality."

Leopold was speaking on behalf of a fraternity of seven nations known as the Oslo States, whose foreign ministers had just completed yet another round of urgent deliberation. Consisting of the Scandinavian states—Norway, Sweden, Finland, Denmark—plus the Low Countries of Belgium, the Netherlands and Luxembourg, the group was bound neither by treaty, nor by trade, nor by shared scientific and cultural interests. The cement that held them together was fear. For three tension-ridden years the Oslo ministers had been crisscrossing northern Europe by train and by plane in quest of a vision they hoped would save them in the war they all saw coming. The name they gave to the vision was neutrality.

In talks with German, French and British statesmen, the Oslo ministers deplored Europe's increasingly blatant preparations for war—massive troop maneuvers in Germany, partial mobilization in France, an alert imposed on the Brit-

A VISION DIMMED

ish fleet—and called for the renunciation of force in international affairs. Told by the British and French that peace depended on Germany—and by the Germans that it depended on England—the ministers found themselves in a thankless role that a Swedish journalist likened to that of a guest who "comes unasked and leaves unthanked." Rebuffed abroad, they tried in vain to define a neutrality that would reconcile their fear of foreign entanglements with their need to stand together against the threat of attack.

The Oslo States, named for the Norwegian capital in which their representatives had first convened in 1930, were not the only nations seeking neutrality on the eve of World War II. The same anxious questions the Oslo ministers posed in one conference after another—how to continue trade, how to ensure a food supply in wartime, how to prevent the transit of troops or planes across their territory, how, in short, to survive—were being asked just as anxiously in capitals all over Europe, and, indeed, throughout much of the world. Nobody was sure that the umbrella of neutrality would protect them from the terrible storm that King Leopold saw gathering—but for many, it was the only shelter they could find.

The paradox of neutrality, as the historian Roderick Ogley has pointed out, is that while its aim is to stay out of war, it can only be appraised and defined under the wartime conditions that threaten it. A further paradox is that while strict neutrality demands complete impartiality, the successful neutral states in World War II all behaved at various times in highly partial and nonneutral ways. And successful or unsuccessful, every neutral learned a hard truth—that in a global war no nation can emerge pristine and unaffected.

The neutrals in their many diverse ways became as much a part of World War II as the belligerents. They not only got involved economically, ideologically and politically but figured largely in the strategic planning of all the warring states. So linked were they to the fortunes of the combatants that an observer tracing the convolutions of their politics could plot the shifting course of the War. Although almost every country in the world hoped to remain aloof from the War, in Europe only six nations—Switzerland, Spain, Portugal, Sweden, Ireland and Turkey—came through with their neutrality intact; in the Western Hemisphere, only Argentina emerged as a determined neutral. The neutrality

practiced by each of them was shaped by the circumstances under which they had to survive—but it also owed much to traditions that stretched back nearly 500 years.

"When the man in the street refers to the necessity of maintaining neutrality," observed the American diplomat Allen W. Dulles in 1934, "all he means is that the United States should avoid being drawn into war." In fact, neutrality has always meant more than that—chiefly because neutral nations must survive economically as well as politically. Hence they have had to steer a perilous course between their own material needs and the attempts of the belligerents to deprive one another of the means of making war. Far from being the simple alternative conceived by Dulles' man in the street, neutrality is a fragile complex of compromises, easily destroyed by the pressures of power politics.

The Great Powers first took note of the thorny problem of neutrality in the late 15th Century, in a set of maritime rules defining the conditions under which neutral ships could carry goods through wartime blockades. Over the next three centuries, nations that proclaimed neutrality were regarded almost as uncommitted allies that for various reasons did not choose to go to war to support their friends. Under that relaxed code, it was common for neutrals to aid one side or another without being accused of unneutral conduct.

That benign approach—it was sometimes called "gentlemen's neutrality"—gradually hardened as wars expanded to involve whole continents and the seas around them. By the end of the Napoleonic Wars in the early 19th Century, the Great Powers were insisting that neutral states be strictly impartial, showing no bias for either side. In a succession of treaties and agreements culminating in the Hague Conventions at the turn of the century, the statesmen of Europe hammered out the basic rules that, in theory at least, govern legalized neutrality still.

According to the Hague Convention of 1907, a formal declaration of neutrality guaranteed that a state's territory would not be invaded and that its right to trade with the belligerents would be respected. On the other hand, neutrals assumed important obligations—including the denial of use of their territory for any act of warfare by any belligerent nation, respect for blockades and embargoes imposed by the belligerents, and the refusal to send troops, war matériel or money to any country at war. The effect of the Conventions was to give neutrality a renewed respectability—and to lull the weaker nations into the belief that they would not be molested if they adhered to the rules.

That dream was rudely shattered on August 4, 1914, when German armies poured across the frontiers of neutral Belgium, in the first great offensive action of World War I. In the four cataclysmic years that followed, neutral rights were so systematically violated that many statesmen wrote off as worthless the provisions of the various Hague Conventions. When the United States entered the War in 1917, President Woodrow Wilson remarked bluntly that "neutrality is no longer feasible or desirable where the peace of the world is involved and the freedom of its peoples."

Between the two World Wars, the underlying principle of neutrality again was called in question, particularly at the League of Nations, based in Geneva, Switzerland, and founded on the principle of collective security and collective moral responsibility. To the small states of Europe anxious to remain neutral in any future conflict, the League at first seemed the ideal solution—a bulwark behind which they could take shelter when shooting began. But it soon became clear that the aims of the League and of the neutrals were quite different. As early as September 1920, the Council of the League announced that "the idea of neutrality of members" was "not compatible with the other principle that all members of the League will have to act in common to cause their covenants to be respected." In effect, the League demanded that if a war occurred all members must support whoever was judged to be in the right, by either military action or economic sanctions against the aggressor.

Almost at once, this principle was indignantly challenged by the practical Swiss, who argued that if they let themselves get involved in joint League actions against aggressors they would be violating a tradition of neutrality and noninvolvement that had kept them secure and prosperous for hundreds of years. The League reluctantly agreed and bent the rules for Switzerland, taking refuge in the dubious assumption that the Swiss "would not stand aside when the high principles of the League have to be defended." But the basic problem of how to reconcile League membership with the declared neutrality of many of its member states was never formally resolved. Instead, a kind of de facto compromise developed, based on the desire of the neutrals for League protection and the desire of the League to attract as close to a universal membership as possible.

Mussolini's invasion of Ethiopia in the fall of 1935 and Hitler's remilitarization of the Rhineland five months later had devastating effects both on the overall concept of neutralism within the League and on the League itself as a haven for small and helpless neutral nations. The Fascist and Nazi aggressions were so blatant, so manifestly illegal and immoral that it became virtually impossible for any right-thinking nation to stand aloof. "Neutrality is finished as a political concept," said the English biologist and writer, Julian Huxley. It was high time, Huxley added, that the minor states of Europe made up their minds to "surrender their sovereign rights of neutrality."

Neutrality was no less an object of scorn among the aggressors. German scholars equated neutrality with weakness and took pride in the fact that the concept could be rendered by no native German word. The German historian Christoph Steding attracted wide attention with a book titled *The Reich and the Sickness of European Culture,* in which he defined Swiss neutrality as a moral disease characterized by weakness of will, sterility and senility.

Equally dismaying to the neutrals was the realization that the League of Nations was an exceedingly flimsy shield. The Germans, who had withdrawn from the League in 1933 and had armed the Rhineland in defiance of possible sanctions, were openly contemptuous. "The veil that concealed the flaws in the face of the lady of Geneva has been rudely torn aside," said one Nazi writer.

The War broke out in September of 1939, just a week after the prophetic Brussels meeting of the Oslo States. It at first involved only four nations—Germany, Poland, France and Great Britain (backed by the Commonwealth countries of Australia, Canada, India, New Zealand and South Africa). Although some statesmen cherished the illusion that the conflict could be contained, the League of Nations proved utterly powerless and the War quickly raged out of control, sucking in previously uncommitted countries regardless of their expressed intent.

The two nations that eventually emerged as the most powerful of the belligerents—the United States and the Soviet Union—both took resoundingly neutral positions in

1939. President Franklin D. Roosevelt assured the American public that he was vigilant against those who would "break down our neutrality," and U.S. Secretary of State Cordell Hull resolutely repeated to Congress that "the nation would at all times avoid entangling alliances and involvements."

In Moscow, Soviet Foreign Minister Vyacheslav Molotov earnestly told assembled party dignitaries that the Soviet Union is "a neutral country which is not interested in the spread of war." He also insisted that it was not the custom of Soviet leaders to "allow our country to be drawn into conflicts by warmongers who are accustomed to having others pull their chestnuts out of the fire for them." The Russians, of course, were in the midst of satisfying their own imperial ambitions; in September, Soviet armies had invaded eastern Poland to join the Nazis in carving up that hapless land, and two months hence the Russians would attack Finland, whose territory they had long coveted. But there was no suggestion that the men in the Kremlin felt anything but coldly neutral toward the British and French in their struggle against the Germans. Neither the Soviet Union nor the United States became heavily involved until it was subjected to surprise attack. Yet even after the Soviet Union joined the Allies in the summer of 1941, it continued to practice a selective neutrality by declaring itself neutral in regard to Japan until the last days of the War.

History will never know what might have happened had Hitler not hurled his panzers at the Russians, and had the Japanese not bombed Pearl Harbor. Both the United States and the U.S.S.R. might have been strong and self-sufficient enough to have stayed out of the War—with consequences impossible to calculate. The smaller neutrals, on the other hand, had far less freedom of choice, and little room for maneuver. Once the shooting started, they were under intense pressures on all sides to drop or modify their neutrality.

These pressures took many forms—from blunt demands that a neutral ally itself with one belligerent or another to requests for the right of passage across neutral territory or insistence that a neutral restrict or abandon its trade in various strategic materials. Some neutrals were pressured because geography had given them assets the belligerents badly needed: deep-water ports on strategic sea-lanes, mid-ocean islands as steppingstones between continents. Other neutrals came under pressure because they possessed raw materials essential to the war production of one or more of the belligerents. And some neutrals were simply unfortunate enough to lie in the path of the juggernaut.

One of the first nations to lose its neutrality was Norway, in whose capital city the Oslo group had first met to declare their pacifism. By 1939, the Norwegians had been at peace for a remarkable 125 years. When asked about foreign commitments, Norwegians liked to quote an opinion of their great poet-politician Björnstjerne Björnson: "The best foreign policy is no foreign policy at all."

In part, this attitude was the result of Norway's physical make-up. A frigid, mountainous and isolated land, one third of which lay beyond the Arctic Circle, Norway could not begin to feed its 3 million people through agriculture; in fact, scarcely 3 per cent of its 119,240 square miles of land area were arable. Norway was thus heavily dependent on fishing and shipping and was forced to import most of its agricultural and industrial products, a situation that made its economy especially vulnerable to wartime pressures.

Feeling safely distant from the centers of European ten-

In a meeting of monarchs, 81-year-old King Gustav V of Sweden (right) welcomes Haakon VII of Norway (left) and Christian X of Denmark to Stockholm in the autumn of 1939. The royal gathering was a symbolic affirmation of Scandinavian union and neutrality.

sion, the Norwegians made virtually no effort to build up their defenses in the turbulent 1930s. Armament, they argued, would only compromise their neutrality and drain money from precious social and economic welfare plans. And who was about to attack them? Unlike the other Scandinavian states, Norway had traditionally good relations with Russia, which had been the first Great Power to recognize independent Norway when it ended its political union with Sweden in 1905. As for England, Norway's faith in its sister democracy was so firm that a Norwegian Prime Minister had candidly proclaimed as a keystone of his foreign policy: "We trust in the British nation."

About Germany there were some doubts, but Norwegian politicians reminded themselves that the German Army had not proved a major threat to Norway's neutrality in World War I. Moreover, many Norwegians had strong personal and cultural links with the Germans. During the terrible famines that afflicted Germany in the 1920s, thousands of German children had been taken in by Norwegian families. In the 1930s, bicultural "Nordic meetings" to which distinguished Norwegians were invited became popular in Germany, while German lecturers, actors, singers and scientists traveled in a steady stream to Norway. If this flourishing Norwegian-German amity were not enough, there was always the British fleet: So long as His Britannic Majesty controlled the North Sea, the Norwegians could not conceive of the Germans' mounting a seaborne invasion.

Norway on the eve of World War II had scarcely 13,000 pitifully ill-equipped men under arms. The Army had no tanks or antitank guns and virtually no antiaircraft artillery. The Navy consisted of a few aged ships designed for coastal defense. The War Ministry took pride in the five fortresses located at strategic points along the coast, but the truth was that their guns were only partially manned and they lacked infantry to support them in case of an enemy landing.

More serious even than the dearth of armaments was the anachronistic thinking of a general staff that, in the derisive words of one critic, "was prepared for the previous war." Norway's military planners failed to notice that Germany had built a new and more flexible Navy, better equipped with submarines and surface raiders, and supported by land-based air power, that made it particularly effective in coastal operations. And in gauging their ability to weather wartime economic pressures, the Norwegians overlooked the fact that the British might have in mind a far tougher strategy than the "blockade by agreement" of the past. As developed in World War I, such blockades allowed neutrals to import certain agreed-upon commodities up to a specified volume, with no control over what was done with the commodities once they were in neutral hands.

As it turned out, the British in World War II demanded that every shipment to a neutral country be accompanied by a certificate—popularly known as a "navicert"—attesting not only that the cargo was within the permissible quota but how it would be used. The burden of proof thus shifted to the neutrals: They had to demonstrate convincingly that a given cargo, before it was allowed to pass through the Allied blockade, would not be transshipped to Germany.

Both Germany and Great Britain promised to respect Norway's neutrality as soon as it was proclaimed by King Haakon VII on September 1, 1939. Within a few weeks, both sides broke their promises. England was concerned about the passage of Swedish iron ore from the northern Norwegian port of Narvik, down the island-shielded waterway known as the Leads, to the North Sea and the gun foundries of the Ruhr. As early as September 19, the British were considering a plan to mine the Leads—which were Norwegian territorial waters—in an effort to force the ore ships out to sea, where they could be picked off by the Royal Navy. That clear violation of Norway's neutrality was avoided with the help of a personal appeal from King Haakon to Britain's King George VI.

The British instead began pressing Norway for commercial agreements that amounted to control of Norway's foreign trade. Britain not only wanted to increase its own trade with Norway—particularly in whale oil and fish products—but insisted on a contraband list that would eliminate much of Norway's trade with Germany. In an effort to throttle any possible reexport of goods to Germany, the British even claimed the right to control Norway's trade with other neutrals. When the Norwegians angrily denounced the claim as an infringement of their neutrality, the British bluntly reminded them that virtually all of Norway's world trade was carried on at the sufferance of the Royal Navy.

To the Norwegians, this tough British attitude came as a

stunning surprise. At the same time, the Germans were applying their own coercive tactics in an effort to force more generous trade concessions. Between November of 1939 and the following February, the Germans sank 51 ships in Norway's territorial waters, causing the loss of 357 Norwegian lives. To accusations that they had violated international law, not to mention Norwegian neutrality, the Germans blandly replied that according to a new rule they had just promulgated, any ship anywhere that was observed zigzagging to avoid being torpedoed, whether it was inside or outside territorial waters, was behaving in a suspicious manner and thus was subject to immediate attack.

Nevertheless, the Norwegians for a time were able to retain a measure of control over their destiny. They did it chiefly by relying on the classic neutral gambit of playing off the demands of one belligerent against those of the other. The one strong counter Norway possessed was its merchant fleet. Knowing that Britain was desperately short of shipping, the Norwegians offered to lease half their fleet to the British—provided the British in turn would relax their embargo enough that Norway could satisfy clamorous German demands for more goods. Grudgingly, the British agreed.

In such three-way swaps, equivalent values were figured to the last detail. In return for the use of 10 Norwegian tankers, for example, the British granted a 50,000-ton increase in Norway's exports of fish to Germany, while Germany in return sent 40 antiaircraft guns to Norway, which was belatedly bolstering its defenses. The gratified Norwegians privately called the deal the "cannon for fish" agreement.

But it was premature for the Norwegians to congratulate themselves. In December and January, the pressures built up rapidly as a result of the Soviet invasion of Finland. The British and French, who sided with the Finns, saw the Winter War as an ideal pretext for an intervention in Norway that would give the Allies direct control over shipping passing through the Leads. The British and French therefore demanded free transit through Norway and Sweden in order to come to the aid of the Finns. Winston Churchill, for one, was confident that "Norwegian and Swedish protestations" could fairly easily be "overborne."

Both the Swedes and the Norwegians flatly refused. Prime Minister Johan Nygaardsvold was so fiercely opposed to a foreign presence in Norway that he vowed to remove all transport from the landing areas should the British arrive. To behave in any other way, Foreign Minister Halvdan Koht explained, would not only be "contrary to the laws of neutrality," but liable to transform Norway into "a battlefield for war of the Great Powers." The Soviet Ambassador in Oslo left Koht in no doubt on this point, calling him to the phone at three in the morning to warn ominously about the disastrous consequences of Norwegian involvement. Dr. Curt Bräuer, the German Minister, contented himself with letting Koht know that there would be "reprisals."

The end of the Winter War in March 1940 left the Norwegians in an even more dangerous situation than before. The Finnish war had not only started the British thinking of invasion but had helped revive German interest in a plan proposed by Grand Admiral Erich Raeder to extend the range of German naval operations northward by establishing bases on the Norwegian coast. Raeder wanted to obtain the bases by negotiation, if possible, or by force if necessary. Mildly interested at first, Hitler began studying the plan in detail only after the Finnish war raised the possibility of British intervention in Norway. "It is essential that Norway does not fall into British hands," Raeder wrote him in a memo. "There is danger that volunteers from Britain, in disguise,

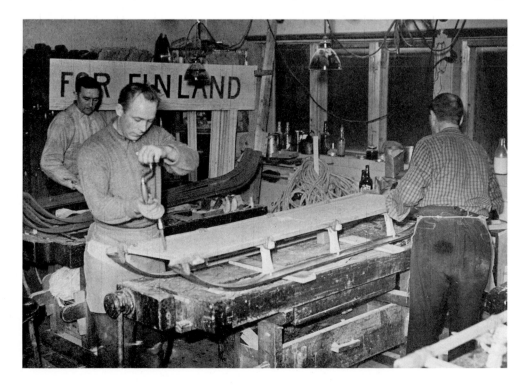

Craftsmen in Oslo work on one of the 500 sleds that Norway shipped to Finland during the 1939-1940 Winter War. The Finnish Army used the sleds to transport its wounded through otherwise impassable snow.

THE AMERICAS' PRO-AXIS NEUTRAL

Within weeks after the Japanese attack on Pearl Harbor punctured the Western Hemisphere's isolation and neutrality, all but two of the 21 Latin American republics had either suspended relations with the Axis powers or joined the United States in declaring war. By the autumn of 1942 such countries as Brazil, Mexico and the Caribbean states were cooperating with the United States in protecting Allied shipping from German U-boat attacks, and Axis agents were being hounded out of all of South America except the southern tier formed by Chile and Argentina.

These countries, declared Undersecretary of State Sumner Welles, were still allowing their territory "to be utilized by the officials and the subversive agents of the Axis as bases for hostile activities against their neighbors." In 1943, after counterintelligence operatives exposed a Nazi spy ring in Valparaiso that had kept the German U-boat command advised of Allied ship movements, Chile belatedly rounded up the Axis agents and broke off relations.

But the maverick Argentines remained stubbornly out of step with their sister republics. Tradition, trade and immigration tied them more closely to Europe than to the Americas. Early European settlers had massacred or driven out virtually all of the Indians they found in Argentina instead of assimilating them, and their descendants held themselves aloof from their mixed-race neighbors. More recent immigrants remained European in fact as well as ancestry: Fully a third of the residents of Buenos Aires held foreign passports. In some provinces whole towns were dominated by German settlers whose social, political and educational institutions were slavish copies of Nazi models.

Although most Argentines favored the Allies, a minority loudly espoused Nazi notions of anti-Semitism and racial superiority. The Army, German trained and German equipped, was a goose-stepping miniature of Hitler's legions, and its leaders counted on an Axis victory. Ethnic ties and political affinity with Falangist Spain and Fascist Italy had eroded the nation's democratic traditions, and the military-run government nurtured a frustrated ambition to displace U.S. influence and dominate the southern half of the hemisphere.

For these reasons, the rulers of Argentina clung to a pro-Axis neutrality and resisted United States efforts to close the circle of hemispheric solidarity. Throughout the War, Argentina would remain an outpost of Fascism and a haven for Axis agents expelled from other South American countries, even after pressure from the Allies finally forced it to adopt a token belligerency toward Germany in 1944.

Members of Argentina's proto-Fascist Alliance of Nationalist Youth rally in 1942 underneath an Andean condor symbol reminiscent of the Nazi eagle.

will carry out an unobtrusive occupation of Norway. Therefore it is necessary to be prepared."

Adding to the German sense of urgency was the testimony of an ambitious politician named Vidkun Quisling. Leader of a tiny splinter party that modeled itself on the Nazis, Quisling had been trying for years to obtain clandestine Nazi support. Now, suddenly, he found that the Nazis were listening. On December 14, 1939, he even secured an audience with Hitler. He told the Führer that the pro-British faction in Norway under Parliamentary leader Carl Hambro (whom he described, incorrectly, as "the Jew Hambro") was plotting to let the British establish bases in Norway. If Hitler would launch a preemptive strike, Quisling would aid him by taking power in Norway through a coup.

Quisling saw Hitler at five o'clock in the afternoon. By six, a directive had gone out from the Führer's headquarters to start planning for an assault on Norway and Denmark. The subsequent plan was designated *Weserubung* (Weser Exercise), so named for the estuary outside Bremerhaven from which the German forces were to sail.

The British too were mulling over a preemptive strike. Concerned about the consequences of a possible German attack, Churchill decided that the time had come for Britain to drop its policy of "honorable correctitude." The Leads would be mined whether Norway objected or not, and British forces would be held ready to rush into Norway in response to any military reprisals Germany might make. Churchill's rationale for this hard line was that "small nations must not tie our hands when we are fighting for their rights and freedom." That attitude infuriated Norway's Foreign Minister Koht, but he failed to heed its warning. Koht confided to the German Minister in Oslo that Churchill was nothing more than "a demagogue and a windbag."

One other factor influenced planners in both Britain and Germany. It was Norway's reaction to the so-called *Altmark* incident on February 16, 1940. A supply vessel being used to reprovision German warships at sea, the *Altmark* was passing through Norwegian territorial waters on its way back from service with the pocket battleship *Admiral Graf Spee*. In the *Altmark's* hold were more than 300 British seamen taken prisoner when the *Admiral Graf Spee* sank their ships. A British naval force boarded the *Altmark* and liberated the seamen, despite protests from the captains of two

Norwegian torpedo boats on the scene. The British public applauded the action and the Germans protested bitterly. But the real importance of the incident was that it convinced the Germans that the British were quite willing to violate Norwegian neutrality. It also demonstrated to both British and Germans that the Norwegians either could not or would not actively defend their neutrality.

Weserubung now became a top priority of the German High Command. "We can under no circumstances afford to lose the Swedish ore," said Hitler. "If we do, we will soon have to wage the War with wooden sticks." In the last days of March and the first days of April, Norway received numerous warnings that a crisis was near. The Norwegian Minister in London cabled that the British were preparing to mine the Leads. From Norway's Embassy in Berlin came word that a German invasion was imminent. An even more pointed warning came from Dr. Bräuer, the German Minister in Oslo. On April 5 he invited prominent members of the Norwegian government to the German Legation to view a film newly arrived from Germany. "The guests were horrified," recalled Halvdan Koht. "The film was a representation of the German conquest of Poland, culminating with gruesome pictures of the bombing of Warsaw, accompanied by the text: 'For this they could thank their English and French friends.' Undoubtedly it was meant to show the Norwegians what would be the result of resisting Germany."

Despite these warnings, the Norwegian government refused to believe that an invasion was near. Much of the minuscule Army was not even mobilized; nor were the coastal defenses placed on any sort of alert. When urged to question the Germans about invasion rumors, Foreign Minister Koht blandly replied that either the rumors were not true, in which case it was pointless to ask about them, or they were indeed true, in which case the Germans would deny them.

On the morning of April 8, the British officially informed Norway that they were mining the Leads. The Norwegian Cabinet met in emergency session and angrily voted to sweep the mines from the sea as fast as the British laid them. In the afternoon, even more disquieting news reached Oslo. Two German ships had been torpedoed off the Norwegian coast by Allied submarines. German survivors in field-gray uniforms were picked up by Norwegian fishing boats, and they volunteered the information that "at the request of the Norwegian government," they were bound for the port of Bergen to help repel an Allied invasion.

Incredibly, Koht still failed, in his own words, "to put two and two together." While the Chief of the General Staff urged immediate mobilization, Koht counseled that the activation of two battalions would be sufficient.

Even that limited response came too late. As Koht was returning to his home outside Oslo that evening, the air-raid sirens began to shrill. He assumed at first that it was a test but began to reconsider as the sirens continued. When he got home he telephoned the Foreign Office. He was told that German warships had been sighted in the fjord outside Oslo and that the coastal forts had opened fire. The German invasion had begun, and though desperate and sporadic resistance continued for two months, Oslo and the southern portion of Norway were overrun within days.

In a sense, the Norwegians' long record of peace had worked against them, for it gave them a false sense of security and encouraged them to believe they could solve international differences solely by negotiations, without backing their position by force. Norway suffered conquest because geography made it important to the belligerents and because it lacked the strength to make its neutrality convincing. Each side doubted Norway's ability to defend itself against the other, and each felt impelled to get there first.

"Nowhere did I find a more resolute turning away from war than among the Danes," said American journalist Donovan Richardson, who toured Europe in the summer of 1939. The Danes' attitude was quite simple. Unlike the Norwegians, they were under no illusion that they were immune from attack—their history books reminded them in chilling detail how they had lost the provinces of Schleswig and Holstein to invading Prussians in 1864—but they refused to worry about a situation over which they felt they had little control. They did not build up their military forces because they believed that would only invite attack. Should Germany attack anyway, they would not resist. Richardson found that the Danes were even able to look with a certain fatalistic humor at the looming crisis. And they made no secret of where their sympathies lay: Copenhagen's newsstands abounded with picture postcards of the King and Queen of England.

Denmark had no natural defenses of any kind. The geo-

graphic link between continental Europe and Scandinavia, Denmark projects like a green thumb 200 miles into the Baltic. Its gently rolling, sparsely forested terrain is ideal for dairy farming—and also for mobile troop operations. In the north, Danish ports strategically dominate the Skagerrak and Kattegat, the two narrow passages between the North Sea and the Baltic. In the south, Denmark is linked to Germany by a narrow neck of land 30 miles wide. From the frontier it is only 250 miles to Berlin.

Even Churchill was willing to concede Denmark's vulnerability. "I cannot blame Denmark," he told a group of Scandinavian journalists in London early in 1940. "The others have at least a ditch across which they can defy the tiger. Denmark is so terribly close to Germany that it would be impossible to help her." And he added, almost as an afterthought: "I do not doubt that the Germans would not hesitate to overrun her on the day it suits them."

Forewarned by earlier, similarly blunt assessments from British diplomats that it could expect no help from the Western powers, Denmark in May 1939 became the only Scandinavian state to accept Germany's offer of a nonaggression pact. Putting the best face on the matter, Danish Prime Minister Thorvald Stauning proclaimed that as a result of the pact "our neutrality has been underlined." The country, he said, now enjoyed "a special feeling of security."

Denmark in fact had the dubious distinction of being the only nation in Europe to reduce its armed forces after the outbreak of war. Despite strenuous objections from the military, the government in the first six months of the War cut ground forces by 50 per cent, to fewer than 15,000 men. That curious action was taken partly to placate the Germans, but partly also out of a defeatist attitude that increasingly infected the government of Prime Minister Stauning and his Foreign Minister, Peter Munch. On January 1, 1940, the Prime Minister gave a radio speech in which he so stressed Denmark's inability to influence events that it became widely known as the "What's the use?" speech.

For a time, the government managed to avoid major confrontations and maintained fairly satisfactory trade relations with both belligerents—partly because Denmark had no strategic materials that either side badly wanted. The Germans tried to pressure Denmark into abandoning its agricultural trade with Britain. But they backed down after the British warned that they would cut off the concentrated animal feed the Danish dairy farmers needed, thus depriving Germany of an important source of its own food supply.

As the War progressed, Denmark leaned more and more away from Britain in its efforts to placate the Germans. When Danish ships were torpedoed, the government deliberately refrained from trying to find out who was responsible. When members of the Danish Nazi Party and other crypto-Nazi organizations openly engaged in pro-German activities, the government looked the other way.

Yet all of these efforts to avoid provocation came to nought. By January 1940, the Danish Admiralty was receiving disquieting intelligence from its naval attaché in Berlin. Captain Frits Hammer Kjolsen reported that the Germans were planning to take over strategic Danish airfields in the north. The Admiralty hesitated before passing the warning on to the Defense Ministry. But Kjolsen's sources were in fact excellent: The information came from the Dutch military attaché in Berlin, Colonel Gijsbertus Sas, who in turn got it from Colonel Hans Oster, an anti-Hitler officer highly placed in German intelligence who regularly leaked military secrets to Western contacts.

As the winter wore on, the information Kjolsen was getting through Colonel Sas became increasingly specific and alarming. By late March, Kjolsen was informed that Germany was planning to invade Denmark and Norway. He relayed this information to his superiors in Copenhagen and heard nothing more. Concerned, he hurried to Copenhagen himself on April 4, and was told to his astonishment that because of the circuitous manner in which he had obtained the information, it could not be taken seriously.

In fact, what Kjolsen had in his hands was the broad outline of the *Weserubung* operation. Knowing that the success of the Norway invasion might hinge on use of the Danish airfields, the Germans had first planned to secure them through diplomatic pressure. But that method seemed both time-consuming and likely to rouse Allied suspicions. It would be simpler, they decided, to include Denmark in the invasion plan. Assigned to the job were two more Army divisions, a motorized rifle brigade, three motorized gun battalions, three light-tank companies, two batteries of heavy artillery and one armored train—some 40,000 troops in all.

The German supply ship Altmark lies aground in the narrow Jossing Fjord on Norway's southern coast after vainly seeking to elude six British warships. On the night of February 16, 1940, a party of 20 British sailors boarded the Altmark, killing seven Germans and freeing 303 British seamen who were imprisoned in the hold of the ship.

As this substantial force began to move into position, reports came flooding in. Major Hans Lunding, a Danish intelligence officer with a network of agents in northern Germany, advised on April 4 that Wehrmacht units were moving toward the Danish frontier. Similar reports came from the drivers of trucks that transported fresh fish from the North Sea to Hamburg. The columns of infantry marching northward, said the drivers, were 30 miles long. Desperately trying to awaken a sleeping Denmark, two senior diplomats at the Danish Embassy in Berlin, acting without authorization, called in the correspondents of two of Denmark's leading newspapers and told them bluntly that a German invasion was under way. The resulting banner headlines seemed to have no effect on the government.

As time ran out for the Danes, Major Lunding grimly reported that German forces would cross the Danish frontier at 4 a.m. on April 9—intelligence that proved to be off by only 10 minutes. A correspondent on the border telephoned his editor in Copenhagen on the evening of April 8 to say that he could hear the German tanks and armored vehicles outside his office window moving into position to attack.

The Danish government was, in fact, neither deaf nor blind to its peril, but it was under intense diplomatic pressure from the Germans. When it was announced on April 8 that the British were laying mines in Norwegian waters, Germany's Ambassador in Copenhagen, Cecil von Renthe-Fink, paid what he termed a friendly "personal" call on Danish Foreign Minister Munch. The Ambassador said that he trusted Denmark would "show understanding" if she were in any way "affected" by Germany's response to the British action. When Munch replied that any violation of Danish neutrality would lead to a general mobilization, Renthe-Fink warned him that this would be most unwise. As a consequence of that meeting, Munch issued a soothing statement saying that in case of unforeseen difficulties the Danish government would "strive to eliminate them in the same friendly spirit in which complicated questions between Denmark and Germany have hitherto been solved."

On the evening of April 8, conversation at the royal dinner table in Copenhagen's Amalienborg Palace centered on whether the Germans were indeed about to invade Norway. A guest wondered if they might assault Denmark as well. King Christian X smiled and said he could not "really believe that." He was still in a "confident and happy mood," recalled one of his bodyguards, when he left for a performance of *The Merry Wives of Windsor* at the Royal Theater.

When King Christian's guests next heard from him, he was broadcasting to the nation at 6:20 the next morning that the government had capitulated to the invading Germans. "God save you all, God save Denmark," he concluded.

No defense forces a country Denmark's size could muster would have deterred the Germans for long. Although the Allies wanted the Danes to remain neutral, they were in no position to protect them. Lacking any strategic resources to

use as bargaining chips, Denmark ultimately was dependent on the simple good will of the belligerents. The lesson it had for other neutrals was that in the face of overriding military imperatives, good will is worth very little.

On August 23, 1939, when Germany and the Soviet Union announced to a stunned world that they had signed a non-aggression pact, Prime Minister Dirk Jan de Geer of the Netherlands was vacationing in Germany's Black Forest. His worried government called him back to The Hague, where members of the Cabinet were debating whether to order a full-scale mobilization. Buying up all the newspapers he could find, the Prime Minister boarded the crack Rheingold Express. As the train sped north, de Geer alternately read and chatted with his fellow passengers. "Do you think the situation is really as bad as the papers say?" he repeatedly asked them. Weighing their replies, he decided that it was not. He got off the train near the border and resumed his vacation in the Dutch resort town of Velp.

Not all the Dutch were as confidently blasé as de Geer. Queen Wilhelmina, for one, was deeply concerned. Yet by and large the Dutch shared the Norwegians' and the Danes' illusion that if they behaved correctly they would be left alone. Unlike their neighbors the Belgians, they had survived World War I with their neutrality intact. They saw no reason why they could not do the same in World War II.

The Dutch scrupulously accorded equal treatment to both the Allies and the Germans and kept their resentments to themselves when their rights were infringed. It was one of the unwritten precepts of Dutch diplomacy never to express publicly any fear of German aggression, and never to hold precautionary staff talks with any potential ally for fear of arousing Germany. This principle was applied with particular care to Belgium; Dutch officials were agreed privately that because Belgium lay directly in the path of German armies bound for France, it would be invaded no matter what it said or did. The Dutch feared that if they held staff talks with the Belgians, Holland too might be included in the German invasion plans. On the other hand, if the Dutch refused military entanglements with their neighbors, the Germans would probably leave them alone on the theory they were an important channel for imports from abroad, as was the case in World War I.

But the Dutch were determined to fight if the Germans did attack. Their strategy was draconian. They planned to open their dikes to the sea, flood one fifth of the nation and assemble their forces behind this vast lake to form a "Fortress Holland" that they reckoned could hold out for several months at least. The Dutch Chief of Staff, General Izaak H. Reijnders, was bitterly criticized for this plan. But he insisted there was no other way for a small country like Holland to survive in a showdown with the German Wehrmacht.

To bolster the Fortress Holland strategy, the Dutch government aimed at building up what Foreign Minister Eelco Van Kleffens called "a reasonable scale of national armament so as not to offer any avoidable temptation to anyone to invade." But the program was a sham. Although a quarter of a million Dutchmen were under arms at the outbreak of war, they were poorly trained and equipped. For all their strong intentions and sound strategy, the Dutch never followed through with funds enough to build a credible fighting force. The Army had no tanks and only 18 armored cars. Artillery was drawn by horses. Infantrymen were issued three hand grenades apiece, and the average infantry regiment had only six mortars—compared with 45 mortars in German regiments. Standard-issue clothing was in such short supply that recruits were asked to bring their own underwear and shoes when they reported for duty.

More important, perhaps, than the material shortages was a critical lack of professional officers—there were only 15 per regiment of 4,000 men—and an overall confusion in planning and procurement. The commander of Holland's northern territories was astonished to learn that the vital telephone and telegraph lines by which he communicated with headquarters and with units in the field were strung over the Ijssel railway bridge—which was to be blown up at the first sign of attack. Pilots of the 170 obsolete planes that constituted the Dutch Air Force discovered as soon as they were mobilized that their bombs were not properly fused and that their guns jammed at high altitudes because they were lubricated with the wrong kind of oil.

The breakdown in planning extended even to the inundation scheme on which the Netherlands relied as its ultimate deterrent. Inundation in the southern part of the country, for example, was impossible in summer because the level of the Rhine was too low then and a planned bombproof

Crouched behind a makeshift roadblock, Danish soldiers lie in wait on April 9, 1940—the day Germany invaded. The Germans began crossing the frontier and landing along the coast shortly after 4 a.m. Two hours later, after 16 Danish soldiers had been killed, Denmark surrendered.

THE VATICAN'S DELICATE BALANCE

Vatican City, an independent enclave occupying 108 acres within Rome, maintained its neutrality throughout the War even though it was surrounded in succession by Fascist, Nazi and Allied armies.

As the leader of 400 million Catholics in both Allied and Axis nations, Pope Pius XII walked a careful line. In radio addresses, he rebuked those "forgetful of moral ties and bent on replacing right by force," yet he invited criticism in the West by refusing to indict the Axis powers by name.

In his actions, the Pope was compassionate and evenhanded. He welcomed envoys from 40 nations. He established a clearinghouse to answer almost 10 million inquiries about POWs of all countries, while he closed an eye to the harboring of Allied and Jewish fugitives in Church properties. And when Rome was bombed, the Pope visited the sites and turned many churches into refuges for the homeless.

Beneath a sculpture of Christ being lowered from the Cross, bombed-out Italians find refuge at Castel Gandolfo, the Pope's summer villa.

Arms outstretched, Pope Pius XII prays for peace amid a Roman street throng gathered

at the site of a bombing by Allied planes in July of 1943. During later air raids over Rome, a few bombs fell on the Vatican, but the damage was slight.

pumping station had never been completed. Moreover, there was no coherent plan to evacuate the populace or to coordinate the flooding with evacuation. In the southwestern province of Zeeland, a small-scale inundation caused panic in November 1939 when sea water poured into the fields at dawn without any prior warning to the public.

On the diplomatic front, confusion and anxiety were rampant. Unlike Denmark, the Netherlands was subjected to intense pressures almost from the outbreak of war. Dutch ships were held up by the British in the North Sea and by the Germans in the Baltic. By mid-November of 1939 the nation was suffering serious losses from U-boats and mines. The Dutch tanker *Burgerdijk,* bound from the United States to Rotterdam, was stopped and then sunk by a U-boat commander who told her skipper that he was not interested in the ship's papers—thus totally ignoring the fact that the *Burgerdijk* was a neutral vessel carrying a neutral cargo intended only for neutral consumption. In the same month, the large Dutch passenger steamer *Simon Bolivar* struck two magnetic mines off the British coast and sank with the loss of 83 lives. With great self-control, the Dutch asked the Germans, at that time sole possessors of the magnetic mine, whether they had laid mines in the area—taking care simultaneously to ask the same question of the British.

With the Germans claiming open season on any ship, neutral or not, crossing the North Sea, and with the British claiming the right to seize cargoes of German ownership or origin, under whatever flag, Holland's muted protests went unheeded. Briefly the Dutch considered sending ships in convoy escorted by naval vessels, but the plan was abandoned because it clearly meant war. Dutch shippers told a London *Times* correspondent that Holland would continue to ply its vital carrying trade, even though it was clearly caught between the devil and the deep sea. *"You,"* they told the Englishman bluntly, "are the deep sea."

One consequence of the sea war was that Holland, heavily dependent on foreign trade, quickly experienced shortages of foodstuffs and other consumer goods. Sugar and gasoline were rationed almost immediately.

The first firm reports that Germany planned to invade the Low Countries came from Colonel Gijsbertus Sas, the Dutch attaché in Berlin who later would warn of an impending attack on Denmark. This time, through his anti-Hitler informant in the Wehrmacht, Sas stated categorically that the Nazis intended to invade at dawn on November 12, 1939.

Reconnaissance of the southeast frontier areas disclosed that the Germans were massing troops, establishing munitions dumps, laying out pontoons for river crossings and hastily building airfields. Dutch intelligence learned that the Germans had been smuggling into Germany all kinds of Dutch uniforms belonging to the Army, the police, the postal service and the rail system—presumably with the idea of creating confusion during an attack. The Dutch quickly voted new funds for defense, speeded up preparations for inundations and proclaimed a state of siege in eight of the country's 11 provinces.

Yet as in Norway and Denmark, there was a curious reluctance in high places to believe fully in the threat. Though he had devised the Dutch strategy of flood and fortress, General Reijnders was among those who seemed paralyzed by the thought of putting it into action. He announced that he did not trust Colonel Sas's judgment. The Colonel had a reputation for being nervous, and Reijnders thought he was merely being used as part of the Germans' *Nervenkrieg,* or

war of nerves. The ostentatious preparations at the border, said General Reijnders, were to goad the Dutch into taking their positions, thus disclosing their defensive plans.

Prime Minister de Geer was equally skeptical. When November 12 passed without incident, he went on the radio to recall World War I, when similar fears of invasion had proved equally unfounded. Then he quoted an old Dutch proverb: "Man suffers more than God gives him to bear when he surrenders to fears that never come to pass."

One result of the November 12 scare was that Queen Wilhelmina approached King Leopold of Belgium to ask if he would join her in an appeal for peace. The two monarchs were under no illusion that their appeal would be heeded, but they reasoned, pragmatically enough, that it would be morally difficult for Hitler to attack them when they were heading a peace movement. At the very least they felt that they would be buying time until the full onset of winter weather made an invasion all but impossible.

Another consequence of the scare was that England and France began urgently pressing the Low Countries to coordinate their military planning with Allied commanders so that Allied armies could quickly come to their aid in the event of an attack. The Dutch, of course, were extremely reluctant to do this; it ran counter to their long-standing policy of offering no possible offense to anyone, and they feared that word would leak out and provide the Germans with a pretext for invasion. As a compromise, sealed letters detailing the Dutch campaign plan were sent to Dutch Embassies in London, Paris and Brussels. The letters were to be opened and presented to local military leaders only when enemy forces crossed the Dutch frontier.

The next serious alarm came on January 12, 1940, when the Belgians informed the Dutch that they had come into possession of German plans for a general attack on the West, beginning with Belgium on January 17. General Reijnders remained unconvinced. "I don't believe a thing of it," he said, pointing out that the orders might well be a cleverly contrived plant. He decided to "act as if nothing has happened," an attitude that infuriated Queen Wilhelmina and Defense Minister Adriaan Q. H. Dyxhoorn. Disregarding General Reijnders, the government ordered all furloughs canceled, strategic bridges wired for demolition and inundation areas prepared for flooding. But after a week in which nothing happened, the measures were revoked.

In fact, the alarm of January 12 was not a hoax—nor were the 18 other alarms sounded from Berlin by Colonel Sas during that winter. On each occasion, the Germans fully planned to invade but were deterred either by a sudden worsening of the weather or by the need to detach forces for the strikes at Norway and Denmark. With each false alarm, the Dutch became perilously more confident.

The Germans, for their part, played a skillful game of alternately heightening and relaxing tension. In February 1940, for example, German propagandists spoke menacingly of "the approaching decision." But that same month a delegation of German businessmen on a commercial tour of the Netherlands insisted genially in public interviews that a resumption of normal peacetime trade was the sole aim of German policy toward the Dutch.

General Reijnders listened to the German assurances and seemed oblivious to the threats. He even instructed Dutch Army intelligence to stop sending Queen Wilhelmina and Defense Minister Dyxhoorn copies of the alarming reports coming from Colonel Sas in Berlin. He had noticed, ex-

Dutch soldiers struggle to free a horse-drawn artillery piece in late 1939. The gun had been dragged deliberately into the flooded field as a test of the Netherlands' plan to stymie an invader by opening the nation's dikes.

Charging on ice skates, Dutch soldiers on maneuvers cross a frozen field that earlier was flooded as a precaution against invasion. The skater at center carries a light machine gun.

plained Reijnders, that the gloomy tone of the reports only served "to make the Queen nervous and induce the Defense Minister to meddle with our business."

At this point the Dutch Cabinet decided that General Reijnders must be replaced. While refusing to credit the reports of German intentions, he had at the same time been agitating for wider military control over civilian life, which the Cabinet was unwilling to grant. To fill his post, the Defense Minister recalled General Henri Winkelman from retirement. Although General Winkelman did not entirely trust the Sas reports, he took the German threat seriously enough to begin cautious discussions with Belgium, France and Britain on a common strategy in case of attack. The Dutch Navy's Rear Admiral Johannes T. Furstner arranged with London to evacuate the Royal Family in an emergency. He also worked out with the British a plan for escort ships to convoy the Dutch gold reserves to safety in England.

All of this was cloaked in deepest secrecy—partly out of fear of the Germans, but also out of concern over the effect on influential members of the Dutch government. "Given the existing mentality," noted Admiral Furstner, there was a good chance that these cautious initiatives "would have

been refused." Indeed, as winter gave way to spring and the weather grew promising for military movement, a strange mood almost of nonchalance gripped the government and the country. The Dutch behaved as if the evil would go away if they chose not to see it.

The German invasion of Norway and Denmark on April 9 brought Holland rudely awake. Now the threat was graphically real, and the government tried belatedly to react. A state of siege was proclaimed, military leaves were canceled, newspapers were censored, the Amsterdam airport was closed to foreign aircraft, and arrests of suspected spies were ordered. On May 4 came word from Colonel Sas in Berlin that an invasion of the Netherlands could be expected in a matter of days. It was the Colonel's 19th warning, and this time the government trembled in expectation.

Thursday, May 9, was a quiet day in The Hague. As Foreign Minister van Kleffens was returning to his home from an after-dinner walk with his wife, he was summoned to the phone to hear yet another message from Colonel Sas. This one was chillingly brief: "Tomorrow at dawn; hold tight."

All that night, members of the Cabinet sat in van Kleffens' study with the shutters closed so that passersby would not

be alarmed by the lights. Reports came in that the Germans had not cleared away the barbed wire along the border, and the ministers began to feel cautiously hopeful. Then, shortly after 4 a.m., they heard a droning sound. Van Kleffens opened the shutters. A moment later, he recalled, "hell burst loose around us" as wave after wave of inbound German bombers roared overhead. The invasion was on.

In neighboring Belgium, the mood had been somber from the beginning. As early as 1936, the Belgian government had stressed that it was operating under a policy it called "realistic neutrality." This meant that the Belgians were determined to forgo alliances and look out for themselves, regardless of what befell the rest of Europe. "We must follow a foreign policy exclusively and entirely Belgian," said King Leopold, adding that such a policy "should aim resolutely at placing us apart from the conflicts of our neighbors."

This policy extended even to Belgium's relations with the other Oslo States. The Belgian foreign office was not opposed to consultations on common principles, but it was vehemently opposed to defensive alliances—or any obligation that might affect Belgium's freedom of action.

The sole considerations shaping Belgium's foreign policy were the merciless realities of power politics. The Belgians, in fact, probably had fewer illusions than almost any other neutral people. The Belgians' sympathies were with the Allies, but they doubted the assurances of both sides that their territorial integrity would be respected. They knew their country was a corridor perfectly suited to any German drive, and they knew as well that the French would vastly prefer to fight World War II on Belgian rather than French soil. They resisted French and British pressures to hold defensive military discussions; the real aim of the Allies, they suspected, was to secure Belgian bases for launching an attack on the Ruhr. They modified this view slightly and agreed to consult with Allied military staffs, after the German invasion scare of November 12, which the Belgians took far more seriously than the Dutch did. Yet even at that critical time, the Belgians insisted that the French send them written "suggestions" about their common defense, to which they would make only verbal replies.

The economic situation was equally delicate. Although Belgium had a much larger industrial base than the Nether-lands, its trade was almost entirely with the Allies, making it extremely difficult for the Belgians to be economically independent during a war. Concerned that Germany would use Belgium as a channel for German imports, the British from the beginning kept a tight rein on Belgian trade, virtually dictating the nature and size of Belgian imports and listing as contraband strategic materials such as diamonds and tungsten that were of critical importance to German industry. The British pressures prompted German threats to take over "protection" of Belgian neutrality or to cut off vital exports of coal and coke to Belgium.

Belgium's gently rolling lowlands were no better suited to defense than the flatlands of Holland, and Belgium lacked the option of flooding large areas to discourage attack. The principal line of defense consisted of a string of powerful forts on the eastern frontier facing Germany. These followed the line of the Albert Canal and the Meuse and were to be backed up by a second, interior line of forts that existed only on paper when the War began.

Belgium's first mobilization, in August 1939, produced an army of 400,000 men; by the spring of 1940 the total had risen to 650,000. This considerable force was equipped with 3,500 field guns and supported by an air force of 200 planes. But the numbers were misleading: Many of the field guns were obsolete, and only 20 of the planes were modern enough to compete on equal terms with the planes of the Luftwaffe. Equipped with only six tanks, a few trucks and very little motorized artillery, the Army was trained for defensive warfare and was incapable of rapid movement.

Any lingering illusions the Belgians may have had about German intentions were dispelled on January 10, when a German plane carrying two staff officers was obliged to make a forced landing in a meadow inside the Belgian frontier. Despite one German's efforts to burn the papers he was carrying, Belgian police were able to salvage some of them. They detailed plans for German seizure of the Meuse bridges south of Namur as part of the overall strategy for invading Belgium, Holland and Luxembourg, the 999-square-mile duchy and Oslo group member perilously surrounded by Belgium, France and Germany.

The capture of the papers, observed Baron Pierre van Zuylen, head of the Political Department of the Belgian Foreign Ministry, "was so extraordinary that it appeared unbe-

In an open carriage, King Leopold of Belgium and a well-bundled Queen Wilhelmina of the Netherlands ride through The Hague in November 1939. Leopold traveled to the Dutch city at Wilhelmina's request to join her in a last, forlorn effort to mediate the two-month-old war in Europe.

lievable." Indeed, many Belgian political officers were convinced that the papers were fakes. Then the usually careful Germans made a second blunder. The German military attaché in Brussels, Rabe von Pappenheim, asked and was granted an interview with the downed German fliers. Pretending that he had misplaced his pencil, Pappenheim politely asked the Belgian officer present if he would get him one. While the officer was out of the room, Pappenheim urgently demanded to know whether the two German officers had destroyed the papers they were carrying. The hasty exchange was recorded via concealed microphone, confirming that the captured documents were not only genuine but vitally important to the German High Command.

Alarmed by this revelation, the British and French demanded the right of "preventive entry" into Belgium to set up a common defense. Still the Belgian government refused. Instead, Belgian forces were ordered to a state of readiness and the government informed the Germans that Belgium was aware of their plans to attack. By "showing the Führer that he was found out," van Zuylen and his colleagues reasoned, they would force Hitler at least to delay the attack and perhaps to abandon it. When Foreign Minister Paul-Henri Spaak demanded an explanation of the captured documents, the German Ambassador was so confused that he blurted out they were merely part of the *Nervenkrieg*, and not to be taken seriously. "War of nerves!" shouted the outraged Spaak. "Against whom? Against us!" He ushered the German out of his office.

Several days later, the Belgian military attaché in Berlin reported that the movements of German troops toward the frontier had stopped: The crisis was over. Yet the Belgians knew that it was only a reprieve. Throughout the bleak winter, they took each successive alert seriously; the Belgians did not fall prey to the optimism that falsely buoyed the Dutch. In the Belgian view, the question was not whether the Germans would invade, but when. Their only hope, they felt, was to try to delay German action on the slim chance there would be a negotiated end to the War.

After the German invasion of Norway and Denmark, the Allies made one last attempt to persuade the Belgians to plan a coordinated defense and permit Allied forces to cross the frontier. The Belgian government once again turned them down. The King's military adviser, General Raoul van Overstraeten, noted prophetically that Belgian refusal might be saving the Allies from military disaster, since the Germans would undoubtedly like to lure them into Belgium "in order to crush them by an enveloping movement debouching from the Grand Duchy of Luxembourg."

The Belgians were more willing to listen to requests for consultations with the Dutch, although they could not finally reach agreement. Holland's General Winkelman wanted the Belgians to close a 25-mile gap between a defense line in northern Holland and the Belgian line along the Albert Canal. But the Belgians wanted to extend their line much farther west than the Dutch wanted. Moreover, their plans called for them to fall back to the southwest rather than to the northwest, as the Dutch wanted them to do.

These tactical differences were still being argued when yet another warning of invasion came on May 9 from the Belgian Embassy in Berlin. And in Brussels it was noted that the German Ambassador was burning his papers.

On the evening of May 9, 1940, the French Embassy in Luxembourg was host to the Ambassadors of the Netherlands and Belgium, the Foreign Minister of Luxembourg and the Consul-General of the United States at a formal dinner. As the diplomats were finishing the fish course, an aide came in and whispered in the ear of the French Ambassador. He excused himself and left, not to reappear. At intervals during the next half hour the Foreign Minister of Luxembourg and the Dutch and Belgian Ambassadors were called to the telephone, and they also disappeared.

The American, George Platt Waller, was left alone at the table with the ladies. After dinner, he politely escorted each of them home. It was only when he got home himself that he received a telephone call from the duty officer at the United States Consulate telling him that German armies had crossed the Luxembourg frontier.

The experience of the Low Countries, like that of Norway and Denmark, demonstrated once again that neutrality is not an absolute but an aspiration—and one that often fails. But to declare that neutrality was impossible, as some statesmen did in the spring of 1940, was premature. A handful of nations were soon to prove that it was an attainable goal—in forms as varied as the contrasting traditions and loyalties of each of the countries that sought it.

Invading the Dutch border city of Maastricht in May 1940, German troops cross the Meuse River on planks laid over rubber boats and scale the ruins of the St. Servaas Bridge, blown up by the defenders.

SWITZERLAND IN ARMS

Fervently raising their right hands, and clutching rifles at their sides, Swiss militiamen in Zurich swear to defend their homeland against invasion in 1940.

A VIGILANT ARMY OF CITIZEN-SOLDIERS

The reasons why Switzerland succeeded in preserving its peace while so many other dedicated neutrals failed are numerous and complex. But one major reason, certainly, was that the tiny Alpine nation, surrounded on all sides by belligerents, presented itself as a nut too tough to crack—or at least not worth the effort.

Switzerland's formidable geography, with its towering mountains and easily blocked passes, was a great natural asset. Yet it would have meant little without a Swiss Army that was an effective fighting machine. The full-time force was small, made up mostly of instructors, senior officers, front-line pilots and border guards. But behind their cadre stood a superbly trained militia composed of every able-bodied Swiss male between the ages of 20 and 60. Every militiaman kept his uniform, personal weapon and ammunition at home, cleaned and ready. Within 48 hours, the nation could mobilize nearly half a million men.

Commanding these citizen-soldiers was a highly regarded officer named Henri Guisan. Guisan quickly rallied the nation to resist an anticipated blitzkrieg. He ordered arms stockpiled and military training expanded. And he improved Switzerland's already-extensive defenses, building fortifications to dominate the mountain passes and manning them with elite ski troops. At his behest, every bridge and highway into Switzerland was mined, as were the railroads that carried vital traffic between Germany and Italy.

Guisan also devised a strategy for last-ditch defense. It called for a 100,000-man force to slow an attack at the border while the bulk of the Army gathered inside the National Redoubt—a congeries of mountain strongholds and underground storerooms in the Alps. Even if half of the country's territory, all of its major cities and three quarters of its population were conquered, Switzerland itself would endure.

The strategy was never put to the test because Switzerland was never invaded. Yet one branch of its bristling defense—the tiny Air Force—got all the action it could handle. By accident and by design, Axis and Allied planes committed 6,501 violations of Swiss air space. The Swiss could not deal totally with such massive overflights. But during the War, Swiss fighters shot down 16 intruders and forced scores more to land at Swiss bases for internment.

Swiss airmen scramble to their Messerschmitts. Nazi pilots cutting across Switzerland bitterly resented being opposed by the excellent German-made craft.

Summoned by General Henri Guisan after France fell, 650 officers rally at Rütli Meadow on the Lake of Lucerne, birthplace of the Swiss Confederation.

A woman distributing papers draws a crowd with the ominous news: war for Europe, mobilization for the Swiss.

A CLOCKWORK MOBILIZATION

When Germany invaded Poland on September 1, 1939, Switzerland mobilized its Army for the first time in 25 years. Frontier units—called to arms three days earlier—already had occupied forts and were laying mines at strategic bridges and passes. Now farmers and bankers, laborers and merchants took up their weapons and reported for duty.

No nation in Europe, indeed the world, had a greater percentage of its male population under arms. By September 3, when France and Britain declared war on Germany, the 4.2 million Swiss were fully mobilized, with more than 1 out of every 10 citizens in the Army and another half million in voluntary auxiliaries, serving as civil-defense workers, ambulance drivers and even as airplane mechanics.

After the call to arms, militiamen are issued supplementary ammunition from a Swiss Army depot.

Fully outfitted Swiss soldiers emerge from a railway station in the city of Lausanne on the way to their assigned bases. Switzerland's border defenses were manned by citizens who lived along the frontier and could get from their homes and jobs to military posts in less than one hour.

TRAINING HARD TO BUILD CONFIDENCE

By law, every Swiss boy had to learn how to handle a rifle while in grade school. The training continued throughout his education until the age of 20, when each youth spent three months in the Army undergoing basic training. Then the militiaman returned annually for a three-week refresher course, until he was permitted to retire to the inactive reserve at the age of 48.

But with the threat of war, the requirements intensified. Basic training was increased to four months and the age limits were expanded to 19 and 60. The already-experienced militiamen, mobilized in September of 1939, worked hard to sharpen their skills as riflemen, machine gunners and artillerymen; they particularly emphasized hand-to-hand combat. Among the toughening physical routines was one in which the soldier dived over a rank of bayonet-tipped rifles *(right)*—a drill based on the legendary valor of a 14th Century Swiss patriot, Arnold von Winkelried, who impaled himself on a mass of Austrian pikes, thus breaking a hole in their formation. His sacrifice inspired his comrades to victory and independence.

Border troops in 1939 prepared for their own sacrificial mission—to delay an invasion at whatever cost. They manned an interlocking system of blockhouses near bridges primed to be blown up at the first sign of war; their only retreat would be to ford or swim the icy rivers, and this they assiduously practiced. The Germans on the other side of the frontier would sometimes harangue them with insults through loudspeakers. Yet Swiss morale remained high. "Some of the men seemed to look forward to a real fight," one officer wrote of his troops. "Others seemed to think that such a thing simply could not happen to us. But nobody looked scared."

A soldier in training dives boldly over a row of bayonets in a traditional Swiss Army exercise. The soldiers propping up the rifles with a board were prepared to lower the deadly hurdle if necessary; no one was supposed to get hurt, but the symbolism of daring and sacrifice was an important element in preparing soldiers for actual combat.

MAKING EVERY VILLAGE A STRONGHOLD

Assessing the Swiss fortifications, a German observer wrote that "almost every village in Switzerland has been turned into a stronghold of defense." The Swiss government spent almost $250 million transforming the country into a deathtrap for an invader. Thousands of cannon-equipped bunkers and machine-gun posts were constructed, laced together by minefields and barbed wire. But the peaceable Swiss were psychologically unable to live in a place that looked so much like an armed camp.

To encourage a mood of normalcy after the initial mobilization, the fortifications in populated areas were designed to be as inconspicuous as possible. Machine-gun bunkers intended as a means of controlling the approaches to key buildings were placed a discreet distance away. Wooden barricades jutted only halfway into the streets, thus providing cover for infantrymen while allowing automobiles and pedestrians to pass. And even the traps built to stop tanks were ingeniously fashioned (*opposite*) so they would not interfere with traffic until the alarm sounded.

At a bunker in Basel, on the German and French borders, a machine gun guarding the train station is sighted past pedestrians and an antitank barricade.

Swiss soldiers create a trap for tanks by emplacing steel girders in a road.

A car maneuvers around log barricades on the outskirts of a Swiss village.

Bicyclists and pedestrians cross a bridge that could be readily converted into a tank barrier by fitting spikes into the capped holes in the surface of the road.

A TINY AIR FORCE THAT REFUSED TO FLINCH

Patrolling Swiss air space was an impossible task for a force that had only 300 pilots and 210 planes early in 1940. Swiss flags with their distinctive white cross marked the border and held down accidental violations. But if incursions appeared to be deliberate—such as entire formations—the lilliputian Air Force had orders to intercept, and shoot if necessary.

Swiss pilots flew Dutch observation aircraft, French and German fighters, and their own home-built attack planes. The backbone of the force were 90 German Messerschmitt-109s; they shot down three Heinkel-111s in the first three weeks after Germany's invasion of France. Infuriated, Luftwaffe chief Hermann Göring sent his own Messerschmitts to escort the German bombers across Switzerland. One result was a massive air battle that pitted 38 German fighters against just 14 Swiss Messerschmitts. The Swiss never flinched, shooting down four of the invaders and losing only one plane themselves.

A frontier guard keeps watch high above a rooftop clearly marked with a large Swiss flag.

Swiss workers assemble Morane-Saulnier fighter planes in a factory near Lucerne. The French-designed Moranes were built in Switzerland under license.

Banking high above the snow-capped Alps, a Swiss Messerschmitt-109—capable of flying at 22,000 feet—patrols against planes crossing Swiss territory.

Dizzyingly high above a valley floor, two Swiss soldiers are transported to their mountain station in an open cable car.

A MOUNTAIN REDOUBT TO WITHSTAND THE WORST

Preparing the National Redoubt to withstand a German siege was a massive job. Fortifications were built high in the mountains and heavy guns were hoisted to defend them. More than 100 cable cars were installed to bring up troops. Caverns were blasted in the rock for use as storerooms, and stocks of food, fuel and ammunition were laid in. The nation's gold reserves were hidden away in mountain vaults.

The main force of the Swiss Army was posted to protect the so-called Doors to the Redoubt—seven valleys that cut deep into the mountains and were vulnerable to armored assault. Small detachments of motorized troops and artillery guarded the valleys to repel paratroop landings. Three great fortresses anchored the Redoubt's flanks and guarded the main rail lines between Germany and Italy. If necessary, the Swiss were prepared to destroy these precious railroads, blasting shut their long mountain tunnels—and thus denying the use of them to the Axis for years to come.

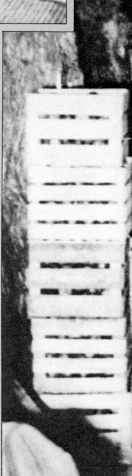

A gun turret is about to be hoisted into its fortress position.

40

Swiss workers stack munitions in a mountain shelter. The shells were carried by underground conveyor belts to the guns that bristled around the Alpine fortress.

SURE-FOOTED BRIGADES TO DEFEND THE ALPS

As they prepared to defend their National Redoubt, the Swiss took heart from the experience of Finland, whose outnumbered soldiers used their skill at fighting in familiar, snowbound forests to bedevil the Red Army in the 1939-1940 Winter War.

The Swiss hoped to benefit similarly from their own Alpine expertise. The Army established a three-week mountain training course that was taught by the most proficient skiers, mountaineers and guides in Switzerland. Students were taught to camp high among the peaks, to maintain their weapons in foul weather and to traverse the roughest terrain.

Graduates of the course joined the Swiss Mountain Brigades. The best went on to advanced training in Alpine maneuver and assault. They also practiced plumbing the snow with poles to locate buried equipment—and lost comrades—should reverberating gunfire, or the capricious Alps themselves, trigger an avalanche.

Swiss soldiers carry spools of communication wire used in connecting isolated mountain units.

In white uniforms blending with the snow, Swiss mountain troops advance with short-handled entrenching tools and avalanche poles to test the footing.

Roped together, a patrol ascends a nearly vertical mountain wall. Alpine soldiers won the coveted High-Mountain Badge after leading a similar patrol.

Amid Alpine peaks, soldiers of the Swiss 10th Mountain Brigade carry their skis along a ridge 9,357 feet high overlooking Tubang Pass during the winter of

1940. The mission of the mountain troops was to swoop down by surprise on the flanks of any enemy soldier who tried to make his way through the high passes.

2

A last holiday among the Alps
The dangerous magnet of outside allegiances
A gentleman-farmer elected general
Watching the Rhine with 10,000 eyes
A last redoubt among the peaks
Shooting down German bombers with Messerschmitts
Nazi threats to eliminate the "Swiss porcupine"
The death penalty revived for turncoats
A tolerant base for every nation's spies
Growing more food in a near-vertical land
Landlocked Basel becomes a seaport
Smuggling watch parts to Britain
Chance bombings not always by chance
"Our little lifeboat is full"

Of all the neutrals, Switzerland has the greatest right to distinction. She has been the sole international force linking the hideously sundered nations and ourselves. She has been a democratic state, standing for freedom in self-defense among her mountains.

—Winston Churchill, 1944.

Switzerland is a haven for Fascists from Germany and Italy. The Swiss became wealthy from World War II while we were expending our blood and our treasure.

—U.S. Congressman Stephen M. Young, 1949.

No neutral state stirred more violently contrary feelings than Switzerland. To some, the Swiss were cynical opportunists who trimmed their sails to the fortunes of war with no other thought than profit. To others, they were a people of humanitarian instincts, whose courage and will kept alive the glimmer of free institutions in a continental Europe that otherwise would have been in darkness. To critics and supporters alike, tiny Switzerland often loomed larger than life, summarizing all the defects and virtues they attributed to neutrality in general.

Partly this was because Switzerland was the professional neutral of Europe—a country whose security had been guaranteed by the Great Powers ever since the end of the Napoleonic Wars in 1815, and whose declared neutrality dated back two centuries before that. If neutrality was a valid concept, then Switzerland was the nation to which the world looked for confirmation. And if neutrality was a fraud and a delusion, Switzerland again was the barometer by which the world measured and judged its failure.

During World War II, Switzerland came under pressures more intense, more varied and more sustained than any other neutral, and was forced to make more frequent concessions. No other neutral state was surrounded by Axis-controlled territory, without any direct access to the sea. One consequence of this stark geopolitical reality was that by 1942—despite mounting Allied protests—Swiss exports to Nazi Germany had nearly tripled over what they had been on the eve of war.

The geography and financial capabilities of Switzerland forced on it a gamut of wartime roles that were both sensi-

THE PERPETUAL NEUTRAL

tive and contradictory. Swiss activities were at the same time humanitarian, diplomatic and commercial. The nation was a haven for the dispossessed, a representative of the interests of countries in murderous conflict, and a banker for the Nazis and for all of occupied Europe. The Swiss deplored the savagery of the Nazis' drive to conquest, but through their banks flowed much of the gold that fueled the Nazi war machine and made the conquests possible.

When news of the outbreak of war reached Switzerland on September 1, 1939, much of the country was celebrating. It had been a glorious summer—an unbroken succession of high, crystalline skies of the kind that drew tourists to this Alpine enclave from all over Europe. Starting in the spring, there had been an extraordinary number of local fetes and festivals culminating in the National Exhibition in Zurich, a gigantic celebration of Swiss solidarity and industry.

It seemed, recalled the journalist Pierre Béguin, as though the entire country were on one last holiday, knowing that the time of holidays was about to end. For Switzerland was well aware—despite its festive mood—that for Europe and perhaps the world the celebrations were almost over. Closer to Germany, both geographically and ethnically, than any of the other neutrals, the Swiss had few illusions about the brutality of the Nazi regime or its warlike intentions.

At the National Exhibition itself, Béguin remembered, all the male employees had been briefed on what to do in case of national emergency. Within hours of news that German troops had crossed the Polish border, much of the Exhibition staff had left to report to mobilization centers. The news came to the vacationing public in the form of a loudspeaker announcement summoning all rowboats on Lake Zurich back to their landings. The cable lifts stopped operating, and red placards went up at the model Swiss village saying that until further notice the National Exhibition was closed.

Switzerland was fully mobilized 41 hours before France could even formally declare war on Germany—and 35 hours before Britain could do so. That admirably swift mustering of national forces was the result of years of watching a bellicose Germany try to bully its way into Swiss affairs. As a loose confederation of three major national groups speaking three different languages—French, German and Italian—Switzerland had always been sensitive to the pull of outside sympathies and allegiances. The cultural and commercial ties of German-speaking Switzerland with Germany were particularly close. Many of the inhabitants of Basel, Bern and Zurich had relatives in Germany. Students from the three cities often attended German universities, and Swiss musicians and actors were well known to German audiences. Indeed, one of the railroad stations in Basel, which was directly on the German border, was a German exclave by right of treaty, and was patrolled by German police.

Almost immediately after the Nazis came to power in 1933, they printed maps showing Switzerland's German-speaking cantons, in the north, as part of an expanded Germany. The Nazis in fact behaved as though they had already annexed the cantons. In a number of celebrated incidents during the 1930s, Nazi agents brazenly crossed the frontier to seize political refugees who had fled Germany, and German newspapers kept up a drumfire of criticism against Switzerland as a haven for "Jews and Marxists."

When Swiss papers replied with criticism of the Nazis, German propaganda insisted that Swiss neutrality must encompass not only the acts of the government but the attitudes of individuals (*Volksneutralität*), and that the newspapers and other channels of "Jewish venom" must be restrained. The Swiss government's rejection of such demands led to violent confrontations, including a much-publicized attack by pro-Nazi groups in Zurich on a cabaret featuring an anti-Nazi revue staged by Erika Mann, daughter of refugee German novelist Thomas Mann.

German citizens residing in Switzerland—there were about 40,000 of them on the eve of war—were pressured by propaganda and open threats to organize themselves into a National Socialist organization modeled after the National Socialist Party and its various branches in Germany. Soon Switzerland had its own Hitler Youth, its own German Maidens and other German student organizations. The elite were given special paramilitary training and formed into "sports groups" that were in reality local strong-arm squads. The staff overseeing these multiple activities was housed in a Nazi Party office building in Basel.

In addition, there were at least a dozen indigenous Swiss pro-Nazi movements that at their height attracted an estimated 40,000 followers. At first, the Swiss government felt that most of these movements were too lunatic to be concerned about—one group sponsored an assassination attempt against Hitler because it felt that he was neither anti-Communist nor anti-Semitic enough. But evidence accumulated that the German National Socialists were collaborating with their Swiss counterparts to gather information on political and military matters of interest to the Reich, and to meddle illegally in Swiss politics.

Not long after Hitler came to power, German smugglers were caught crossing Lake Constance into Switzerland with explosives, presumably for acts of sabotage. In 1936, a Jewish medical student at the University of Bern shot and killed Wilhelm Gustloff, head of the National Socialist Party in Switzerland. The assassination touched off ugly reprisals against Jewish merchants and was seized upon by the Nazis as the occasion for a massive state funeral in Schwerin, Germany, celebrating the ideal of a pan-Germanism that would one day embrace all peoples of German blood.

Thoroughly alarmed by these signs of German interference in Swiss affairs, the government refused the National Socialists permission to appoint a successor to Gustloff. The Swiss took the even more extreme step of establishing a Federal Political Police Force for the first time in history. Its mandate was to combat all subversive forces endangering the state from within.

Simultaneously, the government began looking to its economic and military readiness, in anxious anticipation of the European war that many Swiss statesmen now saw as inevitable. What worried them most was Switzerland's enormous dependence on foreign trade. How, they asked, could a country with virtually no natural resources survive as a neutral state when its markets and its sources of supply were overwhelmed by war? There was no simple answer, but the government decided as a preliminary step to require importers to stockpile "goods of vital necessity" and families to lay in a two-month supply of critical foodstuffs. The government itself purchased large reserve stocks of coal.

At the same time, the government started building new fortifications along Switzerland's Rhine frontier, floated a national loan for strengthening defenses, and lengthened the period of required military training in a militia that numbered nearly 500,000 men.

But what concerned the Swiss Defense Ministry most was a crucial shortage of equipment. Swiss factories could produce ammunition, machine guns, field artillery, even fighter planes, but they were just gearing up to war production in the late 1930s, and the expansion of the armed forces outpaced by a wide margin the matériel on which defense planning depended. At the outbreak of war the Swiss Air Force had only 86 fighter planes of various ages and a few reconnaissance planes; there were no bombers or ground-attack planes. Antiaircraft units were equipped with only 23 heavy 75mm guns, and even these were ineffectual against modern bombers at high altitudes. Much of the field artillery dated from the 19th Century, and antitank units were short of both weapons and ammunition.

At the head of Switzerland's well-trained but ill-equipped

A visiting German sports group receives a Nazi greeting from members of Switzerland's National Socialist Party upon entering a Zurich stadium for an athletic festival.

forces was General Henri Guisan, who was 65 years old. Elected to the supreme command less than 48 hours before Germany invaded Poland, Guisan was a French-speaking gentleman-farmer who had pursued an Army career intermittently since World War I, rising to the command of an Army corps. Although he had not completely given up farming to join the professional corps of officers until he was 52, he had quickly become known as a brilliant strategist and one of the few on the General Staff to understand the changing demands of mechanized war.

The first test for Guisan and his forces came not in the fall of 1939 but the following spring, when Germany unleashed its blitzkrieg in the West. The Swiss had used the intervening months, the period of the "phony war," to strengthen their defenses, both internal and external. After Germany's invasion of Norway and Denmark in April, Swiss police so increased their vigilance against possible saboteurs and agents that it was not uncommon to be stopped a dozen times for identity checks on the 60-mile highway from Zurich to Bern. When news came of the attack on the Netherlands and Belgium in May, the Swiss closed their borders to road and rail traffic and ordered all foreigners possessing firearms to surrender them to the police.

A young officer named Urs Schwarz, commanding an antiaircraft battery, recalled the tension that seized Swiss troops at word of the Nazi drive into the Low Countries: "Ten thousand eyes looked across the Rhine or from mountain peaks and passes into the neighboring land where German forces were supposed to be massing." What the Swiss feared was a German attack across the Rhine and through Switzerland as part of a flanking movement around the southern wing of France's Maginot Line.

Swiss military-intelligence agents began reporting from Black Forest villages just north of the Swiss border that as many as 30 German divisions were on the move toward the Rhine. It was said that portable bridges were being prepared and that all German road signs in the region now gave the exact distance to the frontier as guidance to troops on the march. Intelligence was convinced that the attack was to be launched at 2 a.m. on May 15.

Responding to rumors, Swiss civilians by the thousands fled the frontier region and made their way south, clogging roads that the Swiss Army badly needed for defense operations. Urs Schwarz watched from his command post as "a long, almost unbroken line of automobiles rolled past, heavily packed with women and children, some even with a mattress slung over the top, which the occupants fondly hoped would protect against strafing." Resort hotels in the Bernese Alps and around Lake Geneva that had been deserted by foreign tourists were suddenly filled to capacity.

At the end of the long night, the Germans had not yet arrived—nor did they come in the following days. The Germans indeed had a contingency plan to invade Switzerland—it was code-named *Tannenbaum*—but no date had been set, and the maneuvers of mid-May turned out to be part of an elaborate feint to pin down French forces that were badly needed to the north. Although the immediate threat of invasion receded after Germany's rapid conquest of Belgium and the Netherlands, the Swiss felt only momentary relief. With the fall of France in June, they were isolated in a continent dominated by dictators.

At this anguished moment, the President of Switzerland, Marcel Pilet-Golaz, addressed the nation by radio. A socially stiff but politically pliant man who had once confided that if he could not be a lion he would at least like to be a fox, Pilet-Golaz had been awed by the successive triumphs of the German Army. Now he welcomed with "profound relief" the lull that followed the crushing of France. He suggested that the time had come for Switzerland to take its place in a new European balance of power. To demonstrate

Flanked by members of Switzerland's Federal Council, General Henri Guisan salutes a cheering crowd outside the Federal Palace in Bern immediately after his election as Army Commander in Chief on the 30th of August, 1939—two days before World War II began.

Switzerland's good will toward Germany, he forced on General Guisan a partial demobilization that reduced the size of the Swiss Army by two thirds.

Much of Switzerland was outraged—a General Staff officer told the writer Denis de Rougemont that for the first time in his life he was ashamed to be Swiss—but there was also a sizable body of opinion that agreed with Pilet-Golaz. According to this view, the Axis powers were going to dominate Europe for a long time, and it was only prudent to come to terms with them. There was much talk of *Erneuerung* (renewal) and *Anpassung* (adaptation) of Swiss institutions and politics. Some Swiss business interests were obviously looking to their profits, but there were also idealists who believed that the so-called New Europe the Nazis spoke of might be organized along the lines of Switzerland itself—which after all was an amicable confederation of different national groups.

Whatever their reasoning, the groups that supported Pilet-Golaz contributed to a general mood of accommodation in the summer of 1940, a feeling that there was no way to resist German domination. To combat this mood, General Guisan on July 25 summoned his ranking officers to a meeting at Rütli Meadow, a historic spot surrounded by sheer cliffs at one end of the Lake of Lucerne, where the Swiss Confederation had been formed in 1291. To get there, the officers steamed down the lake on a tourist sight-seeing boat, escorted by armed motor launches carrying a battalion of mountain infantry.

Standing on a grassy slope, Guisan pledged his 650 assembled officers to unconditional resistance in the face of any invader. He then explained the defense strategy he was about to adopt. His plan was, of course, based on the formidable natural obstacles that Switzerland's mountainous terrain presented to would-be intruders.

The only vulnerable point in the country's mountain shield was the so-called Swiss Plateau, a relatively flat expanse of country between Lakes Constance and Geneva. General Guisan proposed strengthening existing lines of fortifications across the plateau—one line near the border and one farther back. Here his men would fight a holding action to give the Army time to mobilize fully and fall back to its ultimate defensive position—a chain of fortifications burrowed into the Swiss Alps in a great ellipse surrounding the whole central Alpine region. By holding on to this mountain redoubt, the Swiss would deny the enemy two vital railroad lines linking the Axis partners—the lines through the Saint Gotthard Tunnel and the Simplon Tunnel, over which moved nearly all of Italy's coal supply from Germany.

General Guisan was confident that in such a position his forces could hold out indefinitely—with artillery placed in the massive cliffs, food and ammunition supplies hidden in glacial ice caves, and Alpine troops specially trained to exploit the hazardous terrain. And if the enemy should eventually break through, the Swiss were prepared to blow up the essential north-south rail routes through the Alps, leaving Italy tied to Germany by only a single major line, over the Brenner Pass in Austria.

Many of the fortifications were already in place, built as part of a defense program the Swiss had initiated in the 1930s. The military advantages of linking all these local defenses into one vast mountain redoubt were obvious. But Guisan and his aides were less certain about how the public would react to a plan that envisioned abandoning to the en-

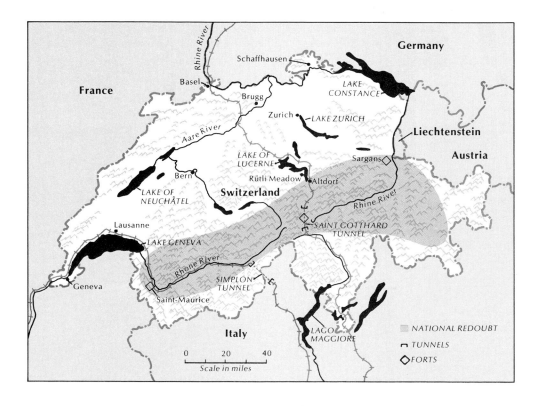

Switzerland's National Redoubt (shaded area), an Alpine bastion against invasion, stretched from Fortress Saint-Maurice in the west to Fortress Sargans in the east. A third stronghold, Fortress Saint Gotthard, protected a nine-mile-long tunnel (inverted brackets) on one of the key rail routes between Italy and Germany.

emy more than half the national territory, three quarters of the population and all of the larger cities, including Bern, the capital. To test the public mood, the government commissioned a team of psychological researchers to take samplings of opinion. Most of the Swiss, the researchers found, were not only weary of German threats but anxious to support any practical form of resistance. Indeed, Guisan's Rütli speech visibly raised Swiss morale and at least temporarily silenced those who counseled renewal and adaptation.

The speech also affected the Germans, who tabled any immediate plans for an invasion as too costly. But they continued to exert strong pressures on the Swiss—and to win important concessions. One of these had to do with Swiss air defenses. In the month following the German invasion of the Low Countries, Swiss airspace was violated 197 times, in almost every case by German bombers or fighters. Most of these intrusions were challenged by Switzerland's harried

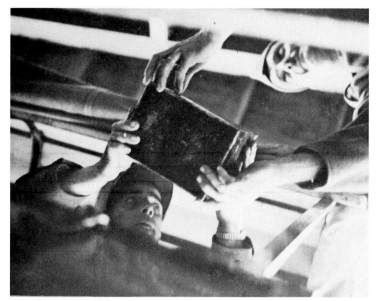

and inadequate air-patrol units. In fact, only five minutes after Germany's Belgian offensive began, Swiss fighter pilot Hans Thurnheer encountered a German bomber between Brugg and Basel. He ordered the bomber to land, and when it opened fire, he shot it down.

In the ensuing days the Swiss shot down four more bombers, so alarming the Luftwaffe command that it ordered a long-range fighter escort for all bombers intentionally crossing Swiss airspace. Flying single-engined Messerschmitt-109s purchased from Germany before the War, Swiss pilots continued to perform exceptionally well against the twin-engined but less maneuverable Messerschmitt-110s flown by the Luftwaffe. By June 8, they had brought down 10 German bombers and fighters, losing only two Swiss planes.

Enraged that German equipment was being used to kill German pilots, Hitler personally intervened, letting it be known that if the Swiss shot down another German plane the Reich would cease talking and would protest "in another manner." Faced with that threat, General Guisan abolished patrols of the frontier areas and instructed Swiss pilots to intervene only when a flight of three or more planes penetrated deep into Swiss airspace.

Soon Swiss airspace was being violated by flights far larger than that, as British bombers passed over en route to Italy. Since the British flew at night and the Swiss had no night fighters, the Swiss Air Force could not intervene. But the Germans complained that Switzerland's brightly lighted cities provided the British with excellent navigational beacons. Under pressure, the government agreed to a total

Swiss Army specialists (left) rig a demolition charge 25 miles east of Zurich in August 1940. General Henri Guisan (second from right, below) returns to his train during an inspection tour of Swiss preparations for the destruction of railroads and key highways in the event of invasion.

INCIDENT AT DÜBENDORF

Among the many Allied and Axis airplanes interned by the Swiss, one proved especially controversial. On the night of April 28, 1944, a three-seated German Me-110 fighter strayed into Swiss airspace after being shot up by a British Lancaster bomber over southern Germany. Swiss antiaircraft crews at Dübendorf Air Base near Zurich fixed searchlights on the plane and signaled for it to land by firing red and green flares. The Germans indicated compliance—and then made a break for it; on flashed the searchlights again, a dozen of them, blinding the pilot, Lieutenant Wilhelm Johnen, and forcing him down.

The Germans had good reason for trying to escape. Their plane was equipped with the latest night-flying radar, the Lichtenstein SN-2, which could track aircraft at a distance of more than four miles. It also carried an important new weapon that was nicknamed Slanted Music, a pair of top-mounted cannon for attacking the vulnerable underside of Allied bombers. Moreover, the Messerschmitt's radio operator, Joachim Kamprath, had disobeyed regulations and brought along a set of secret Luftwaffe code books.

Once they were on the ground, the crew tried desperately to destroy the equipment. Kamprath kicked ineffectually at the radar. Gunner Paul Mahle, who was also the builder of the upward-firing cannon, started to take them apart. The Germans were interrupted by a knock on the cockpit, and a voice instructing them firmly in German: "Please get out. You are in Switzerland. You are interned." The crewmen quickly crammed the code books into their pockets and climbed out. They were surrounded by 20 Swiss militiamen.

After smoking a cigarette with the amiable guards, gunner Mahle asked for permission to return to the plane to retrieve "something personal," then left without waiting for a reply. Moments later he was pulled leg first out of the plane while stretching to set off a timed detonation device. The forbearing Swiss then escorted their captives to the base canteen. While sharing food, wine and war stories with some interned Allied airmen there, the Germans managed to flush pages from the code books down the toilet.

By the next day, Berlin was in a high-level flap. The Swiss refused to return the plane, and the German command naturally feared that its top-secret equipment might find its way into Allied hands. The Gestapo suspected betrayal from within and arrested the families of the downed airmen; SS chief Heinrich Himmler even suggested using German agents in Switzerland to assassinate the three men. Reich Marshal Hermann Göring dismissed the idea, but instead proposed bombing the Dübendorf Air Base. Then SS Major Otto Skorzeny, famous for having freed Mussolini from Italian captivity several months earlier, was called upon to plan a commando raid to destroy the plane.

But the Messerschmitt-110 had already been hidden deep within a secret Alpine shelter. So any raid would have been futile—and might well have meant war with Switzerland. After three weeks of impasse, the two nations struck a deal. At 10 p.m. on May 17, 1944, as the German military attaché looked on, both the plane and its special equipment were burned at Dübendorf. In return, the Swiss were allowed to buy a dozen of another high-performance German fighter, the Me-109G, complete with arms, ammunition and a license to build more of the planes in Switzerland.

As part of the agreement the three airmen were repatriated to Germany, taking with them 400 tins that contained 20,000 Swiss cigarettes, almost impossible to obtain at home. The men were exonerated of blame (Hitler personally apologized for the arrest of their families) and reported back to their squadron, where the Swiss cigarettes helped ensure that they would receive a warm welcome.

Sprouting night-radar antennas on its nose, a German Me-110 sits on a runway at Dübendorf Air Base in Switzerland after being forced down in April 1944.

blackout that for many Swiss was an ominous symbol of their country's increasing isolation.

The Germans also increased pressures to curb the Swiss press. With few exceptions, Swiss editors had been outspokenly critical of the Nazi regime. The day after the invasion of the Low Countries, banner headlines in Switzerland spoke of "barbarism unleashed," and of the Nazis' "rage for conquest." Now newspapers were subjected to a kind of precensorship that prohibited coverage of national defense or criticism of a foreign state. In Berlin the press chief of the German Foreign Ministry chose this moment to warn Swiss correspondents, among others, that there would be no place in the New Europe for journalists hostile to the Axis cause. He pointedly called to the attention of the Swiss a remark attributed to Bismarck: "Governments often have to pay for windowpanes smashed by their newspapermen."

In scores of ways, Switzerland was reminded that it continued to exist only at the sufferance of the Reich. On radio programs beamed from Germany, the Swiss heard a new patriotic song sung by a Hitler Youth choir, with the words: "Homeward bound from our front lines / We'll get you, too, Swiss porcupine!" Hitler called Switzerland "an anachronism" and the Swiss "renegade Germans," and he spoke pointedly of bourgeois states that would not survive the War. The Nazi press reminded Switzerland that before confederation it had been part of Germany, and called it a "nasty dog" for refusing to acknowledge its allegiance. A German diplomat in Bern, in similar vein, compared Switzerland to a fly in a concert hall, and warned: "You Swiss would be wise not to annoy people with your buzzing— otherwise, someone might decide to kill the fly."

Emboldened by German successes, the various Swiss pro-Nazi groups joined forces after the fall of France to form a single party called the National Movement of Switzerland. Although their most visible activity was the distribution of pro-German propaganda, their ultimate aim was to overthrow the government by force, on signal from Berlin. Quickly judged a political danger, they were banned in November 1940 along with the Communist Party.

But even after this crackdown, the problem of maintaining internal security became increasingly difficult for the Swiss. The National Socialist Party had placed the command of its operations under the diplomatic cover of the German Embassy in Bern and was stronger than ever. At the onset of war there were some 16,000 German citizens in Switzerland who were members of the Swiss National Socialist Party and at the same time liable for service in the German Army. Only slightly more than 3,000 of them were called up. Some of the remainder were physically unfit, but many were exempted because they were more valuable to Germany in their civilian jobs, as conduits of Nazi influence and subversion in Switzerland.

Sabotage was on the increase. One case particularly aroused the ire of the Swiss public because it involved two Swiss traitors. Along with seven other trained saboteurs, the two Swiss slipped into Switzerland from Germany on the 16th of June, 1940, with orders to blow up the munitions factory at Altdorf and to set charges at two major airfields. Once past the frontier, the saboteurs boarded a train and sat in different compartments. However, an alert conductor noted that although they were traveling separately, they all carried the same type of mountaineer's bag, wore the same kind of shoes and had bills of similarly large denomination. At the next station he summoned police, who arrested the men after finding that they were carrying explosive charges and forged papers.

Such cases led to a rapid hardening of the Swiss espionage and treason laws, and demands for the death penalty, which had been abolished in Swiss civil law several years earlier but still existed in military law. The government compromised, reserving to itself the right to review appeals in all treason cases but delegating to the Army the responsibility for trial and punishment. As a result, 17 Swiss citizens were executed by military firing squads for crimes ranging from the theft of newly developed artillery shells to copying the plans of top-secret fortifications.

The executions came as a shock to the Swiss, who had naïvely assumed that the only internal threat came from foreigners—mainly Germans—living in Switzerland. Even more shocking was the revelation that the Germans had set up a special training school for Swiss turncoats in Stuttgart. Its graduates were supposed to be experts in espionage and terrorism—for the Germans had a theory that a concerted terrorist campaign, if combined with the threat of invasion, would make the Swiss collapse without firing a shot.

The Swiss counterespionage service estimated that 60 per cent of the agents spying on Switzerland during the War were Swiss citizens. Most of these were apprehended or kept under surveillance, as were the German agents who slipped across the frontier. In fact, Swiss counterespionage was so outstandingly successful that the Germans came to regard it as the best in Europe. There were many times during the War, recalled a German intelligence officer, when all his agents in Switzerland "had either been caught or were so compromised that they could not be used."

Considering the efficiency with which they operated, the Swiss intelligence services were surprisingly small. The espionage and counterespionage branches, which were under the same command, numbered only 10 officers at the outbreak of war; eventually the combined staffs grew to 120 officers—a ridiculously low number when compared with the 3,000 agents the Germans had in their counterespionage service alone.

The mission of Swiss military intelligence was essentially defensive—to keep track of German intentions and movements and warn of a possible attack. To carry out this task with a limited staff, the Swiss relied on secret agents hired for specific assignments, on banking sources with long histories of commercial dealings in Germany, and on the vast pool of German and other refugees who had sought asylum in Switzerland. In addition, the Swiss used the services of a private organization established before the War by Swiss businessman Hans Hausamann to gather and disseminate information on the dangers that Nazism posed to Switzerland. Gradually, Hausamann's group evolved into an intelligence unit, and when war came it was integrated into the Swiss Army's intelligence network. Hausamann's informa-

tion was particularly valued because he had excellent connections with key figures in German industry.

In time, Swiss intelligence became so proficient that it knew every move German forces were making in a "critical zone" of Germany extending back 180 miles from the Swiss frontier. Through informers at the highest levels of the German command—one of whom was an officer in the communications center at Hitler's headquarters—Swiss intelligence often knew Wehrmacht operational orders before they went out to troops in the field.

Sometimes intelligence almost literally fell into the laps of the Swiss because of their strategic location. In 1943 a German plane crash-landed in Switzerland bearing a portfolio of specifications on the newest German fighter aircraft. On another occasion, a French intelligence officer who had crossed the Swiss frontier with his unit after the French surrender asked and was given permission to slip back into France. There he retrieved from a hiding place secret documents on operational procedures of the German Army, which he turned over to the Swiss.

Other valuable information came from the intelligence networks of other countries operating in Switzerland. Although such operations were prohibited by Swiss law, the Swiss tolerated—and even tacitly encouraged—an international swarm of spies. They not only provided valuable information but contributed in an odd way to Swiss security—for Switzerland realized full well that one reason for its survival as a neutral was its usefulness to the belligerents as a listening post in the center of Europe.

Every belligerent had its agents in Switzerland, many of whom operated out of legations to take advantage of diplomatic cover. The Germans had three parallel intelligence networks—run by the National Socialists, the Wehrmacht and the Gestapo—that together employed as many as 1,000 agents. The Americans had a branch of the Office of Strategic Services, run by Allen Dulles, who had arrived in Bern at the end of 1941. Dulles not only managed to get in touch with dissident groups within Germany but established contacts with the partisans in northern Italy and with the French Resistance, which used the American Consulate as a channel for communicating between Resistance groups in the field and their sources of supply. Officially ignorant of Dulles' activities—he was supposed to be a legal assistant

Helmeted Swiss soldiers collect stacks of rifles from troops of the French XLV Army Corps who retreated into Switzerland on June 19, 1940. All told, about 30,000 French soldiers were interned by the Swiss.

A Swiss soldier stands guard at a World War I memorial in the border town of Le Locle. Beyond him, a short passage known as the Tunnel of the Virgin leads to occupied France, marked with a Nazi flag.

to the U.S. Ambassador—the Swiss obligingly put a secret speech-scrambling device into his transatlantic telephone line so that he could hold sensitive talks undetected.

Japan was probably the only country that had two intelligence services working at cross-purposes in Switzerland, both of them within the Japanese Embassy. The Army Intelligence Service was identified with the most intransigent prowar groups in Japan, and it exchanged intelligence regularly with the Germans. Navy intelligence, on the other hand, had ties to Japanese diplomats who toward the end of the War were cautiously exploring a separate peace with the United States. The Navy intelligence group courted Swiss diplomats, and even leaked valuable data to them because it had plans one day to use the Swiss as intermediaries with the Americans.

As for the Russians, they had no diplomatic relations with Switzerland and hence were the only Great Power without an embassy in Bern. They were therefore forced to operate from a cover organization—in this case, a Catholic publishing firm in Lucerne. From this address, and using the code name Lucy, a German resident named Rudolf Rössler fun-neled valuable military intelligence to the Russians that apparently came from the inner circles of the German High Command. The shrewd Rössler was careful to share his information with Swiss military intelligence as well.

In this frenetic atmosphere of intrigue and counterintrigue, it was said that one could not walk into Basel's German railway station, the Reichsbahnhof, or stroll through the dark arcades of Bern in the blackout, without bumping into a spy. Yet most Swiss citizens were hardly aware of the espionage campaign raging around them. Far more worrisome, in their view, were the increasing privations imposed on the public by a double blockade.

After the fall of France, strict rationing was enforced in Switzerland, and the food situation became serious. Dairy products virtually disappeared from the market; meat supplies became so scarce that the government declared two meatless days a week. Figuring on 3,200 calories as the average daily nourishment, government planners first set the Swiss ration at 3,000 calories, then reduced it to 2,400. At the same time, they began looking for ways to increase the

meager production of foodstuffs in a land where much of the terrain was more vertical than horizontal.

At great expense, marshlands were drained, forests were leveled and the total of livestock was drastically reduced to provide more cropland. Visitors to wartime Switzerland were surprised to see the citizens growing food on soccer fields and in parks, along roadsides and railroad embankments and even on their front lawns. By such efforts the Swiss nearly doubled the amount of land under cultivation, although much of the new acreage did not begin to yield crops until late in the War.

The Swiss also experienced serious shortages in other commodities, notably coal and heating oil, which soon were so scarce that the average household could keep only one room heated in winter. To conserve meager supplies of iron and steel the government published a list of items for which their use was prohibited—including signposts, bandstands and weather vanes. Private automobiles all but disappeared from the road for lack of gasoline.

Switzerland had two basic problems of supply: First, the European transport system had virtually fallen apart in the wake of war; and second, Switzerland was caught in the vise of a double blockade, between Germany and Britain, and could not tilt in one direction without feeling pressure from the other.

So devastated was the transport system by 1942 that landlocked Switzerland bought 10 freighters, designated Basel as the Swiss "seaport" for the registry of vessels, and contracted to use the ports of Genoa, Marseilles, Barcelona and Lisbon for the unloading of cargoes. But since there was almost no reliable train service, the Swiss were obliged to send their own freight cars, or sometimes trucks, to the foreign ports. The system was costly, hazardous and enormously time-consuming. In one fairly typical case, a shipment of 6,000 tons of peanuts bound for Switzerland left India in April 1940 and was passed from one Mediterranean port to another before being transferred in Cádiz to a train that was halted by a dynamited railroad bridge in France; the shipment arrived in Geneva by truck six months after it had left India.

Still, it was better to receive goods late than not to receive them at all—which is what happened to Switzerland inter-

mittently as it antagonized either the Germans or the British. Although the Swiss liked to tell themselves that they had an evenhanded trade policy, the fact is that they swung wildly with the winds of war, grossly favoring the Germans in the first years and the Allies at the end.

Given the contrary aims, it was inevitable that Switzerland would become involved in a three-way tug of war. The Allies wanted essential war materials from the Swiss, and were determined to deny them to the Germans. Faced with shortages of coal, iron and oil, the Germans wanted to reduce the export of these materials to Switzerland while increasing imports of strategic Swiss-manufactured goods. As for the Swiss, they wanted to maintain their neutrality, feed their people and carry on a lively trade. In support of their aims, the Allies had their sea blockade, the Germans a land-and-sea blockade and the threat of force, and the Swiss little more than guile and a genius for procrastination.

Until 1942, the Germans had things pretty much their way. Immediately after the fall of France they cut off all coal supplies to Switzerland and refused to budge until the Swiss signed a new trade agreement. Under its terms, the Germans got more arms (the excellent Oerlikon light antiaircraft gun), more aluminum and dairy products—and broad credit terms to pay for them, an important consideration for a country like Germany that was critically short of foreign currency. The Germans also asked for more electric power to run their factories, and the Swiss agreed to sell them huge additional quantities. Finally, the Germans wanted an increase in the transit of goods moving to and from Italy over Swiss railroads; by agreement, the traffic was increased by nearly 40 per cent over the prewar level.

The Allies bitterly protested these concessions, and were tempted to impose a total blockade, cutting off Switzerland from its overseas imports. What restrained them was the knowledge that this would put Switzerland completely under Axis control. In addition, Allied factories needed the special machine tools, precision instruments and timing devices that the Swiss alone could provide.

The wonder is that during this period of German ascendancy the Swiss were able to export to the Allies at all. They managed it by arguing that if their trade with the Allies were severed they would no longer have access to the raw materials they needed to make the bearings, fuses, electrical

Bystanders watch from the field's edge as urban farmers harvest wheat in a Zurich park. To increase domestic production of food, the Swiss also cultivated schoolyards, athletic fields and even amusement parks.

A civilian pours hot tea for artillerymen on maneuvers in December of 1942. To reduce the financial hardship of military duty, mobilized soldiers were paid according to their civilian salaries and family size.

machinery and other equipment they exported to Germany.

Reluctantly, the Germans agreed. A German industrial commission drew up a list of products for which it was prepared to issue *Geleitscheine*—transit permits equivalent to the British navicerts. Most items on the list were of no direct military value—Swiss typewriters, for example, which were available at Macy's department store in New York throughout the War. But the Germans also had to include a certain quantity of industrial products such as machine tools and instruments, which they knew would aid the Allied war effort. In return, the British sent the Swiss copper, rubber, nickel, tinplate and steel sheets—all potentially useful in the manufacture of goods for Germany.

In 1942 the Germans restricted Swiss trade with the Allies to a value not exceeding $125,000 per month. A vigorous smuggling traffic arose, however, in goods that the Germans refused to pass. A British attaché in Bern, John Lomax, devoted all his time to the smuggling traffic. He smuggled out manufactured goods via businessmen and diplomats, and sometimes even by mail, after disguising the items involved. Thus the inner movements of high-precision stop watches were smuggled in ordinary watchcases, and delicate machine parts used in the manufacture of RAF bomb winches were installed in phonographs. Jewel bearings were concealed in recesses in rolled-up newspapers that were sent to cover addresses in Lisbon, and from there to London.

Yet the disproportion in Switzerland's trade with the belligerents remained enormous. Swiss arms exports to Germany in 1941 were four times what they had been before the War, while arms exports to the Allies, not surprisingly, fell to zero. Even counting Switzerland's increased trade with the Allies in the later years of the War, total Swiss exports to Germany were triple those to the Allies. That imbalance—plus the apparent eagerness with which some Swiss manufacturers and bankers catered to German interests—

caused angry feelings on the Allied side, compounded by a sense of helplessness. For much of the War, the only option for Allied negotiators, one of them recalled, was to "combat Nazi force with moral suasion—an unequal contest." The Swiss themselves felt pangs of guilt. A popular Swiss adage had it that "six days a week we work for the Germans; on the seventh day we pray for the Allies."

The situation began to change at the end of 1942, with the Germans retreating in Africa and stalled in the East. Step by step, the Allies began to force reductions of Swiss exports to Germany, using the pressure of the blockade as well as the threat of black-listing individual Swiss firms. Recognizing that the initiative in the War was shifting to the Allies, the Swiss made some adjustments—as deliberately as possible, for at this point no one could be sure that the pendulum might not swing back to the Axis. Export of fuses to Germany was cut by one fourth, for example, and exports of gas and diesel engines were reduced. Wringing such concessions, recalled Dean Acheson, then an Assistant U.S. Secretary of State, was a task that "moved at a glacial rate." But toward the end of 1943 the Allied military situation improved markedly, and pressures on the Swiss increased accordingly. Now they agreed to cut back their most important strategic exports to Germany by 60 per cent.

At midwar, the Swiss were beset by many pressures other than economic ones. For one thing, Switzerland was increasingly in physical jeopardy. As the Allied air offensive mounted in intensity, so did violations of Swiss airspace, and some of the planes dropped their bombs on Swiss territory. Such incidents were usually the result of navigational error—but not always. In the summer of 1943, when the Allies were putting the Swiss under particularly heavy pressure to cut back on their exports to Germany, RAF planes dropped several bombs near a ball-bearing factory in Zurich, an act that enraged but duly warned the Swiss.

In general, both Allies and Axis were unrepentant about such incidents, whether accidental or deliberate. Apologizing in 1941 for two RAF bombings of Swiss villages, British Foreign Minister Anthony Eden managed not to apologize at all: "Fighting as they are for the traditions of freedom, of which the Swiss Confederation has in former times been the protagonist in European history," said Eden blandly, "His Majesty's government feels entitled to claim the forbearance of the Swiss people."

Forbearing or merely cautious, the Swiss refrained from loud public criticism of Allied bombing incidents until April 1, 1944, when 20 American planes dropped 400 bombs on the Swiss border town of Schaffhausen, causing 150 casualties and leaving 50 buildings in rubble. The outraged Swiss President called in the U.S. Ambassador and charged that the attack had been deliberate. In fact, the American crews had been aiming for the nearby German city of Tuttlingen: The two cities were only 21 miles apart. The United States apologized and promised compensation, which was set at $62 million. Before the sum was paid in 1949, the ever-practical Swiss antagonized the Allies once again by demanding—and receiving—payment of interest from the day of the bombing.

According to the meticulous bookkeeping of the Swiss air command, foreign aircraft violated Swiss airspace 6,501 times during the War—and 268 planes were forced to land

Civilian and military fire fighters attempt to extinguish the flames in Basel's railroad station after an accidental bombing by the Royal Air Force in December 1940. The ancient border city was bombed once more by Allied aircraft in March of 1945.

Smoke rises from Schaffhausen after the Swiss town was hit by U.S. bombs on April 1, 1944. The Americans mistook Schaffhausen for German territory because of its location north of the Rhine River, which forms a long stretch of the Swiss-German border.

and accept internment. How many times Switzerland's ground frontiers were violated nobody knows—but in the War's early years the Swiss were at extraordinary pains to protect them. Because of its central, isolated position in Europe, Switzerland became the goal for countless multitudes fleeing war and persecution. Faced with hordes of foreigners trying to cross their borders, the Swiss were torn between a desire to help and a desire to protect their jobs and the character of their insular society.

A stream of refugees made their way to Switzerland all through the 1930s, but the first mass influx occurred only with the fall of France. Waves of French soldiers and civilians sought temporary refuge that the Swiss usually granted. Then Vichy France declared 170,000 French Jews "undesirable," and the Swiss, fearing a new influx, decided their country could absorb no more than 7,000 displaced persons—and they must be "political" refugees. "Our little lifeboat is full," said one Swiss official.

Under these stringent restrictions, Swiss border guards turned back thousands of French Jews desperately fleeing deportation roundups. When some committed suicide rather than return, Swiss officers began refusing to expel those who had managed to slip over the border. The Chief of the Federal Police himself went to the frontier, witnessed the bands of desperate people trying to cross and ordered that the ban be lifted.

Soon public protest meetings throughout the country forced the Swiss government to liberalize its refugee policy: After 1942, the number of incoming refugees mounted steadily. The Italian surrender in 1943 prompted 4,000 Italian Jews to flee to Switzerland rather than risk death under the occupying Germans. At the same time, 20,000 Allied prisoners of war who had fled from Italian prison camps swarmed over the Swiss border. By the last months of the War there were 115,000 refugees in camps in Switzerland and thousands more living in hotels and pensions or being cared for by private relief organizations and friends. It was estimated that 300,000 refugees and immigrants had found temporary or permanent Swiss asylum.

Switzerland's humanitarian record outside its borders was in some ways better—or at least more coherent—than it was at home. From the beginning of the fighting, Switzerland had the often-thankless task of serving as the "protecting power" representing the interests of numerous countries

A Swiss fighter—its wing tip visible at right—guides down a stray American B-24 bomber.

INTERNING A FLEET OF TRESPASSERS

As the air war over Europe intensified, the number of violations of Swiss airspace increased dramatically—in April of 1944 alone there were 650 incursions. And by now, most of the violators were American daylight raiders.

Some of the American overflights were accidents of navigation. Others, though peaceful, were deliberate—as when U.S. pilots flew into Switzerland with damaged planes or wounded crewmen that could not survive the trip home. The Swiss had orders first to warn the intruders by radio, flares or a shot across the nose, instructing them to follow and land. If the warnings were ignored, the Swiss were authorized to open fire with intent to shoot down.

Eventually, 150 American B-17s and B-24s were interned. The planes were lined up in neat rows at Swiss air bases, and their crews were housed in Alpine resort hotels made vacant by the War.

As many as a dozen bombers landed at Dübendorf Air Base near Zurich in a single day. Most came passively, but a few had to be forced down. More than one—mistaking German-built Swiss Messerschmitts for Luftwaffe fighters—opened fire before receiving the Swiss warning.

The crew of one undamaged Flying Fortress landed so willingly that the Swiss were baffled. It turned out the Americans had mistaken the markings on the Swiss fighters—a white cross on a red field—for another, similar insignia in which the colors were reversed. Thus, when a Swiss officer asked the bomber pilot why he had not resisted, the American was offended. "Why," he said, "it would never occur to me to shoot at a Red Cross plane!"

American B-17s and twin-ruddered B-24s crowd a field at Dübendorf in May of 1945. The Swiss held the planes until after Japan surrendered.

American airmen stroll on the picturesque main street of Adelboden, a ski resort outside Bern where almost 600 fliers were interned.

at war with one another—including the interests of the United States in Germany and of Germany in the United States. The Swiss looked after diplomatic property, arranged the exchange of interned civilians and diplomatic personnel—900 Americans interned in Germany and Italy were exchanged for a similar number of Germans and Italians interned in America—and arranged for the transfer of funds from families to displaced persons in foreign countries. For performing these services Switzerland received scant thanks. The Germans always suspected that Switzerland favored the United States in its representations between the two countries, and the American press accused Switzerland of being an agent of the Nazis.

One of Switzerland's prime tasks as a protecting power was the inspection of prison camps in both Germany and the United States—a duty it shared with the International Committee of the Red Cross (pages 186-203). This was in some ways fortunate, for the committee had its headquarters in Geneva, which permitted unusually close cooperation between its delegates (all of whom were Swiss) and the

Swiss government. Prison-camp inspections, according to the Geneva Convention of 1929, were supposed to be the responsibility of the protecting powers, but in fact the Red Cross very quickly became involved through its program of distributing relief parcels to prisoners. Some countries— Germany for one—elected to have their camps inspected by the International Committee rather than by the protecting power on the ground that it infringed their sovereignty less to be scrutinized by a private organization than by a foreign government.

As a place of haven, Switzerland appealed to the Germans as well as to the Allies—but for different reasons. Nazi leaders saw it as an ideal hiding place for assets plundered from occupied Europe. In the waning months of the War, the interest of the Allied economic negotiators began to shift from Swiss exports to Germany, which were decreasing rapidly, and to focus on enemy holdings in Switzerland—especially the gold that had flowed from Germany into Swiss banks. The Allies suspected that the financial services of Switzerland were far more important to

Germany than Swiss exports. Indeed, the Germans' need for the Swiss financial and gold markets was thought to be one of the main reasons they had failed to invade.

Allied negotiators began pressing the Swiss hard for information about individual and corporate German assets being held by Swiss banks. The problem was that Swiss bankers were protected both by law and by long tradition from divulging the secrets of their clients, whoever they might be. Indeed, Switzerland's bank-secrecy law makes it a crime for banks to reveal to anyone, even the Swiss government, the holdings and transactions of their customers. Accordingly, the Swiss refused the Allies' initial demands. In retaliation, the U.S. government froze Swiss funds in America, amounting to $1.5 billion.

Because they feared permanently losing the American market—and of being accused by the rest of Europe of economic collaboration with Germany—the Swiss reluctantly agreed in March 1945 to make an inventory of all foreign holdings. But they insisted that although they would turn their findings over to the Allies, no foreign agencies would be allowed to assist in the inventory. Thus the Allies had to accept on faith what information the Swiss gave them. This immediately became a new point of contention—for the Swiss put German assets at $250 million, whereas the Allies said they must be at least three times as much.

The situation was further complicated by the fact that the Allies were now claiming title to all German-owned assets in neutral countries, to be used for reparations. Switzerland vigorously denied that the Allies had any right to property within Swiss borders. After strenuous negotiations, the Swiss agreed to a 50-50 split of German assets—half to go to the Allies and half to be retained by the Swiss against debts owed Switzerland by Germany.

There arose next the separate question of the looted gold that Germans had plundered from occupied Europe and passed on to Swiss banks. Allied investigators knew that Germany had $40 million in gold assets at the start of the War. But Switzerland alone was thought to have purchased $300 million worth of German gold in exchange for Swiss francs. The excess obviously must have been stolen from government or private holdings.

Tracing the gold was no easy task; much of it had been melted and recast, with new dates placed on the bars. Still, the Germans found it difficult to use plundered gold openly in monetary transactions, for the Allies had declared that in international financial dealings they would recognize no gold thought to be German loot. This made other nations reluctant to handle gold that might possibly be traced to Germany. But Switzerland—with its secretive banks—was an obvious clearinghouse through which such gold could pass undetected. With the Swiss francs they obtained in exchange, the Germans bought vital ores in Turkey, Spain and Portugal, supported an anti-British uprising in Iraq and propped up the currency of Greece to enable it to sustain German-occupation costs.

Although the Swiss would give no figures for the gold they had received from Germany, they insisted that the $300 million the Allies claimed was grossly exaggerated. The only gold that the Swiss would acknowledge was $58 million known to have been plundered by the Germans from the national banks of Belgium and France. This sum they agreed to pay back in settlement of all claims for looted gold in Switzerland.

Although the Allies revised their original estimate of Swiss holdings downward by $100 million and more, they were by no means satisfied that the Swiss had surrendered all the Nazi gold they possessed. When the dispute was at its hottest in early 1946, Switzerland was suddenly flooded with 20-franc gold coins bearing the dates 1935 and 1937—leading to Allied speculation that the Swiss were minting new coins and predating them to unburden themselves of some of their excess Nazi gold. But Allied investigators never were able to prove that Switzerland held more gold than it had acknowledged, and ultimately the case was closed.

In their financial dealings throughout the War, noted the Swiss historian Heinz K. Meier, the Swiss were guided by "the principle so dear to them, that private property was inviolate." If their insistence on that principle to the exclusion of moral judgments sometimes maddened the Allies, their humanitarian activities won them the grudging admiration of both Allies and Axis. One Swiss writer observed that his countrymen "exercised resistance spiritually and collaboration materially"—a formula that to their own considerable surprise enabled the Swiss to survive in the most exposed position occupied by any of the neutral states.

Clustered behind concertina wire, refugees in April of 1945 await entrance to Switzerland at Ramsen on the German border. The Swiss let in almost 300,000 refugees during the War, including 29,000 Jews.

SPAIN'S BITTER LEGACY

Guernica, Pablo Picasso's mural masterpiece depicting a Basque town torn asunder by bombs, evokes the destructive heritage of the Spanish Civil War.

RESTORING A DIVIDED NATION

The onset of World War II found Spain a nation already physically and emotionally shattered. The trials of Generalissimo Francisco Franco's Nationalists were only beginning when they completed the rout of Spain's Republican government early in 1939. After almost three years of merciless Civil War, the Spanish people were hungry, in large part homeless, and still bitterly divided. Life was so hard and rife with disappointment, one mother recalled, that her young son "forgot how to cry."

The new government's most pressing problem was to feed the people. The Civil War had left Spanish agriculture prostrate. Hundreds of thousands of work animals—horses, mules and oxen—had been slaughtered for food, making the planting and harvesting of crops especially arduous. Then a persistent series of droughts turned much of the arable Spanish countryside to dust.

As a result, Spain had to seek millions of tons of grain and other foodstuffs from foreign sources in the years that coincided with World War II. The task was complicated by Britain's wartime naval blockade, which limited imports of food to Spain so Franco could not send surpluses to the Axis. The food that got through was barely enough to keep the nation alive. "Your stomach hurt so much you couldn't stand up straight," said a peasant in Spanish Andalusia. "People fell down and died in the streets, just like that."

Many people also lacked shelter. Large sections of Madrid, Barcelona and other cities were in ruins, and scores of smaller towns had been utterly destroyed. The Nationalists, operating with a war-depleted treasury, did what they could to restore the hardest-hit communities, paying special attention to Guernica, the town that Picasso's mural had immortalized as a symbol of war's brutality.

But for the defeated Republicans there was no amnesty. A soldier returning to his devastated village encountered the omnipresent Guardia Civil, or national police. If the Guardia found a man's name on a nebulous "enemies" list, he was arrested and summarily tried. The verdict was usually death by firing squad, or at best a prison term.

Republican soldiers of the International Brigade, defeated by Franco, tearfully render their clenched-fist salute at a final muster in Barcelona.

Nationalists give a Fascist salute at a ceremony in the debris-strewn courtyard of Toledo's Alcazar Palace, where they withstood a 71-day Republican siege.

"ENDURING THE HUNGRIEST YEARS"

By 1940, many thousands of Spaniards had died of starvation—victims of the terrible drought's scorched fields and withered crops. Oranges were so precious that grove owners hired guards to shoot poachers. "We have always been a hungry nation," said a priest, "but those years were the hungriest and the hardest of our lives."

Though they toiled mightily during the barren years, Spain's farmers were hampered because much of the irrigation system had been destroyed in the Civil War, and many nitrate-fertilizer plants had been converted to gunpowder production—in case Spain entered the war in Europe.

The government sought food from every quarter and began constructing new irrigation canals. Still, Spain went hungry. New droughts seared the country from 1942 to 1944, and strict rationing was necessary until 1952.

Under the scrutiny of guards, political prisoners dig an irrigation canal near Seville.

After three consecutive years of drought, the Manzanares River, which normally supplied water to Madrid, is reduced in the fall of 1945 to a muddy trickle.

Beneath a portrait of Generalissimo Francisco Franco, women and children wait in line with pails for their daily ration of milk. After the Civil War, the government rationed more than 80 different food items.

In a Valencia prison, inmates assemble for Mass in 1943. The government considered Republicans anticlerical and attempted to reindoctrinate them.

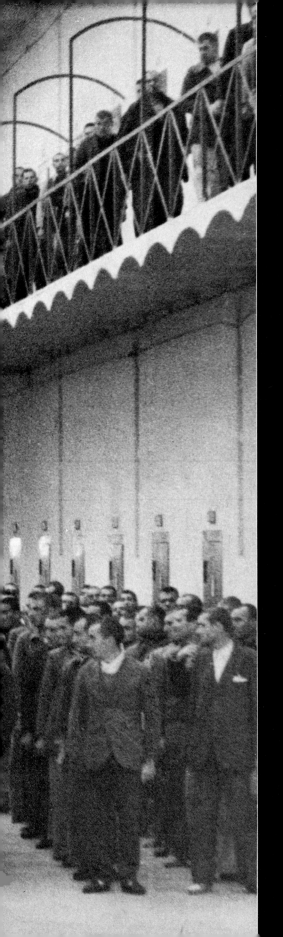

Women inmates (top) enjoy an hour in the sun with their children, who lived in prison with their mothers until they were five years old, when they were transferred to state institutions. Twice a year the children were allowed to visit their fathers, who were in separate prisons (bottom).

A POLICY OF REVENGE AND "REDEMPTION"

The Nationalists wanted to put their Civil War foes to work rebuilding Spain, but first they intended to exact revenge. An Italian diplomat visiting Spain in July 1939 reported "a great number of shootings. In Madrid alone, between 200 and 250 a day, in Barcelona 150, in Seville 80."

Although the political executions continued for several years, Franco did offer a program of "redemption": Prisoners who worked for the state could earn a reduction of two days in their sentences for each day of labor. The program was largely a failure, however, because the government required participants first to undergo a rigid reeducation that included public admission of their ideological sins. The Republicans remained so embittered toward their Nationalist captors that few of them chose to recant, and by 1941 only 8 per cent of Spain's 233,373 political prisoners had been put to work.

On a battle-ravaged hillside in central Spain, pick-wielding workers begin the job of reconstruction. The government paid such laborers the equivalent of 80 cents a day—just enough to feed a family of four.

plants made such reclamation projects necessary in every Spanish city.

BUILDING A "NEW SPAIN" FROM THE GROUND UP

The Civil War left much of Spain a rubble heap. More than half a million homes were uninhabitable, 2,000 churches were in ruins, 3 out of 4 bridges were unusable, and 173 towns were so devastated they had to be rebuilt from the ground up.

The Nationalist government "adopted" 90 of the wrecked towns, giving them priority for reconstruction so they could stand as showpieces of Franco's España Nueva—New Spain. Elsewhere, the rebuilding of Spain went on in fits and starts. In most towns, the central plazas and public buildings were restored first. The financially strained government could not construct new housing units quickly enough to meet the shortage, and for years the poor were forced to live in the streets, or in makeshift shelters (overleaf).

HOMES FOR THE DISPOSSESSED

Members of an impoverished Madrid family (above) assemble outside their home, an abandoned crypt they have made habitable by breaking down partitions between individual burial niches. By 1940, the government was able to move thousands of Madrileños out of such makeshift dwellings into raw but solid new developments (right).

3

Generalissimo Franco's moment of triumph
Reflected glory for Portugal's Salazar
A "nonbelligerent" tilt toward Berlin
Secret Spanish bases for German U-boats
The bloodless conquest of Tangier
An invitation to share the invasion of Gibraltar
A Nazi plot to unseat the Caudillo
Hitler's praise for "the only tough Latins"
Lisbon's fears of a Spanish invasion
A U.S. airliner saved by Germany's spy chief
The Portuguese islands that everybody wanted

In the spring of 1939, the peoples of the Iberian Peninsula watched anxiously as the Great Powers edged toward war. Since the days of Napoleon they had lived in virtual isolation from the European mainstream, and now they had special reasons to avoid the looming conflict. Spain was just emerging from its own terrible Civil War, while Portugal was prospering modestly under its first stable government in two generations. Behind the barriers imposed by the Atlantic and the Mediterranean and by the rugged Pyrenees, the leaders of both nations hoped to remain isolated politically as well as geographically.

But neither Germany nor Great Britain was prepared to allow them an easy neutrality. Spain and Portugal contained Europe's only large quantities of wolfram ore, which was crucial in the production of armor-piercing shells. And, despite Iberia's relative isolation, each country held a vital position on the map of Europe. Spain was an uneasy neighbor to British Gibraltar, the massive rock fortress that controlled the western entrance to the Mediterranean; Portugal ruled the Azores, an Atlantic island chain whose possession could give an aggressive navy control of the southern shipping lanes between Europe and America.

Spain's Generalissimo Francisco Franco y Bahamonde and Portugal's Prime Minister António de Oliveira Salazar both realized that their countries were tempting targets for an aggressor. And they knew that if one Iberian country was drawn into war, the other would inevitably be sucked into the maelstrom. Their only course was a careful, mutually supportive neutrality—a policy that each man stretched so deftly that neither warring side was provoked into invading the peninsula.

On the morning of May 19, 1939, Francisco Franco appeared on a platform crowded with dignitaries, overlooking Madrid's expansive main boulevard, the Paseo Castellano. Behind him rose an ornate arch etched with his name and with the word *victoria*—victory. At that moment, the 47-year-old conservative revolutionary was master of all he surveyed. For two-and-a-half years, he had led the Nationalists—a coalition of military men, landowners, middle-class businessmen, Church leaders and monarchists—in a brutal Civil War against Spain's Republican regime, which had the backing of trade-unionists, peasant farmers, Communists and Socialists. With substantial military help from

DICTATORS ON A HIGH WIRE

Germany and Italy, Franco's Nationalists had prevailed over the Soviet-backed Republicans. Now, the *Caudillo,* or Leader, stood to receive the salute of his Army.

The city of Madrid, which had suffered until very recently under Nationalist siege, was gilded splendidly for the occasion. Roses and carnations carpeted the parade route and balconies were draped with colorful flags and banners. On orders of their new government, hundreds of thousands of Madrileños lined the Paseo Castellano to watch the five-hour spectacle.

Significantly, a battalion of Italians led the parade·of victorious troops. Italian dictator Benito Mussolini had contributed 40,000 men as well as planes and tanks to the Nationalist cause. Various units of the Spanish Army followed, including foreign legionnaires, fierce-visaged Moroccans and members of the Falange, the right-wing political party that had supported Franco's rise to power. At one point, a score of warplanes flew low over the city that lately had been a target for their bombs.

Nazi Germany's Condor Legion, 6,000 strong, was the last unit to pass. The Germans' position, like the Italians', was one of honor, earned in battle. Franco had recently signed a treaty of friendship with Hitler and had taken pains to reassure him of "the friendship of a people who in their hardest hours discovered their true friends."

No matter how grand, the victory celebration could not hide the fact that the ordeal of Civil War had brought Spain to its knees, shattering its people, laying waste its fields and paralyzing its industry. An estimated 500,000 men, women and children had died and two million more had been wounded. In May of 1939, Spain's 26 million surviving citizens were faced with malnutrition and the very real possibility of starvation, for the Civil War had hit the farmers with particular ferocity. Nearly 40 per cent of the country's horses and 25 per cent of its cattle had perished during the conflict. The Republicans had destroyed much of the mechanized farm equipment owned by the rich landowners, and in many areas men and women had to drag plows to rend the sere earth for planting. Spanish agriculture, lamented one farmer, had "reverted to the Middle Ages."

Indeed, the Spanish were beginning a period they would remember as the "Years of Hunger," in which the nation's countless poor would survive by eating a thick porridge of potato peels, known as San Antonio *puré,* and a watery soup made from wild grass.

Though Franco desperately needed to import large quantities of food, he could not pay for it with cash. Spain's treasury was as bare as its larder: The Republicans had used the nation's gold reserves to buy arms from the Soviet Union, and the Nationalists had fallen deep into debt to Germany and Italy for the same reason. In all, the Civil War had cost Spain more than nine billion dollars. But Franco could acquire food in trade for one of Spain's few remaining resources, wolfram ore, which contained tungsten, an element that was used to harden steel for artillery shells and had countless other military applications; the Germans also needed tungsten steel to make precision tools. The Spanish leader deemed it wise to sell the precious ore to both Germany and Britain. Germany's help during the Civil War and the potency of its Army—as demonstrated by the Condor Legion—were reason enough to send the ore to Hitler. And if he excluded the British, Franco feared Spain would be blockaded by the Royal Navy. Winston Churchill in fact had warned earlier in 1939 that if Spain sided with Germany "General Franco's government would never be able to send another ship to sea nor receive another cargo."

Francisco Franco had labored hard to become Spain's strongman. And now, though he had dreams of empire—visions that Hitler promised to help fulfill—Franco sensed that joining the Axis at the War's outset would be a rash, if not suicidal, act. Spain needed time to recover, time Franco would gain by keeping Hitler at arm's length.

In Lisbon, Prime Minister Salazar had hailed Franco's victory in the Civil War as a victory for Portugal as well. During the years of conflict, Salazar had kept Portugal neutral in word, but in deed he had given Franco his complete support. He had allowed Germany and Italy to channel supplies through Portugal to the Nationalists and he had sent thousands of "volunteers" to fight for the rebels. He also had obliged Franco by deporting thousands of Republican refugees back to Spain—and almost certain imprisonment or death. Now Salazar basked in reflected glory. "In every sphere where our action was not restricted," he told the National Assembly, "we helped as much as possible Spanish nationalism and Christian civilization. We expended effort, lost lives, ran risks, shared suffering and we have no claims to make nor any little bills to present. We won, that is all.''

Most important, the deeply conservative Salazar regarded the Franco regime as ''a barrier between Portugal and Iberian Communism,'' which he saw as a disease that might infect Portugal and weaken the stable rule he had imposed over the past six years.

Before Salazar joined the government, Portugal had suffered a dizzying succession of rulers; nearly 50 different governments had come and gone between 1910 and 1928. Portugal was a country, wrote a British journalist, ''where anarchy had a free hand.'' Such instability had reduced Portugal to virtual bankruptcy. In April of 1928, the junta then in power invited Salazar, a widely respected professor of economics at Coimbra University, to become Minister of Finance. The 39-year-old Salazar, whom one contemporary described as ''a hermetic man with a tendency to austerity,'' agreed to take the post—but only if he were given control of all government spending. ''I must be obeyed without question,'' he told the politicians who had summoned him to Lisbon. ''If you do not agree, remember that three hours on the train will take me back to Coimbra.''

The junta agreed to Salazar's terms. He began boldly, decreeing that any bureaucrat who exceeded his budget

would be thrown in prison. The threat evidently worked, for by the end of 1929 Portugal had a balanced budget. Four years later, when Salazar became Prime Minister, he established syndicates of workers and employers modeled on those in Fascist Italy. In the process, he turned Portugal into a totalitarian state that he could describe proudly in 1939 as ''antiparliamentarian, antidemocratic and antiliberal.''

On March 17, 1939, Salazar and Franco signed a treaty called informally the Iberian Pact. Under its terms, the two neighbors agreed that neither one would aid a country that attacked the other and that each would respect their 750-mile-long common border. Salazar praised the agreement as creating ''a true zone of peace in the peninsula.'' His statement was at least part rhetoric, however. For as both Franco and Salazar realized, Iberian neutrality depended almost entirely on the good will of both Britain and Germany and on the thrust of events elsewhere.

Six months later, on the day Germany invaded Poland, Salazar declared Portuguese neutrality. He told the National Assembly that Hitler had agreed to respect the territorial integrity of both Portugal and its overseas possessions—notably Mozambique and Angola in southern Africa and the Azores and Cape Verde Islands in the eastern Atlantic. Great Britain had made similar assurances, said Salazar, and had agreed not to invoke the treaty of Windsor, which since 1386 had bound the two countries to mutual assistance. The British had last used the treaty to draw Portugal into the First World War, at a cost of 7,222 Portuguese lives.

Franco quickly followed Salazar's lead. On September 3, he broadcast an appeal for peace to Great Britain and Germany, ''whose hands could unchain a catastrophe unparalleled in history.'' He called on the two sides ''to spare other people the sufferings and tragedies that befell Spain'' and decreed ''the strictest neutrality for all Spanish subjects.''

Franco's decree was for public and diplomatic consumption. He sent private assurances to Berlin that he would tilt Spanish neutrality in favor of Germany whenever he could. Salazar, for his part, took steps to distance himself from Britain, declaring that ''Portugal claims as a neutral the right to trade with other neutrals and with the belligerents, to look for supplies wherever we consider it convenient.'' Thus the two Iberian dictators walked out onto a diplomatic high

From the highest point on a stage filled with dignitaries, Generalissimo Francisco Franco y Bahamonde returns the salute of a motorcycle formation in the vanguard of more than 100,000 troops he reviewed on the 19th of May, 1939, to celebrate his victory in Spain's Civil War.

wire, one on which the slightest misstep by either might send both Spain and Portugal tumbling into war.

For a few months, Franco diligently curried favor with both sides. In January 1940 he signed a trade agreement with France for wheat, phosphates and automobiles in exchange for oranges, iron ore, lead, zinc and mercury, and he got a $10-million credit from Great Britain to purchase goods within the British Commonwealth. At the same time, he agreed to allow Germany to reprovision and refuel submarines in Spanish ports. The only condition he laid down was that the Germans had to conduct their operations in secret, lest the British take reprisals against Spain.

The *U-25* was the first submarine to use a Spanish port, gliding into Cádiz harbor on the evening of January 3, and mooring alongside the German merchant ship *Thalia*. Four hours later, the restocked *U-25* slipped back out to sea. Elated by the ease of the event, the Germans rapidly extended their refueling operations to the ports of Vigo on the Atlantic, Las Palmas in the Canary Islands and Cartagena in the Mediterranean. They also stocked the Spanish Navy base at Cartagena with a supply of U-boat parts.

Franco soon granted the Germans more concessions, allowing them to set up a radio station at La Coruña, in northern Spain, and to fly their own weather reconnaissance planes from Spanish bases under Spanish insignia. Franco's largesse, however, was not enough for Luftwaffe chief Hermann Göring, who complained to a Spanish general visiting Berlin that ''Spain's behavior is super-neutral'' and demanded to know when Spain would enter the War.

The general, Air Minister Fernando Barrón y Ortiz, had no answer. In all likelihood, Franco himself was not sure if and when he would become Hitler's comrade-in-arms, but he seemed noticeably impressed by Germany's initial military triumphs. When the Germans rolled through the Netherlands, Belgium and Luxembourg and crossed into France, Franco remarked admiringly to an aide, ''The Germans have a good eye. They always pick the right time and place.'' And he wrote in flowery terms to Hitler, ''I do not need to reassure you how great is my desire not to remain aloof from your cares.''

Then on June 10, with France about to fall, Italy declared war; three days later, Franco changed Spain's status from neutral to ''nonbelligerent.'' He liked the term because he

had seen Mussolini use it adroitly during the preceding winter, when Italy was giving loud verbal support to Hitler but declining to enter the War. The appeal of nonbelligerency to both Franco and Mussolini was that it was a kind of neutrality without legal rights or obligations—permitting them to take a pro-Axis line without risking military involvement. Publicly, Franco explained the shift by saying that now that Italy, a fellow Mediterranean nation, was at war, ''Spain needs greater freedom of action.''

On June 14, the day that Paris fell to the Germans, Franco exploited that freedom. He sent a 3,000-man force across the Strait of Gibraltar to occupy the Moroccan port of Tangier, which a seven-nation council had administered since 1923 as an international city. The bloodless undertaking buoyed the nation to dreams of further expansion. The slogan ''Algiers and Oran for Spain'' appeared on Spanish walls, and Britain's Ambassador to Madrid, Sir Samuel Hoare, was greeted wherever he went with shouts of ''*Gibraltar para España*''—''Gibraltar for Spain.'' A few weeks later, Franco gave permission for a German military team to visit Spain. Their mission: to lay the groundwork for a joint Spanish-German invasion of Gibraltar.

Admiral Wilhelm Canaris, the chief of German military intelligence, led the five-man team that traveled to Spain in late July to plan the assault on Gibraltar—code-named Operation *Felix*. Canaris' top aides were Lieut. Colonel Hans Mikosch and Captain Rudolf Witzig, heroes of the recent

Portugal's austere Prime Minister António de Oliveira Salazar wears a bowler to a 1944 political gathering in Lisbon. Though little-traveled and not a career soldier, Salazar also took the titles of Foreign Minister and War Minister to ensure his total control over Portugal's neutral course.

MOLDING A GENERATION OF ORPHANS

The Spanish Civil War produced a generation of orphans. Thousands of children whose parents had been killed or imprisoned wandered the streets in search of food and shelter. Many of them eventually were taken into custody by the Auxilio Social, the women's auxiliary of the Falange Party. The Auxilio established its first orphanage in 1936 at Valladolid, outside Madrid. By the end of the Civil War, the women's organization was running dozens of such orphanages, called family centers, where thousands of destitute children were fed, clothed and raised.

Many of those taken in were the children of the regime's Republican foes, an irony not lost on dissident Spaniards, who noted that, "First the fathers are shot, then the children get charity." Indeed, the Falange was determined to sway the children of those who had spurned its doctrines. The family centers were run with a precision its instructors had learned by studying Germany's Hitler Youth program.

The children's day began at dawn with a bugle call and an icy shower, followed by a spartan breakfast and hours of classes and exercises. The girls were taught domestic skills, while the boys drilled and paraded—all in preparation, they were told, for the time when they would restore Spain's imperial grandeur.

Street children are taken into custody by social workers. In the orphanages they would, said one critic, get "a bath, a uniform and a life of Fascist training."

At a family center in the town of Vallecas, young girls perform a Spanish folk dance as part of what their teachers referred to as ''a complete moral and physical education.''

Spanish boys in uniform salute as the flag is lowered at sundown in a government-operated school. Students at the family centers were encouraged to become members of the paramilitary Falange Youth.

commando-like German attack on the great Belgian fortress of Eban Emael. At Franco's orders, the Germans received a free hand. Mikosch tugged on an ill-fitting Spanish Army uniform and strolled close to the barbed wire and minefields that separated Gibraltar from the Spanish towns of Algeciras and La Línea. And he had a Spanish airliner fly as close to Gibraltar as the pilot dared without alarming the British. Other members of the team made their observations from villas overlooking the Rock.

The Germans were impressed by what they saw: a 1,400-foot-high limestone mountain bristling with gun emplacements. Though they could not see inside, the Germans knew Gibraltar was honeycombed with 10 miles of tunnels and guarded by 12,500 soldiers. Storming it would be a daunting task, but the Germans were confident that they could succeed if they made a large enough investment in manpower and equipment. Canaris' team estimated that the assault would take exactly 65,383 men, 13,179 tons of ammunition, 9,000 tons of fuel and 136 tons of food per day.

The attack was to begin with a 24-hour artillery barrage, followed by dive bombers. Then assault troops would sprint through the maelstrom of fire and dust toward the Rock. They would be aided by an experimental device consisting of a container of coal dust and methane gas; when detonated, the bomb caused a firedamp, which all miners fear because it absorbs oxygen so quickly that it causes almost instantaneous suffocation. The new explosive seemed perfect for the tunnels of Gibraltar.

In mid-August, Hitler agreed to Canaris' plan, and named Lieut. General Huertz Lanz, a crusty mountain trooper, to head the operation. Lanz assembled a cadre of 16,500 at a training camp near Besançon in occupied France, where he had found a craggy hill that somewhat resembled Gibraltar.

Hitler, in the meantime, continued to press Franco to enter the War at once. In reply, Franco sent his Chief of Staff, General Juan Vigón, to Berlin with a letter for the Führer. In it, Franco lavished praise on Hitler as a great general, but he also recited a litany of his country's troubles: Spain was starving and exhausted and if it entered the War, the British would seize the Canary Islands, a Spanish possession off the coast of Africa. Still, Franco wrote, he would declare war if Hitler guaranteed that Spain could have as spoils Gibraltar, French Morocco and part of French Equatorial Africa.

Franco felt he was safe in making such a sweeping list of preconditions. He knew Hitler could not cede French Morocco to Spain without upsetting the collaborationist French government in Vichy, and he was aware that Hitler coveted most of North Africa for himself. Predictably, Hitler was vexed by Franco's letter, complaining to Italy's visiting Foreign Minister Count Galeazzo Ciano that Spanish participation in the War "would cost more than it is worth."

Even as he held Hitler off, Franco made reassuring noises to the British and the Americans. He secretly sent notes to London and Washington promising that he would stay out of the War, thus keeping open the possibility of trading with them for more wheat, petroleum, rubber and cotton.

Hitler decided that it would require a personal appeal to get Franco to enter the War. He asked for a face-to-face conference, and Franco agreed to meet him on October 23, 1940, at Hendaye on the French-Spanish border. The Spanish leader arrived at 3 p.m., more than an hour late. His tardiness was deliberate. "This is the most important meeting of my life," Franco told an aide. "I'll have to use every trick I can, and this is one of them. If I make Hitler wait, he

will be at a psychological disadvantage from the start."

The two dictators greeted each other warmly, then retired to Hitler's private railroad car for talks that would stretch out more than nine hours. Franco began by again praising Hitler lavishly. Spain would gladly enter the War alongside Germany, he said, but only at the proper moment.

Now was the proper moment, Hitler insisted. The British were already defeated, they simply did not realize it yet. Hitler suggested that Franco sign a treaty that would bind him to declare war on Britain in January 1941. At that time, German panzer units and mountain troops would cross the Pyrenees and join Spanish forces in a swift conquest of Gibraltar. Spain would get the fortress, Hitler said, and perhaps parts of Africa, too.

Franco sat for a moment considering his reply. "His expression was impenetrable," recalled Paul Schmidt, Hitler's personal interpreter. "But it was clear to me that Franco, a prudent negotiator, was not going to be nailed down."

Schmidt proved to be an accurate prophet. Franco answered with a fresh recital of Spain's troubles: the terrible shock of the Civil War, the country's lack of food and modern armaments, and the British navicert system of granting shipping "passports," which enabled them to control neutral sea trade. Furthermore, Franco told Hitler, the War was not over. "The British will fight until they are worn out," he said. "Even if Great Britain is invaded, they will continue to fight in their colonies, in Canada, everywhere." Franco also reminded the Führer that the United States, in spite of its neutrality, possessed "a great potential for war."

As Franco talked, Hitler became increasingly restless. At one point, he rose to leave, telling Franco there was no use continuing the conversation. But he immediately sat down again and took a different tack. Spain, he reminded Franco, owed Germany a great debt for its help during the Civil War. Now was the time to repay that debt.

Franco agreed. Spain would fight, he said, if Germany supplied him with one million tons of wheat and let him set the time for Spain to become a belligerent. After dinner, Franco kept Hitler waiting for an hour while he took a nap. Finally, the two agreed to a secret protocol under which Germany promised to meet Spain's military and agricultural needs, and Spain promised eventually to enter the War. Spain also was to get unspecified territory in Africa.

Hitler had come to Hendaye to pin down Franco, but he left only with a vaguely worded piece of paper that Franco would twist to his own ends. "Hitler was terribly disappointed," Franco later recalled. "His greeting had been warm. His good-by was icy." In Franco, the Führer had met his diplomatic match.

When December came, Hitler sent Admiral Canaris back to Madrid to demand that Spain enter the War on January 10, 1941. In reply, Franco pointed out that he had not received so much as a bushel of grain from Hitler. His forces were preparing for combat, Franco said, but he refused to commit himself to a date for joining the Axis or for storming Gibraltar. Canaris' report was the last straw. Hitler canceled Operation *Felix* and turned to the air to battle the British in the Mediterranean, sending several crack Luftwaffe units to Sicily to bedevil the Royal Navy.

Twice more, in 1941, Hitler tried to prod Franco to act. First, he sent Mussolini to plead with him. But Mussolini had little stomach for his task, being more concerned with the battering his armies were taking in Greece and in North Africa. According to Franco, at one point he asked the Italian dictator bluntly, " 'Duce, if you could get out of the War, would you?' He started to laugh, raised his arms to the sky and cried, 'If only I could, if only I could.' "

Then Hitler wrote Franco an impassioned letter, promising to ship Spain 100,000 tons of grain on the day Franco set a date for the Gibraltar operation. But Franco kept increasing the ante, and the time was coming when Hitler could spare only words, not goods. Soon he would have to rescue Mussolini's reeling forces, and then he would become embroiled in the fateful invasion of the Soviet Union.

Despite Franco's adroit refusals to enter the War, he showed a pronounced tilt toward Germany that increased dramatically after the fall of France. Factories in Barcelona, Seville and Valencia turned out war goods for the Germans, including submarine engines, rifle cartridges, parachutes and uniforms. The Spanish also shipped large quantities of both wolfram and mercury to the Reich; in return they received a handful of modern aircraft and artillery pieces. In April of 1941 Spain agreed to send 100,000 workers to Germany—a figure Franco eventually whittled down to 20,000.

The British were quite aware that Spain was helping to

Citizens of Tangier (far left) greet an invading column of Spanish cavalry with the Falange Party salute. In June 1940, Spain sent a detachment of 3,000 troops, including the Moroccan desert fighters at near left, to occupy the strategic North African city opposite Gibraltar.

fuel the German war machine; nevertheless, they gave Franco a credit of $12.5 million that spring to buy food and raw materials and they eased their navicert system in Spain's favor. To do otherwise, Ambassador Hoare told his superiors, "would definitely play into Hitler's hands."

On June 22, Hitler invaded the Soviet Union, and Franco responded vigorously by calling for Spanish volunteers "to destroy Communism, the nightmare of our generation." Within three weeks, the first of 47,000 men who formed a force known as the Blue Division (pages 92-105) entrained for the long journey to the Russian front. By sending the Blue Division to fight as part of the Wehrmacht, Franco had satisfied Hitler's demands for Spanish participation in the War. Yet he had not actually declared war, which mollified Great Britain, for London continued both diplomatic relations and economic aid. Once again, Franco had maintained his equilibrium on the high wire.

In December, when Japan attacked Pearl Harbor and the United States entered the War, Franco allowed the Spanish press to rant against the Americans. But in private he told American diplomat Myron Taylor that not one but three wars were now being waged across the globe. First, he said, there was the war in Western Europe—a war of commercial and imperial interests—which Spain wanted desperately to avoid. Then there was the war between Germany and the Soviet Union; here he felt bound to side with Hitler against Russia's "Godless hordes." Lastly, there was the war in the Pacific. This, said Franco, was a struggle between the United States, the defender of the Philippines' Spanish culture, and the "barbarian hordes" of Japan. And in this conflict, Spain's sympathies lay with the United States.

Franco believed fervently in this three-war theory, which he communicated to Taylor in his study in the Pardo Palace, flanked by portraits of Hitler, Mussolini and Pope Pius XII. But he was not at all sure he had convinced the Allies of his good intentions toward them. Rather, he feared that they might invade Spain at any moment. Early in 1942 he sought reassurance from Portugal's Salazar, who had so far maintained more cordial relations with the Western Allies.

The two men met on February 12 in the Spanish city of Badajoz. Franco was worried, he told Salazar, that an Anglo-American force was about to land on the Portuguese Azores as a prelude to an invasion of Portugal and Spain. Salazar, who served as his own foreign minister, assured Franco that he had met recently with the British Ambassador to Lisbon. From his conversations, he was certain that all of Iberia was safe from Allied invasion.

Franco's relief was obvious. The next day he made his first public trip through Spain since the Civil War. In Seville he told a gathering of Army officers that "if one day the road to Berlin lay open, it would not be a mere division of volunteers but a million men who would offer themselves to defend it against the Red hordes." With Spain apparently safe from Allied attack, such words were a cheap price to pay if they kept Hitler happy and maintained the status quo.

Franco's rhetoric may have soothed Hitler, but it did not have the same effect on German Foreign Minister Joachim von Ribbentrop or SS Brigadier General Walter Schellenberg, Chief of Foreign Intelligence. Tired of Franco's wavering, they began plotting his overthrow. Their plan centered on replacing Franco with General Agustín Muñoz Grandes, the respected leader of the Blue Division.

Muñoz Grandes became a willing accomplice to the plot, for he was eager to bring Spain into the War and to drive the British from Gibraltar. "I am prepared to stake everything, even myself, for friendship with Germany," he informed Ribbentrop in June. "My driving force is hatred for England, which has oppressed my country for centuries."

According to the scenario, Muñoz Grandes would return home in triumph from his exploits against the Russians and demand that Spain join the Axis. If Franco stalled, the Germans would underline Muñoz Grandes' demands by bombing Madrid. And if even that did not persuade Franco to declare war, Muñoz Grandes would organize a coup and form a new government that would.

Somehow, Franco heard of the German plot to unseat him; as in his dealings with Hitler, his reaction was slow and calculating. In August, he fired his brother-in-law, Foreign Minister Ramón Serrano Súñer, the most pro-German member of the Cabinet. Franco did not know whether Serrano Súñer was plotting against him, but he was taking no chances. He replaced Serrano Súñer with General Count Francisco Jordana, a well-known Anglophile. For the moment, he left Muñoz Grandes in place.

If Franco was looking for an excuse to put more distance

between himself and Hitler, the German plot provided it. A few weeks later, the Nazis angered Franco further when a U-boat sank the Spanish freighter *Monte Gorbea* off Martinique, sending thousands of tons of Argentine wheat destined for Spain to the bottom of the Caribbean. In retaliation, Franco ordered the Germans to halt their secret submarine resupply operations in Spain, and to enforce the order he posted guards on the German merchant ships involved. Then, in November, came an Allied offensive that moved Franco toward genuine neutrality.

On Sunday, November 8, 1942, American Ambassador Carlton Hayes awoke Count Jordana at 1 a.m. and asked for an immediate interview with Franco to relay an urgent message from President Roosevelt. When Jordana told Hayes that Franco was away hunting, the diplomat took Jordana into his confidence and handed him FDR's letter.

The Allies, Roosevelt had written, were in the process of invading North Africa. "These moves are in no shape, manner or form directed against the government of Spain or Spanish Morocco or Spanish territories," he added. "Spain has nothing to fear from the United States."

"I have never seen a man's face change expression so quickly and so completely as Jordana's," Hayes later wrote. "From one of intense anxiety, it was now one of intense relief." Jordana finished the letter and smiled. "Ah," he sighed, "so Spain is not involved."

Over the following days, the Spanish government sought similar assurances from the Germans that they would not try to use Spain as a shortcut to North Africa. Berlin replied that guarantees were not needed among friends—then requested permission to move troops across Spain. Franco refused,

and when the Germans occupied Vichy France on November 11, he mobilized the Army along the French border, fearing that Hitler might decide to enter Spain by force. The thought surely crossed Hitler's mind, but the exploits of the Blue Division in Russia had led him to respect Spanish fighting prowess, so he resisted the temptation. "The Spanish are the only tough Latins," Hitler told his aides, "and they would carry on guerrilla warfare in our rear."

Franco then turned his attention once more to the plot against him. He ordered Muñoz Grandes home from the Russian front, decreeing a state welcome for his return. The entire Spanish Cabinet and scores of dignitaries turned out on December 17 to greet the general when he arrived in Madrid. Only Franco was absent. He summoned Muñoz to the Palace, pinned a medal on him and shuffled him off to the ceremonial post of Commander of the Military Household. The German bombing of Madrid never materialized, and though Franco never accused Muñoz of being in on the plot, it was clear that only his military successes and personal popularity had saved the general from a firing squad.

Seven months later, in July of 1943, Franco decided to bring home the Blue Division itself. The Germans complained when the first Spanish troops began leaving Russia that October, and Franco placated them by advancing Berlin $40-million credit to purchase more wolfram ore. Franco's generosity left the Germans with a sour taste, however, for he balanced his credit grant by sending Hitler a bill for more than twice that much as payment for the services of the Blue Division and for Spanish labor in Germany.

At the same time, Franco took a final step from nonbelligerency back to neutrality. He picked October 1, or the Day of the Caudillo, symbolic because it marked his official ac-

Francisco Franco and Adolf Hitler exchange pleasantries at the start of their only face-to-face encounter, in a railroad car at Hendaye, France, in October of 1940. For nine hours the two men talked "at each other," according to a witness, and although Hitler was at the pinnacle of his power, he was unable to persuade Franco to enter the War.

cession to leadership in 1936. On that day, Franco usually entertained the diplomatic corps at Madrid's Oriente Palace. Ambassador Hayes was startled and pleased by the change from previous gatherings. "The year before, Franco was noticeably cordial to Axis diplomats," Hayes recalled. "This year he greeted them only perfunctorily. The German Ambassador was almost completely isolated."

When Franco spoke, his message was for Allied ears. He did not say that Spain was abandoning nonbelligerency, but he took pains to describe Spain's "vigilant policy of neutrality." For all intents, Franco had ended his long romance with the Axis. As a further sign of his shift he ordered all German agents expelled from Spain, a decree that was hardly enforceable but one he knew would please the Allies. Only in the area of trade did Franco maintain his old ties. Spain continued to produce uniforms, ammunition and parachutes for Germany and tried to keep up the shipments of wolfram—though by now the Allies were outbidding the Germans and buying the ore in great quantities.

Portugal's Salazar also profited by selling wolfram to both sides, although he halted shipments to Germany in June 1944—not coincidentally the month the Allies invaded France. But unlike Spain's pugnacious Caudillo, Salazar never considered entering the War. Throughout, his policy was one of prickly defiance, a stance that somehow kept the belligerents at arm's length. Late in the War, a popular singer of *fado*, blues-tinged Portuguese ballads, paid tribute to Salazar's tactics—"ever repeating, ever retreating, never demurring, always deferring, but nobody's tool."

Salazar realized that his greatest weapon in the struggle to maintain Portugal's neutrality was its location athwart major Atlantic trade and transportation routes—a position that also made it invaluable as a conduit for spies and information to and from the Continent. Curiously, early in the War, Salazar fretted most about the possibility of an invasion by Franco, the Iberian Pact notwithstanding. In June 1940, when Franco changed Spain's status from neutral to nonbelligerent, Salazar feared that his neighbor would join the Axis and march into Portugal. Rumors circulated in Lisbon that Spain was swarming with German "tourists" ready to assist in such an invasion. At the same time, a Spanish magazine editorialized that it was the will of God that Spain and Portugal be reunited in 1940, exactly three centuries

after a 60-year union of the two countries had ended.

If Franco invaded, Salazar knew that he could expect little help from the British, whom the Germans had driven off the Continent. So he turned to diplomacy. He sent Franco a gift of 10,000 tons of wheat and 6,000 tons of corn, and he ordered his Ambassador in Madrid to suggest a strengthening of the Iberian Pact. The Caudillo was willing to oblige, for he had not been contemplating an invasion of his neighbor. Indeed he welcomed a chance to cement relations further and to win an important concession from Salazar. By late July, Franco's brother Nicolás and the Portuguese Ambassador had hammered out a protocol to the pact whereby either nation could call for consultations if threatening circumstances arose. More important, the younger Franco won verbal assurances that Portugal would not interfere if Spain or Germany attacked Gibraltar.

Nevertheless, Salazar felt uncomfortable with the decision for he feared that war would inevitably spread to Portugal. He decided to make contingency plans and ask the British for advice. That December—as Franco was fending off Hitler's demands for immediate action—Salazar held talks with Britain to coordinate strategy should war break out on the Iberian Peninsula. The upshot was that in the event of Nazi invasion, the Portuguese Army would resist just long enough to allow Salazar to move his government to the Azores. Salazar also agreed to a British suggestion that he double the size of the 40,000-man Army and station a large portion of it in the Azores and in the African possessions of Angola and Mozambique in order to maintain a viable fighting force that could contribute to the Allied cause. At the same time, Salazar took pains to safeguard Portugal's gold reserves, shipping most of his bullion to the United States.

While Salazar labored to secure relations with Britain and Spain, the fall of France had transformed Lisbon, the capital, from a sleepy, steamy city of one million into a crossroads of the world. It was now a haven for refugees fleeing across the Pyrenees and Spain from German-dominated Europe and for spies of all nations who filtered through Lisbon's cafés and hotels, exchanging information and sowing rumors and discord. From Lisbon, a refugee fortunate enough to buy a seat could fly Pan American's Clipper to New York or take a British Overseas Airways' flying boat or a DC-3 to

LISBON: EUROPE'S ESCAPE HATCH

Lisbon, the capital of neutral Portugal, was transformed during World War II from a quiet, stately city into a hub of feverish commerce and intrigue. The sunny metropolis on the Atlantic crawled with spies of all nations. It was a city of speculators trading currency on the world's last free money exchange, of black marketeers and government agents dealing in scarce commodities, of International Red Cross workers transshipping relief supplies to POW camps. And Lisbon was also a city of desperate refugees fleeing Nazi domination —the port of last resort where they hoped they could get visas and buy passage to safety in the West.

Obtaining a visa was not a simple matter. At any given time, thousands of applications were on file at Allied embassies, and a refugee who did not have any special influence might have to wait a year or longer for his papers. The result was a life in limbo.

"The poor refugees," wrote American correspondent Eric Sevareid, "droop over sidewalk café tables, munching cold Portuguese beans with their beer. Daily, the same routine: the general delivery window to ask for a letter; the newsstand to speculate on Hitler's next move; then back to the corner café and a listless bed."

Once a refugee secured a visa, he still had to purchase a ticket on an airliner or a ship—an expensive and frequently labyrinthine procedure that entailed bribing agents and ship's masters, who would casually bump one passenger for another if the price was high enough. One fortunate person who managed to bribe his way onto a freighter noted that, in Lisbon, "human distress offers splendid opportunities for speculation."

Travelers disembark from a Pan American Clipper in Lisbon's Tagus River. The 20-seated flying boats made three New York trips weekly.

London. There also were a number of berths available on neutral passenger ships; until the United States entered the War, the American Export Line did a brisk business transporting 600 refugees on three sailings a month.

At one point, wrote American reporter Eric Sevareid, 20,000 refugees were on the waiting list for visas at the American Embassy. Many others were content to linger in Portugal, hopeful that they could outwait the War. Their numbers included several former national leaders whose countries had fallen to Hitler. "In the Palace Hotel," Sevareid observed one day in late 1940, "these men strolled a few feet away: Bech, once Premier of Luxembourg; Pierlot, the last Premier of Belgium; Chautemps, once Premier of France; aged Paderewski, first President of Poland. That very day, a man came in to reserve a suite for the Nazis' latest victim—deposed King Carol of Rumania."

The wait in Portugal was not unduly harsh: There was no food rationing and no blackout. And for the wealthy, there was Estoril, a resort on the Atlantic 15 miles from Lisbon. At Estoril, it seemed that the War did not exist. "Stifle the curiosity that makes you buy a newspaper," wrote British journalist Hugh Muir, "and you can turn back the pages of history to a day when there was no Hitler or toy Caesar."

The sands of Estoril, recalled Muir, "were packed with beach lizards getting roasted to a fashionable brown," and "French beauties in harlequin colors." Policemen with tape measures struck the only serious note; they measured swimsuits and banned bathers of both sexes whose costumes they deemed too skimpy. At night, wealthy refugees went from the beach to the casinos. "You can dance on the lighted floor of the Wonder Bar or you can play roulette or baccarat," said Muir. "Most people do both, sharing their time between rhythm and ruin."

As Lisbon became the escape hatch of Europe, traffic at Sintra field 18 miles outside the city increased dramatically. There, the airlines of Portugal, Spain, Italy, Germany, Great Britain and the United States spun a web of routes that connected the warring nations with the neutrals and—indirectly—with one another.

There was no room for belligerent attitudes at Sintra; often, enemies were situated side by side on the tarmac and inside the terminal. Muir noted on one visit that the British Airways office was less than 20 feet from the Lufthansa counter. "Inside the German office, a Nordic head was bent over a desk," he observed. "Outside the door was a British gathering of passengers and friends; mingling with them was an Italian pilot in a white suit wearing as much gold braid as an admiral."

British airliners flying into and out of Sintra seemed to lead a charmed life, for German warplanes rarely attacked when the airliners flew within their range over the Bay of Biscay. Actually the British owed their safe passage not to luck but to Admiral Canaris, the German intelligence chief, who realized that the flights served German interests almost as much as they did British ones.

At the beginning of the War, Canaris had met secretly in Lisbon with Baron Oswald von Hoiningen-Heune, German Ambassador to Portugal, to discuss the British flights. "We agreed," recalled the Ambassador, "that no diversionary or sabotage actions would be undertaken by German military personnel in Portugal." Canaris undoubtedly made a similar pact with the Luftwaffe, for he realized that German agents in England could use the British flights to send information out of the country, usually with the help of Spanish and Portuguese diplomats who used their country's mail pouches to pass espionage data. Industrial diamonds were smuggled into Germany in the same way, as were quantities of iridium, used in the manufacture of spark plugs for high-performance aircraft engines. And with the connivance of Portuguese news agents, literally tons of British newspapers and periodicals found their way each week to the German Embassy via the British flights.

Canaris himself on one occasion stopped German agents from blowing up a Pan American Clipper lying at anchor in Lisbon's Tagus River. At a staff conference in early 1942, Field Marshal Wilhelm Keitel, Hitler's Chief of Staff, ordered Canaris to sabotage the New York-to-Lisbon flights. Canaris passed the order on to his staff but decided that he would do his best to thwart it. A short time later, he was in Lisbon and learned that German saboteurs had placed a bomb in a Clipper's cargo hold. Canaris ordered the bomb removed, and because the flight was delayed by bad weather, the agents were able to carry out his orders.

But Canaris could not always be on the scene to prevent mayhem in his pursuit of higher interests. On the 1st of June,

Bathers enjoy the beach at Estoril, a short drive from Lisbon on the resort coast known as the "Portuguese Riviera." The serene atmosphere, said an observer, created an "illusion that time has been rolled back."

1943, the Germans shot down a British airliner en route from Lisbon to London—the only one of hundreds of flights the Luftwaffe ever attacked.

For years, no one knew for sure why the Germans shot down that particular plane, British Overseas Airways Corporation Flight 777. Years later, Winston Churchill came forward with an explanation. The Germans, he said, attacked the plane because they believed he was on it.

Flight 777 had left Lisbon just as Churchill was planning to fly home from North Africa, where he had been inspecting British forces. One of the passengers on the British airliner, Churchill wrote, was "a thickset man smoking a cigar." When German agents at the airport spotted him, said Churchill, "they signaled that I was on board." Actually, the man was Alfred Chenhalls, the business manager for actor Leslie Howard, who also was on the plane.

From Lisbon, Churchill surmised, the word went out to shoot down the aircraft. "It is difficult to imagine how anyone in their senses should imagine that I should have flown home, from Lisbon, in broad daylight," he recalled, perhaps forgetting that a year earlier he had returned from Bermuda

on a commercial airliner. Churchill did, in fact, fly home on the night of June 1 in an RAF bomber that veered far out over the Atlantic to avoid German planes.

Flight 777 took off at 9:35 a.m. and climbed to 10,000 feet. Three hours later, a formation of eight Junkers-88s intercepted the DC-3 over the Bay of Biscay and opened fire. The pilot just had time to radio London that "an unidentified aircraft is following me" before his plane went down. As the German formation veered away, one crewman saw the rear door of the passenger plane open. Four men jumped out, clinging to a single parachute. The parachute furled open for an instant, then caught fire. The four men fell into the sea. There were no survivors among the plane's 13 passengers and crew of two.

The nameless agent who signaled that Churchill was on Flight 777 was one of a legion of German spies who planted themselves in Lisbon and popped up like noxious weeds to bedevil the British and Americans—and the Portuguese. Their deeds ranged from sabotage to less evident acts like bribing the office boy of a British news agency to show them dispatches before they were sent. German agents also spent

their time looking for overt signs of pro-British sentiment, which they then complained about to the Portuguese.

Despite their long alliance with Britain, the Portuguese did their best to be evenhanded. If a Portuguese bookseller displayed six British books in his window, he took pains to place six German books alongside them, observed Maximilian Scheer, an American writer who visited Lisbon in 1941. Portuguese newspapers were equally scrupulous in their observance of neutrality. "They attack neither Churchill nor Hitler, neither democrats nor dictators," Scheer reported. When a German warplane crashed in Portugal, "the plane was seized (for England) and the crew escaped (for Hitler)."

The Portuguese government carefully extended its even-handedness to outpourings of public sentiment for one side or the other. When the Duke of Kent visited Lisbon in June of 1940, to help celebrate the 800th anniversary of the Kingdom of Portugal, so many people wore British badges and waved Union Jacks that the Germans protested, and the government outlawed such explicit displays. One ingenious manufacturer got around the ban, however, by making a badge consisting only of a bowler hat and a large cigar.

In early 1941 the British applied pressure of their own

over a far more serious matter. The Portuguese had made several large shipments of wolfram to Germany in 1940 and London insisted that Salazar reduce sales to Berlin or face decreased British shipments of rubber and petroleum. Instead, Salazar cut tin shipments to Germany, which placated the British without deeply offending Hitler, who, Salazar knew, could get the metal from other sources. Nevertheless, the Germans complained bitterly. At the same time, rumors spread through Lisbon that Germany would launch an invasion across the Pyrenees in the spring. In all likelihood, the Germans themselves had started the rumors, both to disguise their preparations for the upcoming invasion of the Soviet Union and to play on Portuguese fears that Britain or the still-neutral United States would soon invade either the Iberian Peninsula or the Atlantic islands. In truth, the British, Americans and Germans had long coveted the Azores and all three had made plans to occupy them.

Hitler first envisioned invading the Azores in coordination with his assault on Gibraltar. To him, the islands were a natural steppingstone to the Western Hemisphere. If the United States entered the War, his bombers could strike at New York City, 2,500 miles distant, from the Azores—he had on the drawing board an Amerika bomber capable of the round trip. More immediately, the Azores would give the German Navy an advance base for its U-boat wolf packs to harass shipping in the Atlantic. Even when he gave up the attack on Gibraltar and turned east toward Russia, Hitler kept alive his plans for the islands. "The Führer is still in favor of occupying the Azores," noted Grand Admiral Erich Raeder in May 1941. "The occasion for this may arise by autumn."

The United States also was eyeing the Azores with interest. President Roosevelt had bound his nation to Great Britain with the Lend-Lease Act and had promised Churchill vast quantities of arms. FDR thought it might be necessary to occupy the Azores to head off the Germans and to keep Atlantic shipping lanes open.

In April 1941, Roosevelt drew up a map that placed the Azores in the Western Hemisphere, implying that the United States would invoke the Monroe Doctrine to defend the islands if the Germans invaded. Roosevelt also told Churchill that the U.S. Navy would patrol in the general area to warn British convoys of German U-boat activity. A short

On an inspection tour in August of 1941, General Oscar Carmona (left), Portugal's figurehead President, addresses the commander of the garrison in the Azores. By 1943, the Portuguese had increased their troop strength on the strategically located islands to 40,000 men.

90

time later, columnist Walter Lippmann suggested in the New York *Herald Tribune* that Germany had to be forestalled in the area—with or without Portuguese assent. And on May 6, Senator Claude Pepper of Florida made a speech calling for an immediate American take-over of the islands.

The Portuguese were mightily alarmed by Pepper's jingoistic speech; they would have been even more upset to learn that in late May, Roosevelt ordered 25,000 U.S. troops made ready to sail for the Azores within a month. When Hitler invaded Russia, the Americans shelved their plans for the expeditionary force, reasoning that the Germans could no longer spare enough troops to assault the islands.

Although Hitler's armies were occupied in the Soviet Union, his U-boats remained a potent force in the North Atlantic. In the first six months of 1941, the Germans sank about three million tons of Allied shipping. The British were not yet ready to invoke their ancient treaty with Portugal and request bases in the Azores, but they did ask the Portuguese to supply them with a complete survey of the islands.

Salazar obliged. In December 1941, he sent a team to survey the islands for the British. For the moment, he would go no further. Then, nearly a year later, he received a telephone call that changed both the course of Portugal's neutrality—and the role of the Azores.

Salazar was dining in his residence behind the National Palace on November 7, 1942, when British Ambassador Sir Ronald Campbell telephoned to ask for an immediate interview. It was already 9:30 and Salazar, who usually went to bed soon after dinner, tried to put Campbell off until morning. When the envoy insisted, Salazar agreed to a 1 a.m. meeting. "Salazar thought something extraordinary must be happening," reported journalist Augusto de Castro, to whom Salazar later related the evening's events. "What could it be? The Prime Minister thought for a moment that Allied troops might have landed in the Azores. That would have swamped Portugal in a wave of disaster."

Instead, Campbell told Salazar—even as U.S. Ambassador Hayes was informing the Spanish government—that Allied forces had begun landing in North Africa. Salazar's reaction was much the same. "I breathed a sigh of relief," he later recalled. Portugal's neutrality was still intact and Portugal's islands were still safe.

Over the next several months, the Azores became increasingly important to the Allies. German U-boats were now making contact with their supply submarines near the westernmost of the islands, out of range of Allied aircraft. Given such a safe area in which to resupply, the Germans could double or triple their usual cruising period—with telling effect on Allied shipping. U-boats accounted for most of the 2.1 million tons sunk in the first half of 1943.

Now, more than ever, the Allies needed air bases on the Azores to counter the U-boats, and in June of 1943 the British finally invoked the treaty of Windsor and requested airfields on the islands. Salazar hesitated momentarily, and Churchill considered taking the islands with or without Lisbon's assent. But British Foreign Minister Anthony Eden persuaded Salazar to sign an accord on August 17; in return for the air bases, Portugal received $30 million, the promise of modern fighter planes and antiaircraft guns, and a British pledge to protect Portugal if the agreement provoked an Axis or Spanish attack.

The first British units landed on the island of Terceira on October 12, 1943. The United States also wanted to establish a base on the Azores, but Salazar refused, for he had stretched his neutrality as far as he dared. When the British insisted, Salazar relented somewhat. American personnel could work on the Azores, he said, but only in British uniforms and on the fiction that they were "on loan to His Majesty's government."

As expected, the Azores agreement upset the Germans. "Salazar has lost his faith in us," raged Propaganda Minister Joseph Goebbels, who also used the occasion to snipe at Franco. "Salazar keeps swaying to and fro between the extremes of the pendulum. The same is true of Franco. The dictators would do far better if they openly took sides with us, for if our side does not win they are lost anyway."

Goebbels' ranting was mere wishful thinking; Germany by now could do little to help, or harm, the Iberians. Hitler's armies were being battered everywhere, and Mussolini's own ministers had ousted him from power in Rome. The ebb of Axis fortunes did not go unnoticed in Madrid, where Franco quietly removed the portraits of Hitler and Mussolini that had occupied places of honor in his study. Or in Lisbon, where Salazar removed the picture of Mussolini that had sat on his desk for years.

A RUSH TO FIGHT COMMUNISM

Two days after the German invasion of Russia in 1941, Spanish Falangists march to the War Ministry in Madrid to volunteer for the fight against Communism.

A DIVISION EAGER TO SETTLE OLD SCORES

Spain's leaders saw in Germany's invasion of Russia on June 22, 1941, a chance to square two accounts at once: By offering a division for Hitler's "crusade against Bolshevism," they could even the score against the hated Soviets, who had opposed them in the Spanish Civil War, and pay back the Germans who had come to their aid. They could also remind Hitler of how well Spaniards fought—in case he harbored any desire to add Spain to his burgeoning empire.

A call for volunteers to fight in Russia elicited a response that bordered on national pandemonium. More than 3,000 students from the University of Madrid rushed to join up. The class of 1941 at the Spanish Military Academy in Saragossa volunteered en masse. Many regular Spanish Army officers took a demotion in rank or enlisted as common soldiers to be sure of being accepted as volunteers.

Within two weeks, the Blue Division (named for the blue shirts the men wore as a symbol of the Falange Party), had more than 40 times the 18,000 volunteers it needed. Only the best were chosen—most of them experienced fighters, veterans of the Civil War. All the officers above the rank of lieutenant were from the regular Army. The troops were first trained in Germany—and then sent to the Eastern Front, where they served as part of the Wehrmacht in order to protect Spain's veneer of neutrality.

For the Spaniards, Prussian discipline proved as hard to adapt to as the Russian climate. The Germans complained that they often failed to salute, dressed sloppily and were too friendly toward the Polish and Russian civilians they met. The volunteers in turn thought the Germans petty and stiff. Hitler, who shared the general German view of the Spaniards as "wildly undisciplined," nonetheless marveled at their prowess as warriors: "One can't imagine more fearless fellows," he said. "They scarcely take cover. They flout death. Our men are glad to have them as neighbors."

The volunteers fought alongside the Germans for two long years—sharing their victories and their eventual reversals. In all, about 47,000 men served in the Blue Division at one time or another. Almost half of them became casualties.

Young Spanish volunteers push forward to join the Blue Division in June of 1941. Many recruiting centers filled their quotas in a single day.

In a boisterous mood, troops of the Blue Division entrain for Bavaria. The soldier at top wears a German Iron Cross awarded during a previous combat tour.

Nazi and Spanish banners adorn a pavilion in Bavaria as the Blue Division is honored at a festive meal during its journey across Germany in July of 1941. The

A HEARTY WELCOME TO GERMANY

The Spanish volunteers who left for Germany on July 13, 1941, had few thoughts of death and none of defeat. The celebrations attending their departure ran on for days. They were remembered in farewell Masses, praised in speeches and saluted in endless toasts. Massive crowds jammed railroad stations to say good-by—and to shout choruses of "Death to Russia!"

As the trains passed through France, French civilians and exiled Spanish Republicans pelted the volunteers with rocks and insults. But once they reached Germany the celebration began anew. About 10,000 Germans turned out at the border to greet the Spaniards, and the towns they visited feted them with elaborate dinners. On July 17 the first volunteers reached the training center at Grafenwöhr in Bavaria. They were sworn into the German Army and exchanged their natty Spanish uniforms for Wehrmacht gray.

En route to Bavaria for training, flower-bedecked Spanish volunteers wave their thanks to a crowd gathered at the Karlsruhe railroad station to welcome them with gifts, including a small picture of Adolf Hitler.

uniformed waitresses serving them are members of the Nazi Women's League.

THE GRUELING HIKE INTO COMBAT

After a month's training in Bavaria, it was time for the Blue Division to taste combat in Russia. This time the trains took the men only partway to their destination: The German command thought that the Spaniards would benefit from a toughening, 625-mile march to the front.

The division snaked eastward in a column 20 miles long, each soldier lugging more than 70 pounds of equipment. The men grew painful blisters and choked on the omnipresent dust—until autumn rains turned the clay roads to mud. They also suffered from the heavy German diet of coarse bread, spiced cabbage and potatoes, which gave many of them gastritis.

The march took 45 days. At its end, the Spaniards were assigned a 25-mile sector of the Leningrad front along the Volkhov River near Novgorod. By mid-October of 1941 they had achieved their first victory, establishing a beachhead on the eastern bank of the Volkhov.

A Russian soldier, killed in the Blue Division's first month of battle, lies in a snowy bunker taken by Spanish troops as they fought their way across the Volkhov River.

With their weapons slung from their necks, Spanish troops enter already-occupied Novgorod, completing a 990-mile journey by train and by foot from Bavaria.

BRINGING LATIN WARMTH TO FRIGID RUSSIA

For the volunteer troops from Mediterranean Spain the most difficult adjustment was to the wicked Russian winter—and the winter of 1941-1942 was the coldest in a century. By Christmas, frostbite had cost the division the services of 725 men—eight more than had been killed in the nine weeks of campaign thus far.

The southerners adapted to survive. Initially, some units had just one overcoat for every 10 men, so they took turns wearing the coat—particularly on freezing guard duty. Smart soldiers wore long underwear outside their uniforms as winter camouflage, and stripped warm, felt-and-leather boots from dead Russian soldiers. The division itself adapted to winter combat by recruiting enough skiers from its ranks to form a special 205-man company. The ski unit soon distinguished itself in a costly raid across frozen Lake Ilmen, breaking through the Soviet lines to relieve a trapped German unit. Thirty-seven Spanish troopers won the Iron Cross—most of them posthumously—in that action alone.

The Spaniards tried to bring a bit of humanity to the Russian front. At Christmas they enjoyed a huge shipment of brandy, cigars and cigarettes from home. They befriended Russian peasants, who in return often warned them of Red Army movements. And many Spanish soldiers found Russian girlfriends—a few of whom were eventually smuggled back to Spain.

Troops from the Spanish ski company head out on patrol. In the fighting across Lake Ilmen in January 1942, the unit suffered nearly 95 per cent casualties.

A young Spanish soldier and his Russian girlfriend try to overcome the language barrier in the doorway of her house near Novgorod.

Warm inside the Russian isba, or wooden hut, where they were quartered, officers of the Blue Division celebrate Christmas in 1941 with brandy, cigars and a decorated tree.

Holding a submachine gun in his mittened hand, a bundled Spanish soldier wears a pair of wicker-work overshoes at the entrance to his bunker—nicknamed Villa Pepinos.

THE GENERAL WHO EARNED HITLER'S RESPECT

The Blue Division's first commander, General Agustín Muñoz Grandes, was a born warrior who carried the scars of nine battle wounds with him to Russia. Although the general thrived on close contact with his men, one observer noted that he made his officers "uncomfortable." With good reason: He had the disturbing habit of asking the men what they thought of their leaders—and listening to the answers.

Muñoz Grandes cared little for ceremony—or for displaying his medals, including a Knight's Cross with Oak Leaves awarded personally by Hitler. But he demanded total dedication from his men. Deserters and those who injured themselves to avoid combat were summarily shot. By contrast, he compassionately sent home men who had lost brothers—lest a family lose not one son but two.

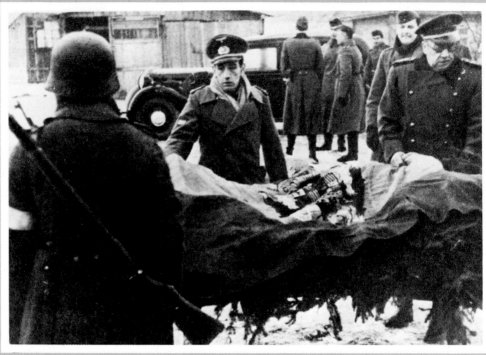

General Agustín Muñoz Grandes (center) unveils a wreath for Spanish dead at a Russian cemetery.

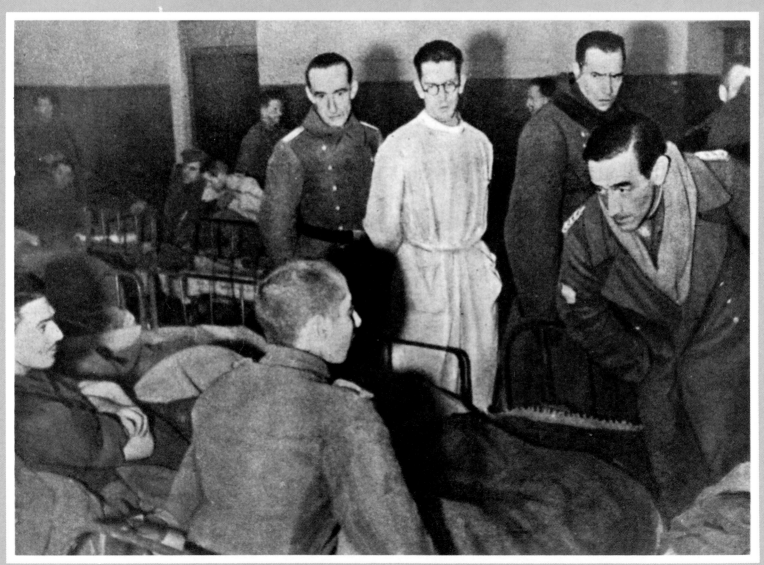

Trailed by aides and doctors, General Muñoz Grandes chats with a wounded soldier at a field hospital following the Blue Division's first combat in 1941.

Adolf Hitler welcomes Muñoz Grandes to the Wolf's Lair, his headquarters in East Prussia, in July of 1942. Hitler had told the Spanish commander that he considered the Blue Division ''equal to the best German divisions.''

General Friedrich von Chappuis, the Spaniards' German leader, awards Muñoz Grandes the Iron Cross.

Kneeling in prayer, Spanish soldiers honor a fallen comrade newly buried in a Wehrmacht cemetery in Russia. The Spaniards had hopes—never realized—of collecting their scattered dead into a single cemetery.

Veterans of the Blue Division, some blinded, one missing a leg, join relatives of the dead at a memorial service in Spain following the division's return.

THE POIGNANT COST OF A COURAGEOUS STAND

The Blue Division faced battle almost daily during the winter of 1942-1943, its second on the Russian front. The fighting was fierce and bloody, and reserves and supplies were scarce. And the enemy was growing stronger: By mid-winter the Soviets had amassed a 9-to-1 manpower advantage in some sectors.

On the 10th of February, 1943—"Black Wednesday"—the Soviets attacked, hoping to encircle and annihilate the troublesome Spaniards near Krasny Bor, about 20 miles below Leningrad. For two deafening hours, 800 heavy guns inflicted an "absolute inferno" upon the Spanish bunkers. Then, while Soviet planes bombed and strafed, the Russians loosed their infantry and tanks. A few Spanish units fought to the last man, blowing up their guns to deny them to the enemy, calling down fire upon their positions when overrun.

For the first time since arriving in Russia, the Blue Division was forced to retreat. Their new lines held, but pressure soon mounted to recall the volunteers to Spain. Families worried about rising casualties, and the Franco government was anxious to put some distance between itself and the crumbling Axis.

The order to withdraw came in October. The battered Blue Division was welcomed back to Spain with great private relief and a minimum of public ceremony: Franco, ever cautious, feared offending the Germans by drawing too much attention to the pullout. Left behind in Russia were almost 5,000 members of the Blue Division, missing or dead.

Attended by flag-bearing Guardia Civil members, a mother, wife and daughter—wearing her Communion dress—mourn a volunteer who died in Russia.

THE PRICE OF NEUTRALITY

Swedish ships languish in the west-coast port of Goteborg—prisoners of a determined German sea blockade that began in 1940 and lasted throughout the War.

"WE ATE LESS AND WE FELT BETTER"

A Swedish iron miner, wearing an air filter on his helmet, takes a break. By 1942, the blockade had cut Sweden's iron exports by about one third.

The Swedes awoke on April 9, 1940—the morning Germany invaded Denmark and Norway—to find themselves cut off from more than their unfortunate neighbors. German ships and air patrols were blockading the Skagerrak, a 100-mile-long strait that separated Sweden from the North Sea, its Western markets, and 70 per cent of its energy supply.

At one stroke, Sweden had become almost totally dependent upon the Nazis for its foreign trade. A few months later Germany relented a bit, allowing five non-Axis ships into Swedish ports each month. These safe-conduct ships came crammed with such necessities as oil, textiles, wheat—and with raw motion-picture film, which enabled the Swedes to avoid a dependence upon Nazi propaganda movies.

But it was not enough, and the blockade forced a drastic reordering of daily life. Private stores of animal fodder were confiscated by the government and redistributed. An incentive program prodded farmers to clear new land and grow scarce grains. Consumption was trimmed by conservation campaigns and by a system of rationing in which as many as 90 ration cards for different items were issued to a single household. Scrap drives salvaged used goods for recycling, and industry produced thinner tires and thinner milk.

Where they could, the Swedes shifted from what was imported, and scarce, to what was domestic and plentiful. Swedish peat heated thousands of homes. Restaurant menus offered hare and reindeer in place of hard-to-get chicken and beef. Swedish steel, famed for its high quality, replaced rubber in conveyor belts and tin in toothpaste tubes. And Sweden's bountiful forests were exploited to yield three times as much timber as before the War. Invention sprang from necessity: Trees were transformed into everything from yeast and soap to a cellulose rayon that was used to make hose for women and uniforms for soldiers.

Curiously, the blockade had a positive side. Some enforced innovations became permanent. Bicycle holidays, in lieu of foreign travel, reintroduced the Swedes to their own country. And the rationing helped them to stay fit. "We ate less," recalled one Swede, "and we felt better."

In Stockholm, a German tourist exhibit asserts the impregnability of Fortress Europe, while the theater next door plays the American film Mrs. Miniver.

In the vast open-pit mine at Kiruna, 90 miles north of the Arctic Circle, a train (foreground) loads up with some of the world's richest iron ore. Sweden stationed

Industrialist Sven Wingqvist, inventor of the ball bearing and founder of a mammoth Swedish company, SKF, inspects one of the high-precision bearings his factories supplied by the hundreds of thousands to both sides.

the bulk of its Army in the far north as a signal that it would fight to hold its great mineral resources.

A VITAL INDUSTRY MADE SELF-SUFFICIENT

Iron ore was one thing that the Swedes had in abundance—and the belligerents badly needed. Steel ball bearings, made from high-quality Swedish iron, were shipped openly to Germany and smuggled to Britain throughout the War.

But to turn the iron into steel and steel products required immense quantities of coal and coke, half of which Sweden had imported from Britain before the blockade. Germany made up some of that deficit. And the Swedes aided themselves by mining inferior domestic coal and converting their blast furnaces to wood or electrical power, thus cutting by two thirds their need for imported coal.

Steel producers came up with processes that substituted Swedish silicon for imported nickel and reduced the need for rare elements like tungsten. Old mines were reopened to dig manganese, another essential element. By 1943, such measures had almost tripled the percentage of domestic materials used in Sweden's metal industry.

STRETCHING THE YIELD OF MEAGER HARVESTS

Even prior to the German blockade, Sweden had to import about 30 per cent of its food supply. Swedish agriculture needed enormous injections of foreign fertilizer, fodder and fuel—a dependence that, according to one expert, made farming in Sweden "only a processing of imported raw materials."

The Swedes found substitutes for some of these imports at home. They put horses back into harness and converted tractors to run on firewood. They flavored fortified wood pulp with molasses to make an ersatz fodder for livestock.

Swedish harvests were down overall by one fifth in 1940 and one third in 1941. The two-year totals for rye and wheat, for example, equaled one good prewar year. The only bright spots were abundant harvests of sugar beets and potatoes. The potatoes, along with barley meal and wood shavings, were mixed with bread grains to stretch the nation's supply of flour.

Five women and a man tend a Swedish potato field. The military draft created a serious labor shortage in Sweden that made the role of women on farms

A farmer shows off her champion sugar beets. The production of beets—unlike that of grain—remained steady throughout the War.

more essential than ever before. Those male farmers spared by the draft were frequently organized into labor brigades to work their farms cooperatively.

REAPING THE BOUNTY OF THE FORESTS

Sweden's salvation was its forests, which covered half the land. During the coal-short, extraordinarily cold wartime winters, wood fires kept millions of Swedes at least passably warm. In the 12 months ending in June 1943, roughly 70 million cubic yards of wood were cut—triple the amount harvested three years earlier.

More than two thirds of the wood was burned as fuel. Most of the remainder was converted to pulp or cellulose fodder, a process that created a myriad of useful by-products. Among them were ethyl alcohol, used to make solvents, fuels and even radiator fluid, and turpentine, which was essential in the mining of copper and zinc. Solid wood resins were used to make glue and dye. Wood sugar was distilled into a kind of schnapps, the popular Swedish drink; the government spent six cents a quart to produce the drink and sold it for $2.25, thus helping to balance the nation's wartime budget.

Grasping a sharp pole, a Swedish lumberjack gingerly picks his way through a bay filled with logs that have been floated downstream to Stockholm. The

Yarn came from paper pulp—much of it recycled after frequent collection drives. Pine stumps were distilled to yield tar, which in turn made substitute oils to lubricate automobile engines. Kilns turned lumber wastes into charcoal. Altogether, the Swedes found use for more than half of every tree they cut—and almost all the rest was water.

Swedish Girl Scouts dump old boots onto a rubber-collection heap.

logs were first cut to length and were then distributed for use as firewood.

Young Swedes pause during a wastepaper drive to read the comics.

A DIET BASED ON FISH AND MILK

By 1943, fully 70 per cent of everything the Swedes ate was stringently rationed. Each adult got about an ounce of meat per day, one egg every two weeks, and five ounces of bread daily, even less than the average Briton or German. Restaurants in fact demanded to see a ration coupon before serving a single slice of bread.

Shortages made the Swedes inventive. They brewed "tea" from barley and oak leaves, and a coffee substitute from beets and acorns that one visiting American pronounced "as potable as a bad English cook would produce with good coffee."

A carrot extract mixed in margarine provided some of the vitamin A usually obtained from high-protein meats. And fish remained relatively plentiful and cheap. But the mainstay of the Swedish diet was milk, which was not rationed. Cheese and butter production was curtailed and cream was banned, so that as other foods grew scarcer, the milk supply doubled.

At an open-air market, Stockholmers queue up to buy fresh fish from the Baltic Sea. Unrationed fish supplied protein for the largely meatless Swedish diet.

A Swedish housewife gazes at her dozens of assorted food coupons. Children, expectant or nursing mothers and manual laborers were all eligible to receive extra rations.

A Swedish North Sea fisherman and his wife dine at home on simple wartime fare: herring, potatoes and a little black bread. Despite the blockade, the Swedes' daily caloric intake by 1942 had declined less than 10 per cent.

CONCOCTING SUBSTITUTES FOR SCARCE FUELS

The blockade by the Germans hit Sweden the hardest by cutting off its imports of oil and gasoline. Private automobiles all but disappeared from Swedish roads, causing one visitor to observe that "the most common vehicles on Stockholm's streets are bicycles and baby buggies."

Most of the fuel brought into Sweden by safe-conduct ships went to the Air Force and Navy, and even they were compelled to cut back on maneuvers. Civilian builders turned to wood and brick instead of cement, which required more fuel to make. Trains powered by electricity and steam carried freight that normally would have gone by ship or truck. Hot water became a luxury for which some hotels charged their guests an extra 10 per cent.

Ambulances and fire engines were always able to get fuel, but other motor vehicles were either parked for the duration or were converted to run on so-called producer gas, made in apparatuses that were attached to their rear ends. The Swedes tried out about 100 different fuel-making models, producing gas from wood, charcoal, methane, coal and other substitutes. The most efficient achieved speeds of 40 miles per hour and gave 80 miles to a four-foot-long sack of wood chips or charcoal.

Bicycles, supplemented by electric trolley cars, dominate the morning rush hour in wartime Stockholm. By 1944, production of new bicycles had grown to five times the prewar level.

In the square outside the 16th Century town hall at Malmo, drivers stand by their cabs—each of which lugs a producer-gas apparatus behind it. Typically, in order to start the engine, charcoal or wood chips were first poured into the apparatus and then stoked with a long iron rod.

During the doleful early years of the War, Winston Churchill gazed frequently at the large map of Scandinavia occupying a corner of the British Cabinet Room. His attention focused on a 950-mile strip of neutral territory, threatened on all sides by belligerent forces. "I stood there and thought of isolated Sweden," Churchill later recalled. "My advice to Sweden was always: to keep quiet and rearm."

Words of wisdom. Sweden, an erstwhile warrior nation that for 125 years had made neutrality a way of life, did in fact rearm to the extent of ensuring that an invasion from any quarter would at best be a bloody and time-consuming business. And throughout the War, Sweden's obvious determination to defend itself was supported by a quiet, stubborn diplomacy that sorely vexed the combatants—Winston Churchill among them.

Sweden's national policy was simplicity itself. The sole aim was to stay out of war at whatever cost, even if that course caused pain to the national conscience. Indeed, the tilt of Swedish neutrality at given times could be read as a barometer of the changing fortunes of global war. For more than three years, while Swedish leaders were understandably convinced that Hitler's armies were invincible, Sweden's bias clearly favored Germany—especially in matters pertaining to strategic trade and the transport of military personnel and war matériel across Swedish territory. But after the February 1943 surrender of the German Sixth Army at Stalingrad and, three months later, the Axis defeat in Tunisia, Sweden increasingly and inexorably inclined toward the Allied nations.

In sum, Swedish neutrality in World War II was a skillful, often courageous yet sometimes ignoble performance by a people who had in ages past stood as a symbol of berserk violence—but were now forced to survive by their wits.

To their victims, the Vikings who swept out of the North in the Ninth Century were distressingly alike. They were savage warriors, superb seamen, restless explorers and, perhaps most significant, shrewd and avid traders. Yet there was a vital difference in Viking outlooks: The Danes and the Norwegians sailed forth mainly westward on their pillaging expeditions—while the Swedes, on the Gulf of Bothnia and the Baltic Sea, moved into the eastern vastness.

Setting out from Birka, their trading center near the site of

4

An early history of berserk violence
The boy king who challenged Peter the Great
A turn toward peace under a marshal of Napoleon
Hitler's design to "close the Baltic bottle"
The reluctant decision to rearm
"Do not disturb the peace of the North"
Draining defense inventories to help the Finns
A daring air shuttle across occupied Norway
The bane and blessing of abundant iron
Weathering the wrath of Hermann Göring
Britain's flotilla of foul-weather freighters
Exploits of a most irregular airline

SWEDEN: A BAROMETER OF WAR

modern Stockholm, Swedish Vikings sailed across the Baltic to the Gulf of Finland, whence they followed a river and lake system deep into a great wilderness inhabited mostly by primitive Slavs, whom the Norsemen subjugated. The merchant-warriors founded Novgorod, a fortified town 100 miles inland, and from there they established trade routes all the way to the Black and the Caspian Seas.

The conquered Slavs called the invaders *Ruotsi,* which was corrupted into *Rus* and eventually gave rise to the name of Russia. Over the years the Slavs assimilated their Swedish colonial masters. Nevertheless, long after the Vikings had faded into history, protection of the Russian trade routes remained a cardinal aim of Swedish policy. During the 1470s the aggressive Muscovites, who had become the dominant power in Russia and were now expanding their domain, annexed Novgorod, the key Swedish outpost. But the Swedes were a prickly people: They fought against Danes, Norwegians and Germans—and they were more than willing to fight Russians. By force of their fierce arms, they clung for more than 200 years to the Gulf of Finland and the Estonian and Livonian coastlines, denying Russia access to the Baltic and levying large tolls on Russian traders.

Then, in 1697, came an event that would lead during nearly two decades of bloody conflict to a permanent change in the balance of power between Russia and Sweden. On April 5, Sweden's King Charles XI died of stomach cancer and was succeeded by his son, a spindly blond 15-year-old who was crowned Charles XII.

Meanwhile, the formidable Muscovite ruler who would become known as Peter the Great watched this transfer of the Swedish crown with hungry fascination. Calculating that young Charles would be easy pickings, Peter entered into an alliance against Sweden with Augustus II, King of Poland and Elector of Saxony, and King Frederick IV of Denmark, both of whom were cousins of Charles.

Rarely have any aggressors been more mistaken about the nature of their opponent. Despite his fragile appearance, there blazed within Charles XII a warlike spirit that would place him among history's great captains. In March of 1700, upon learning that Cousin Augustus had marched into Swedish Livonia, Charles announced with quiet menace: "I have resolved never to begin an unjust war—but also never to end a just war without overcoming my enemy." In alliance with England and Holland, Charles first polished off Denmark, besieging Copenhagen and forcing Cousin Frederick to sign a treaty withdrawing from the war. Then Charles turned his angry attentions to Russia.

Czar Peter's plan was to win his way to the Baltic by seizing the Swedish-held provinces of Karelia and Ingria, on the eastern and southern coasts of the Gulf of Finland, together with the strategic port of Narva. In October 1700, Peter invested Narva with 40,000 troops. On November 20, in the midst of a blinding snowstorm, Charles arrived at the head of a relief army of 10,500 men. The Swedish King hurled his troops directly at the center of the Czar's forces, which outnumbered him by four to one. By nightfall the Russians had been shattered, with a loss of 8,000 men.

The Swedish victory at Narva astonished Europe. And Charles now added to the confusion by turning his back on Russia to dispose of Cousin Augustus, whom he deemed particularly perfidious. For six frustrating years, Charles pursued Augustus back and forth across the immense Polish plain, and ultimately deep into Saxony. But the long campaign was costly. Czar Peter used Charles's preoccupation to make good his own losses—and more. By the time Charles forced Augustus to abdicate the Polish throne, Peter had won his long-sought way to the Baltic and was building his new capital, St. Petersburg, at the mouth of the Neva River. Now, with Augustus and Poland out of the way, Charles would seek his final reckoning with Peter.

And so he did—but in an unexpected manner. Instead of moving to recover his lost Baltic provinces, Charles set out before dawn on the morning of August 27, 1707, at the head of 32,000 men and marched toward Moscow itself.

The Swedes won battle after battle—in one skirmish, the King personally killed two Russians, one with a pistol and the other with his sword—but were unable to bring the enemy to bay. Worse yet, as Peter retreated he left behind a broad swath of scorched earth. Finally, on June 28, 1709, with the pursuing Swedish Army near starvation and short of ammunition, Peter the Great made his stand at the little town of Poltava in the Ukraine. Charles, wounded in the foot by a sniper's bullet several days earlier, was carried into battle on a litter slung between two horses. But his inspirational leadership was missing—and his forces were shattered. Four days later the Swedish Army surrendered.

ROYAL SYMBOLS OF NORMALCY

Sweden's Royal Family was never so visible—or popular—as during the anxious War years. The royal presence was lent to clothing drives, air-raid and evacuation drills, Army and Navy maneuvers. Crown Prince Gustav Adolf sold defense bonds. His brother, Prince Bertil, joined the Navy. Crown Princess Louise helped send gifts to Swedish soldiers. The widower King, Gustav V, though 82 when the War began, stepped up his involvement in both political and charitable activities.

The family served as a reassuring symbol of normalcy. King Gustav continued to play tennis daily and work on his delicate embroidery. In public, at least, the family practiced a careful neutrality. When repatriated POWs passed through Sweden, even British-born Princess Louise called on German and British soldiers alike.

The epitome of a calm, collected Sweden, King Gustav V assiduously applies himself to his needlepoint in September 1942.

Led by Crown Prince Gustav Adolf (second from right), the Swedish Royal Family participates in a defense-fund-raising procession in May of 1940.

Crown Princess Louise (left) convenes a charity meeting at the palace.

Prince Bertil (left) rides the Navy torpedo boat under his command.

Charles XII escaped and survived another nine years, all the while striving singlemindedly to renew his struggle against Russia. But by now every hand was turned against him, and in 1718 he was shot to death while fighting in Norway, which had allied itself with Peter the Great. Charles's legacy to Sweden was neither land nor riches but an ingrained hostility toward Russia that survived for centuries.

With his interminable conflicts, Charles had left Sweden impoverished and in political chaos; there ensued, with rare intervals of relative tranquillity, a prolonged period of near-anarchy during which Sweden lost the last of its territories across the Baltic. In 1809, during yet another bloody war against Russia, the Swedes were driven out of Finland and forced to retire to the borders that define the country still. In the aftermath of that defeat, Sweden took the extraordinary step in 1810 of electing as its Crown Prince and de facto ruler one of Napoleon's marshals—a dashing cavalryman named Jean Baptiste Bernadotte.

Napoleon himself had endorsed Bernadotte's candidacy, and the Swedes hoped the Emperor would support a campaign to win back Finland. But Bernadotte had other ideas. He was convinced that Napoleon's power was waning and that a diminished Sweden lacked the resources to compete for power in the new Europe he saw emerging.

Bernadotte resolved to withdraw from Great Power politics and to concentrate on building Swedish security and economic well-being within the Scandinavian peninsula. To protect his western border, he annexed Norway from Denmark in 1814 after a brief and almost bloodless campaign. By the time he came to the throne as Charles XIV in 1818, Sweden had fought its last war: Ahead lay an era of unparalleled peace and prosperity.

The new King had correctly anticipated that in post-Napoleonic Europe the power of Russia in the East and of Britain in the West would be the counterweights of a new stability. Favored by the half century of Continental peace that followed, Sweden mustered the energies that had gone into war and turned them to building a modern industrial state. Growing rich from its manufactures—notably high-quality steel—the country developed a circumstantial neutrality that gradually hardened into a creed.

Born of misfortune and nourished by peace, Swedish neutrality was protected from internal pressures by the country's ethnic homogeneity—and from external interference by its geographic isolation. Because Sweden's 6.4 million inhabitants were virtually all of the same racial stock, the country had no large dissident minorities urging ethnic allegiance to other lands. And because Sweden was isolated from the mainland of Europe by the Baltic on the south and by icy mountains and bleak tundra in the north, it was able to keep apart from the tensions building in Europe as the emergent German Empire started its expansionist thrust in the later decades of the 19th Century.

There were, to be sure, strident voices inside and outside Sweden urging war against the Germanic Confederation in 1848, against Russia in 1856, and against Prussia and Austria in 1863. But each time the government drew back, increasingly aware of the discrepancy between Sweden's modest military resources and those of the Great Powers. By the turn of the century, Swedish neutrality was regarded both within and without as the keystone of the nation's foreign policy and the guarantor of the national honor.

In 1907, Bernadotte's great-grandson was crowned Gustav V. He was on the throne while Sweden remained neutral during World War I. And he was still there when the shadow of approaching war fell over Europe in the mid-1930s.

From his Renaissance palace in Stockholm, Gustav presided over a constitutional monarchy dominated by the moderate Social Democratic Party. In one generation, Sweden's attitudes toward Germany and England had undergone a radical change. Since the days of Bismarck, Sweden had cultivated German friendship and trade and based many of its fiscal, social and educational policies on German models. During World War I, noted one analyst, Sweden's pro-German sympathies were tempered by "respect for and fear of Great Britain." But the Nazis' obvious thirst for conquest alarmed the Swedes, and by the late 1930s the country's "sympathies for Britain and the democracies were tempered by her fear of and respect for Germany."

Adding to Sweden's fear of Germany was the fact that Britain in 1935 signed a pact that limited Germany's naval strength to one third of Britain's. Intended to restrain German sea power, the pact in fact had the opposite effect. Under the terms of the Versailles Treaty, Germany was allowed a strictly limited Navy, with no submarines. The 1935 pact not only sanctioned submarines but gave Germany's meager Navy a green light to build at full capacity for at least the 10 years it would need to reach the agreed-upon limit. If the Germans built to the limit, noted Winston Churchill, they would become "masters of the Baltic." Hitler understood the pact in the same way. "The Baltic," he boasted, "is now a bottle that we Germans can close."

In the following year began a parade of events that had a profound effect on the nature of Swedish neutrality. Sweden had placed immense faith in the League of Nations as an instrument for preserving peace in general—and protecting the small, neutral Scandinavian nations in particular. But with the failure in 1936 of the League to do more than slap the wrist of Italy's Benito Mussolini with trade sanctions for his Ethiopian adventure came a dawning realization: Sweden could not rely on other nations to safeguard its security. Instead, Sweden would have to look at its own defenses, which had fallen into disrepair.

Swallowing the acid pill of its antimilitary bias, the Social Democratic majority began to rearm Sweden. It went slowly at first: From a pre-1936 level of $31.5 million, the defense budget rose to $37 million in 1936-1937. The pace quickened after Hitler's 1938 march into Austria. For 1938-1939 the defense budget stood at $58.5 million, and Foreign Minister Rickard Sandler offered both an explanation and a warning: "The strengthening of our defenses has but one purpose: Do not disturb the peace of the North."

Guarding the peace was an Army and reserve of modest size—130,000 men—but high professional caliber, with officers who were rated among the best in Europe. Although the Swedes were short of armor, with 64 tanks and 30 armored cars, the General Staff was among the first anywhere to understand the importance of mechanization and was pushing for a more mobile army. The Air Force had 195 planes of mixed quality, with heavy emphasis on torpedo-bomber squadrons that could strike quickly at the supporting units of an invasion force.

Sweden's Navy, by far the most powerful in Scandinavia, was designed for operations in the shallow, shoal-ridden waters of the Baltic. Its heaviest guns were carried by eight large armored vessels unique to the Swedish Navy. Though they had a battleship's 15-inch batteries, they weighed only 7,000 tons—about two thirds the tonnage of a German pocket battleship and less than a fifth that of the full-scale battleships in the British and American fleets. In addition, the Swedes had an excellent strike force of 15 submarines specially built for cruising in the shallows and among the rocky islands of Sweden's 1,400-mile coastline. Swedish naval architects had also designed a destroyer for coastal operations—15 were in service in 1939—that had an excellent top speed of 42 knots and unusual maneuverability.

But the best design in the world was meaningless without the means of production. Realizing at the outbreak of hostilities that they were too dependent for military equipment on Germany, England, Italy and the United States, the Swedes began converting peacetime factories to the production of the materials of war. Automotive manufacturers turned to making tanks, safety-match manufacturers produced ammunition, and makers of hunting rifles built machine guns.

Some of the outstanding weapons of World War II came off Swedish production lines. The famous Bofors 40mm antiaircraft gun, which was prized for its advanced automatic loading and exceptional accuracy, became the standard British and American light antiaircraft weapon. Soon the Swedes were producing an extra-light dive bomber, the Saab B-17, that could outmaneuver the more famous German Stuka while carrying a greater bombload.

A team from Sweden's Voluntary Motor-Boat Fleet—a wartime auxiliary coast guard—searches the hold of a foreign vessel in 1940. Such inspections made it very difficult for smugglers to transport contraband through Sweden to the belligerent nations.

Thus, World War II found Sweden better prepared to defend its neutrality than any other nation in northern Europe. Yet that neutrality very nearly failed in its first major test—a traumatic trial of the Swedish conscience springing not from Nazi aggression in the West but from the November 30, 1939, onslaught by the Soviet Union against Finland.

Historically, Swedes perhaps felt closer to the Finns than to any other national group, including even the Danes and the Norwegians. Moreover, Sweden had long looked upon friendly Finland as a buffer against the ancient Russian enemy. Now, with Finland in deadly peril, Swedish public opinion cried out for military intervention.

Although sympathetic, Sweden's leaders adamantly refused to renounce the neutrality upon which they had staked their survival; for one thing, they feared that Germany, which in August had signed an alliance with the Soviet Union, might seize upon intervention as a pretext for assaulting Sweden.

Still, under popular pressure, the Swedish government moved as far as it dared from the strict dictates of legal neutrality. Operating under a kindly official eye, a purportedly private organization established recruiting stations throughout Sweden to enlist volunteers to fight with the Finns; hundreds of officers and noncoms were even given leave from the Swedish Army to go to Finland. And Sweden's Prime Minister Per Albin Hansson pledged both humanitarian and material assistance to his country's afflicted neighbor.

Such measures satisfied hardly anyone, and as national criticism rose to a crescendo the government found it necessary to call upon King Gustav for a public explanation of Sweden's stance. "With sorrow in our hearts," said Gustav, "we have come to the conclusion that if Sweden now intervened in Finland we would run the gravest risk of being involved not only in the war with Russia but also in the war between Great Britain and Germany, and I cannot take that responsibility upon myself."

By March 13, 1940, when the silence of peace fell upon the Winter War, about 8,800 Swedish volunteers had made their way to Finland. Going into action in the very last days of the War, on a quiet sector of the front, they had suffered 33 killed and 200 wounded. Swedish supplies sent to Finland included not only foodstuffs, clothing and medicine but 84,000 rifles, 575 automatic weapons, 85 antitank guns, 112 field guns and howitzers, 104 antiaircraft guns, 50 million cartridges and even 25 aircraft.

To aid the Finns, Sweden cut deeply into its own Army's inventories. Sweden also sent large supplies of oil and coke to Finland, drawing again on national reserves that it badly needed for home consumption. Finally, Sweden allocated 300 million kronor ($12.6 million) for postwar economic assistance to Finland. All of these moves were highly popular, but they stirred concern among government planners trying to determine how Sweden should allocate its resources to weather the larger war in Europe. Every depletion of its national reserves, the planners knew, placed a further burden on Sweden's overseas trade as the sole source of the economic strength that Sweden would need to survive.

Before the War, the combined total of Swedish imports and exports had amounted to about $935 million a year. For Sweden's exports—minerals, metals and wood products—Great Britain was the best customer, with 24 per cent of the trade, followed by Germany with 18 per cent. For Swedish imports—especially food, solid fuels, petroleum products and artificial fertilizers—the foreign roles were reversed: Germany, with 22 per cent, led both the United States, with 16 per cent, and Britain, with 12 per cent.

Shortly after the outbreak of war, both Germany and Great Britain signed agreements respecting—at least in principle—Sweden's right to trade with whatever country it wished, and during the quiet first seven months of the conflict, Swedish commerce actually increased. Even then there was a price to be paid: During that same period, no fewer than 40 Swedish merchant ships were sunk, most of them by German mines or by U-boats whose skippers operated on the hallowed principle of shooting first and seeking to identify the target later.

The German invasion of Norway and Denmark brought an end to Sweden's precarious trading balance between the belligerents. No sooner had the Wehrmacht moved into Scandinavia in April of 1940 than Germany clamped a blockade on the Skagerrak, the arm of the North Sea separating Norway and Denmark, thereby sealing off the Baltic and the major western Swedish port of Goteborg. For the British, the enemy action brought an unexpected bonus: When the blockade was imposed, about half—some

600,000 tons—of the Swedish merchant fleet was west of the Skagerrak in ports or waters that were controlled by the Allies. Under heavy British pressure—and having little practical choice in the matter—Sweden leased the vessels to the Allies for the duration.

But that was about the only glimmer of light amid the Allied gloom. With Sweden now isolated from the West, its trade with the Allies was cut to a trickle—and even that was maintained only by dangerous or devious designs.

Great Britain desperately needed Swedish-made ball and roller bearings, as well as other precision parts, for its aircraft industry. To obtain such vital items, British Airways operated for the Air Ministry a perilous shuttle route from Scotland's Leuchars airport to Stockholm. The 800-mile run, which took up to eight hours in a lumbering Dakota, stretched for 250 miles over occupied Norway, always at the mercy of German antiaircraft guns and interceptors. Once inside Sweden, the unarmed aircraft had to stay within a narrow corridor on its way to Stockholm's Bromma Airport; if it strayed from the delineated boundaries, it was subject to being shot down by the Swedes.

Flying only at night and preferably in foul weather, to avoid being illuminated by the moon over Norway, the re-

markable air-transport service made a total of 1,200 flights between Scotland and Sweden. In so doing, it carried more than 500 tons of precious parts to Great Britain.

Almost as arduous was the route worked out by Sweden's giant SKF company to transport precision thread taps to Coventry for use in building British aircraft engines. The SKF parts were hauled by rail to Haparanda, on the Swedish-Finnish border, then taken 300 miles by truck on primitive arctic roads to the Finnish port of Petsamo, where they were picked up by legally neutral American vessels, shipped to New York, thence to Liverpool and finally, overland, to their Coventry destination.

In perhaps the boldest venture of all, Great Britain ran the German blockade with ships that would have been utterly helpless had they been discovered in time by enemy sea or air patrols. When the Germans invaded Norway, George Binney, a British businessman, was in Trondheim to purchase steel. And William Waring, a professional accountant, was working on the books of the British Embassy in Oslo. Both made their way to Sweden and were given titles as assistants to the British commercial counselor in Stockholm. In fact, the two were assigned by their government to find ships and crews to break the German blockade.

Throughout the rest of 1940, they labored at their frustrating task, finally rounding up five Norwegian ships, each of about 10,000 tons, that had been stranded at Goteborg by the German conquest of their homeland. To man the vessels, Binney and Waring signed on British merchant seamen who had been caught ashore in Norway by the invasion and had fled to Sweden, along with some Norwegians and Swedes. Loaded with 25,000 tons of Swedish steel, machinery and ball bearings, the unarmed fleet sailed from Goteborg on January 23, 1941.

During the first part of their voyage the ships headed north for 50 miles, hugging the coast in Swedish territorial waters and under the protection of the Swedish Navy. Then, cloaked by night, they turned west and ran for a British Navy escort awaiting them in the North Sea. They were spotted and trailed by a single German aircraft, whose pilot was unsure of their identity. Only when he saw them nearing the escort did he make a strafing attack, killing one man.

When Hitler heard that all five ships with their crucial cargoes had reached England, he furiously reprimanded

As frost forms on their hats and collars, two Swedish volunteers man an antiaircraft gun in northern Finland in January 1940. More than 8,000 Swedes—many of them professional soldiers on leave—fought for Finland in the three-month-long Winter War against the Soviet Union.

Grand Admiral Erich Raeder, Commander in Chief of the German Navy. The German blockade was immediately intensified. Moreover, the German Ambassador in Stockholm warned the Swedes of dire consequences if they allowed future shipments. Since Sweden had no choice but to take the German threats at face value, the effort launched by Binney and Waring was stalled for more than a year.

Sweden's trade with Britain during the early years of the War was thus a matter of catch as catch can, carried out mostly by stealth in the dark of night. Commercial relations with Germany were much more regular—and struck at the very heart of Sweden's status as a free and neutral nation.

As Nazi Germany demonstrated time and time again, it considered neutrality no more than a flimsy legalism, to be shouldered aside whenever military or other considerations seemed to warrant. During naval staff discussions about the invasion of Norway, at least one admiral had argued that rather than risk an attack from the disputed waters of the Norwegian Sea, it would be safer to march overland from territory seized in Sweden.

Hitler, however, had cause to avoid a military confrontation with Sweden, largest and by now the strongest of the Norse nations. His offensive against the Low Countries and France was scheduled for the late spring of 1940, and he had no intention of permitting troops needed for that operation to become tied down in Scandinavia. That Germany could conquer Sweden was taken for granted; yet it was entirely probable that Swedish forces could hold out for a while in their rugged northland, forcing Hitler to expend the commodity he could least afford—time.

Once he had gone ahead with his invasion of Denmark and Norway, Hitler was further discouraged from aggressive notions about Sweden by his suspicious ally, the Soviet Union. While still trying to digest a large part of Finland, the Soviets were willing to countenance the German takeover of Norway and Denmark. But the idea of Sweden—which Russia historically considered to be within its own sphere—in Hitler's hands was more than Josef Stalin could stomach.

On April 14, less than a week after Germany moved against Norway and Denmark, the German Ambassador to Moscow sent home a dispatch marked "Very secret, urgent." In it he reported that Soviet Foreign Minister Vyacheslav Molotov had told him Russia was "vitally interested in preserving Swedish neutrality." The next day, German Foreign Minister Joachim von Ribbentrop replied: "We are determined to respect unconditionally the neutrality of Sweden, as long as Sweden in turn observes strict neutrality."

To the Nazi warlords, "strict neutrality" worked decidedly in favor of Germany. Early in the year, the German Navy had decreed that it must be made "absolutely clear" to Sweden that "pro-German neutrality is the sole road to preservation of its independence." Admiral Raeder had told Hitler that the occupation of Norway would enable Germany "to exert heavy pressures on Sweden, which would then be obliged to meet all our demands."

The first and most ominous pressure was applied by Hitler himself. On April 16 he summoned Admiral Fabian Tamm, the head of a Swedish delegation sent to Berlin to convince the Germans that Sweden was determined to defend its frontiers against any invader. Hitler complained of criticism of his regime by the Swedish press and said he had heard that the Swedish government was hostile to him. British and Norwegian troops, he added, were still fighting in northern Norway; he believed that the British would use their foothold at Narvik to move into northern Sweden and—with Swedish acquiescence—take over that region's strategically priceless iron-ore fields.

Never, replied Tamm. Sweden was committed to defending its neutrality against any and all incursions. "Does that include England?" Hitler shouted. It did indeed, said Tamm. "Who says so?" cried Hitler. "Does the King say so?"

Yes, he did. Upon hearing Tamm's report of the conversation, King Gustav V wrote personally to Hitler: "I solemnly declare to you, Mr. Chancellor, that Sweden will maintain the strictest neutrality. Sweden is firmly determined to oppose with all its power any and every attempt to violate that neutrality." Insofar as he would accept any man's word, Hitler accepted Gustav's. The son of one German princess and the widower of another, Gustav was a known admirer of Germany's culture; beyond that, the monarch shared in his country's historic hatred of Russia.

Nevertheless, Hitler could not resist turning the screws. In his reply to Gustav, Hitler promised that Germany would respect Swedish neutrality—under certain conditions. Of these, the most important was that Sweden continue to sup-

Swedish soldiers scramble to board their trucks during a military exercise in 1940. Within one week of the German invasion of Denmark and Norway, a general mobilization nearly quadrupled the number of Swedes in uniform—from 85,000 to more than 320,000 men.

ply the Nazis with undiminished shipments of iron ore.

Iron. To Sweden it was both bane and blessing, livelihood and life itself. Its possession made larger, more powerful nations eye Sweden hungrily; its location in the frozen North permitted Sweden to hold the ore fields as a trump card, threatening to demolish the mines with high explosives before invading armies could reach the remote region.

The deposits, located in Swedish Lapland, well above the Arctic Circle, were the richest in all Europe (containing about 66 per cent iron against 33 per cent for the French fields in Lorraine), and were estimated to be more than two billion tons. In 1902, Sweden had constructed the state-owned Iron Ore Line, a railroad that connected the producing centers of Kiruna and Gällivare with the ports of Lulea on the Gulf of Bothnia and Narvik in Norway. Sweden and Norway were united at that time under the Swedish crown; three years later, when Norway broke off the relationship, the Swedes attempted to make Lulea the exclusive port for ore shipments. But the idea soon proved impractical; the Gulf of Bothnia is frozen for four or five months of each year, while Narvik, because of its proximity to the warming Gulf Stream, is ice-free throughout the year.

Narvik therefore remained very much in business, burgeoning from a tiny village at the turn of the century to a bustling port of about 10,000 inhabitants, almost all of whom were employed by the Swedish Iron Ore Trust. In a typical prewar year, about three quarters of the Lapland ore was shipped out of Narvik, with more than 1,000 freighters carrying two thirds of the mineral to Germany and the rest to Great Britain, Belgium and other countries.

In the late spring of 1940, after fighting fiercely but failing to win lasting control of Narvik, British and French troops were withdrawn from Norway. With the Skagerrak blockade and the German occupation of Norway, Swedish ore shipments to Britain and other Allies were effectively ended. Even more unfortunate for Sweden, coal and coke from Great Britain were also cut off; before the War, Britain had been the principal supplier of the eight million tons of solid fuel imported annually to heat Swedish homes and run the nation's armament and other industries.

Given that critical situation, Sweden probably needed no threats from Hitler to work out a mutually satisfactory trading arrangement: Sweden would maintain its prewar level—in 1938 it was 9.78 million tons—of ore exports to Germany; in return, the Reich would provide Sweden with coal and coke, which in 1940 came to 5.7 million tons. That was considerably less than the amount Sweden wanted, but enough to get by on. Meanwhile, negotiations

of a much more controversial nature were being conducted.

For as long as German troops were still fighting in Norway, it was clearly more convenient to provide them with arms and ammunition transported by rail across Sweden than by risking sea routes patrolled by the Allies. The Swedes, however, refused to cooperate, citing neutrality as their reason for permitting only the "humanitarian" transit of food and medical supplies. Thwarted, the Nazis resorted to the expedient of smuggling: On May 7, 1940, Swedish customs guards opened 146 crates, each marked with a red cross, in a Narvik-bound railroad car. Instead of medical items, they found nearly 150,000 cartridges and an arsenal of grenades and artillery shells. "The car," announced the chief customs officer, "has been sealed and remains here."

At about the same time, Hermann Göring, soon to become the first and only Reich Marshal of Germany, decided to try his hand at moving munitions. For years, Göring had made Sweden his personal concern. A World War I flying ace, he had emerged from that conflict permanently embittered, earning a meager living as a pilot for Europe's fledgling commercial airways—including the Swedish airline. While in Sweden, he met and married the Baroness Karin von Fock-Kantzow, who until her early death was probably the only thing—woman, man or cause—the cynical Göring ever truly loved. Göring spent much of the years 1924-1926 in and out of Swedish asylums, under treatment for a mental breakdown induced by morphine addiction. He had turned to the drug to alleviate the pain of a nearly fatal bullet wound he suffered in a clash with the police during Hit-ler's abortive attempt to seize power in 1923. As he rose to prominence in Nazi Germany, Göring maintained his Swedish contacts, especially in the aristocratic circles that his marriage had opened to him. Now, on behalf of the Third Reich, he meant to cash in on these connections.

Early in May 1940, while the battle for Narvik and northern Norway was still undecided, Birger Dahlerus, a Swedish engineer, received an urgent request to fly to Berlin to see Göring, his longtime friend. Instead of the benevolent *Unser Hermann* ("our Hermann") he had known, Dahlerus found to his dismay a blustering bully from whose lips the word *Kriegsnotwendigkeit*—"necessities of war," the term used to excuse Nazi aggression and atrocity—fell all too easily.

Pacing angrily to and fro, Göring denounced Sweden in general and its hostile—as he considered it—press in particular. He added ominously that Sweden lay at the mercy of German armies whenever they wished to move.

After this florid display of temper, Göring got down to business. The hard-pressed German soldiers at Narvik, he said, were sorely in need of artillery. He proposed, among other things, that Sweden allow transit of three batteries of artillery in sealed railroad cars with Red Cross markings. When Dahlerus protested that he was not authorized to negotiate any such proposition, Göring demanded that Sweden send a delegation that was so empowered.

The Swedish negotiators, Admiral Tamm and diplomat Gunnar Hägglöf, arrived on May 11. They found Göring preoccupied with Germany's blitzkrieg assault on the Low Countries and France, which had been unleashed only the day before. Nonetheless, Göring soon warmed to his self-

assigned task of browbeating the Swedes. The occupation of Narvik, he said, was a pet project of Hitler's, undertaken against the judgment of his military advisers. If Germany's ''Narvik heroes'' were to suffer because Sweden declined to assist in providing them with artillery, Göring warned, the Führer would neither forgive nor forget.

Calmly the Swedes pointed out that an invasion of their homeland would be costly—if only because explosives were already in place to blow up the northern iron mines and electrical installations in the event of attack. Hägglöf also cited repeated German assurances, including the one from Hitler to King Gustav, that Swedish neutrality would be respected. Sweden, he explained, would breach its own neutrality if it permitted the transport of arms to the troops that had invaded neutral Norway. Göring's patience, never his long suit, was by now exhausted. Pounding a desk with his fist, he said furiously: ''You, Mr. Hägglöf, are a hidebound lawyer and diplomatist; you understand nothing about the fate of nations.''

It required courage of high order to stand up to the wrath of Hermann Göring. But the Swedes steadfastly stuck to their refusal, and Göring suddenly reverted to his pose as Sweden's German champion. Sweden, he said, was like a second homeland to him, and he would never do anything to harm his Swedish friends. But, he added darkly, he could by no means guarantee that Hitler and the rest of the Nazi hierarchy would feel the same way.

Four days later a more aggressive member of that hierarchy, Foreign Minister von Ribbentrop, took over the effort to coerce Sweden into granting transit rights. At the time, Rib-

bentrop was at Hitler's headquarters in Bad Godesberg, on the Rhine, where the Führer was overseeing his armies' thrust into France. To that spa city Ribbentrop summoned Arvid Richert, Sweden's Ambassador in Berlin.

In a windy harangue, Ribbentrop offered the German view of Scandinavian neutrality insofar as it was affected by the conflict in Norway. The struggle around Narvik, he insisted, was entirely between Germany and the combined invasion forces of Britain and France. Since Norwegians were not involved (in fact, they were fighting alongside the Allies), it could hardly be an unfriendly act toward Norway for Sweden to permit the transportation of German arms. Actually, Ribbentrop continued, such transit might be the only way to protect Swedish neutrality—since, unless permission were given, thereby enabling Germany to contain the fighting in Norway, the War might spread to Sweden.

Richert returned to Berlin, where he was confronted by a Ribbentrop underling, Baron Ernst von Weizsäcker, the German Secretary of State. From him, Richert learned that Germany, far from seeking to send three artillery batteries across Sweden, as Göring had said, wanted transit rights for three full trains, each made up of 30 to 40 cars and containing not only ground artillery but antiaircraft guns and communications equipment.

Deeply impressed by the threat implicit in the German demands, Richert warned his government that continued refusal would entail the risk of German military action. The Swedes, however, remained firm: After an emergency session of the Cabinet, the Swedish Council on Foreign Relations on May 18 ruled against the transit of arms, offering as

Four Italian-made destroyers purchased by Sweden are docked in Goteborg after being released by Britain's Royal Navy. The British, fearing that the ships would fall into the hands of the Nazis, had seized them while they were en route to Sweden in June of 1940.

A Swedish civil-defense officer emerges from a tunnel blasted out of solid rock to protect residents of Stockholm in case of an air raid. An air vent rises from the shelter at center left.

a sop its permission to allow the homeward passage across Sweden of some 2,500 German sailors whose ships had been sunk in Norwegian waters.

Having braved the fury of Adolf Hitler, the Swedes braced themselves for a German attack. They were only partly relieved when word came from Germany that the Führer, although enraged, had said that he was too busy with the invasion of France to attend to the Swedes—just yet.

By June 4, with the British evacuation from Dunkirk, the war in France was all but over, and Germany was predicting the imminent withdrawal of Allied troops from Norway as well because they would "soon be so badly needed elsewhere." Four days later, the last British and French forces left the Scandinavian peninsula.

Sweden was now an isolated enclave, beyond the reach of British aid in the event of a German attack. Within the enclave, the Swedes began to live a curiously disjointed existence. Signs of war obtruded everywhere, but people behaved much of the time as if it did not exist. At least one member of virtually every Swedish household was drawn into wartime activity. Some went into the armed forces, others volunteered for special auxiliary units like the civilian Home Guard or the Women's Auxiliary aircraft spotters. At the age of 16, every citizen was required to register for a civil-defense assignment; those who were not enlisted in the armed forces or their auxiliaries were given tasks ranging from the maintenance of air-raid shelters to the manning of field kitchens for troops on maneuvers.

Yet visitors to Sweden found the country almost eerily calm and the leisure habits of the people surprisingly untouched by crisis. Visiting Stockholm in the winter of 1940, American journalist Martha Gellhorn was struck by the lights. "To the east and the south the great cities of Europe lie nightly in darkness," she wrote. "Every night the lights of Stockholm shine on the waters of the Norrstrom and Lake Malar, festoons of lights hang over the main streets, the shop windows and the cafés are brilliant, and the snow gleams under the street lamps."

In Stockholm's Kungsgata amusement area, nightclubs were filled night after night with men and women in evening dress. The Grand Hotel swarmed with businessmen,

speculators, spies and foreign correspondents. Long lines formed to see *Gone with the Wind* and the sentimental English film of home-front heroism, *Mrs. Miniver*. Shakespeare, Chekhov and Ibsen played to full houses at the Royal Dramatic Theater, and tickets to contemporary American plays such as *Our Town* and *The Little Foxes* were hard to find. Looking for something to cheer, Swedes turned out in record numbers to see their world champion Gunder Hägg run the mile and to watch a heavyweight boxer named Olle Tandberg knock out a Dutchman to win the European crown. Reviling such wartime frivolity, German propaganda castigated Sweden as a nation of "dressed-up swine" devoted only to pleasure, who lacked the vigor to join Hitler in the "historical mission" he had undertaken.

The first indication that life in Sweden could not go on quite as it had was the disappearance of private cars from the roads for lack of fuel. Most people took to bicycles or to three-wheelers, while taxis and official vehicles were fitted with bulky, gas-producing charcoal burners invented by a Swedish engineer. A visitor from Britain recalled that her most "alarming experience" in wartime Stockholm was "to watch the chauffeur open the stove on the bonnet or the luggage carrier while flames shot up as he emptied in a sack of fuel." But, she added, "the results were excellent."

Severe shortages of most consumer products began to appear in 1942. Under the double pressure of a German blockade in the Baltic and a British blockade in the North Sea, Sweden found itself forced to ration leather, meat, soap, bread, wool, sugar, eggs, flour. The ingenious Swedes alleviated some of the shortages by finding substitutes. "Sweden wears wood, drinks wood, eats wood, fuels automobiles with wood," wrote a marveling American journalist in 1943. Swedish chemists found a way of combining wood pulp with leather scrap to make a gray, linoleum-like substance that was used to resole shoes. Soldiers' uniforms were 20 per cent wood pulp, and even the popular drink, schnapps, was manufactured out of pulp instead of potatoes. Cows ate wood pulp as fodder, and humans drank a "coffee" that was a mysterious mixture of wood shavings, beets and acorns. Looking back at his wartime experience, a Swedish journalist recalled chiefly the "enormous piles of wood lying everywhere in the cities."

More destructive to Swedish morale than the shortages

was the unemployment in industries stifled by the blockade. In 1940, some 100,000 Swedes were out of work—a situation that would not improve until the armaments industry gradually began to build up. The spectacle of men lined up outside soup kitchens was something new for prosperous Sweden—as was the alarming inflation that drove prices up by 40 per cent during the war years, and real wages down by 10 to 12 per cent. Suddenly Swedes found their taxes nearly doubled, as the government struggled to pay for its rearmament program. With the construction business virtually paralyzed, new housing at any price became almost impossible to find.

For Swedish libertarians, the most disturbing changes were the restrictions placed on individual freedom of action and speech. A number of Communists and other suspected security risks were rounded up and sent to "work camps" for the duration. Even more alarming to some was the censorship imposed in the first year of the War, chiefly to control the widespread expression of anti-German sentiment. Swedish newspapers were confiscated for publishing testimony about the Germans' torture of captured Norwegian resistance fighters, and when a freight train mysteriously exploded in the town of Krylbo, the press could neither identify it as a German train nor reveal that its freight was ammunition. Politically controversial books were banned, as was Charlie Chaplin's poignant film satire on Hitler and Mussolini, *The Great Dictator*. The Allied departure from Norway

A Swedish soldier keeps watch over German troops during a break in the Germans' rail journey across Sweden in boxcars. The transit trains—which for three years carried German soldiers and war matériel to and from occupied Norway—were an embarrassment to most Swedes.

Playwright and entertainer Karl Gerhard appears with a Trojan horse that symbolizes the German fifth column in Sweden. Threatening to close the theater, censors forced Gerhard to tone down his anti-Nazi wit.

THE SWEDE WHO SAVED 100,000 JEWS

A wealthy young Swede, Raoul Wallenberg, arrived in Budapest in July 1944 armed with little more than a fervent desire to rescue the Jews of Nazi-dominated Hungary, who were marked for forced labor and death. His mission had the moral support of the Swedish government, and he had been given diplomatic credentials. Otherwise, he was on his own.

Within weeks, the resourceful Wallenberg was operating on an astonishingly massive scale. He printed up and distributed to Jews thousands of fake Swedish passports. He set up safe houses in Budapest and boldly hung the Swedish flag in front of them. Circulating in Budapest society, he made secret friends in high places, bribed less sympathetic officials and reminded diehard anti-Semites of the reckoning that surely awaited criminals after the War—a warning that restrained the Nazis from destroying the Budapest ghetto as the Red Army approached.

All told, Wallenberg saved the lives of an estimated 100,000 Jews. He seemed to lead a charmed life among the Hungarian Nazis and their German overlords. His undoing, ironically, came at the hands of Hungary's so-called liberators. The Russians took Budapest in January 1945 and evidently saw Wallenberg as a threat to their plans for postwar Hungary. He was escorted to Red Army headquarters and never returned. Despite Soviet claims that he died in 1947, he was later reported alive in Soviet prisons a dozen times.

Wallenberg works in his Budapest office in 1944.

With hands clasped, Raoul Wallenberg (right) patiently tries to persuade Nazi officials to free interned Jews. Those to his right hold false Swedish passports.

made the censors more anxious than ever to ban anything that might rouse the Germans' ire.

The shifting power balance in Scandinavia led to a major shift in Swedish foreign policy. On July 8, the government at last agreed to the transit of war matériel across its territory to the German occupation forces in Norway. And Sweden also gave Germany the right to transport troops—allegedly traveling to or from furlough in Norway—across Swedish soil. The British could only protest helplessly.

Sadly for Sweden, the agreement was no more than an opening German wedge. Troop transit, for example, had been made conditional on the promise that the number of Germans entering Norway on the so-called leave trains would be kept in more or less equal balance with those who were departing on furlough. But by early 1941 the troops moving into Norway by far outnumbered those who were leaving; it was clear that Germany was using the trains to reinforce its army of occupation. When Sweden's Foreign Minister complained, the Nazis discarded all pretense: On March 14, the German High Command announced that it meant to send more than 16,000 additional troops into Norway—and that any Swedish attempt to prevent the movement would result in "a very critical situation."

Behind the increased troop traffic lay Hitler's determination to bolster his forces in Finland in preparation for his cataclysmic invasion of the Soviet Union. With that onslaught, launched on June 22, 1941, came the most staggering blow of all to Sweden's already faltering neutrality. Declaring that refusal would be considered "an unfriendly act," Germany insisted that Sweden authorize the transit of a fully armed infantry division from Norway to Finland.

The Finns, who were understandably eager to recover the territory that they had lost in 1940, had joined in the attack against Russia; they urged Sweden to accede to the German demand. Yet the proposed movement would be a blatant violation of Sweden's neutrality, and Prime Minister Hansson's effort to push through the concession to Germany—and, as he argued, to Finland—caused a Cabinet crisis. It was resolved only after rumors spread that King Gustav had threatened to abdicate unless the Cabinet agreed to the Reich's mandate. (Despite his known admiration for Germany and hostility toward Russia, it remains open to question whether the King actually intervened in such a way.)

The Cabinet gave way, and on June 26 the German 163rd Infantry Division began to roll across Sweden at a rate of four trainloads per day. It was a massive operation, for the Germans took with them large quantities of munitions in anticipation of an eastern offensive. After two weeks, 15,000 officers and men, along with all their weapons and supplies, had been deposited in Finland, ready to join the assault on the Soviet Union, which was now one of the Allies.

The Swedes would have preferred to keep quiet about the transit operation, but it stirred such controversy within the government that it was soon common knowledge. Details appeared in the German press, and the Swedish government acknowledged it in a public announcement.

The outcry was immediate. Britain and the Soviet Union formally protested to Stockholm. In Norway, Sweden was bitterly dubbed "Transitania." In Sweden itself, the respected journalist Torgny Segerstedt mourned his country's shameful servility. "Once it was possible to be proud of being a Swede," he wrote. "Once Sweden was a kingdom."

Against the clamor, the Swedish Foreign Ministry lamely explained that the reason for the government's decision was Sweden's "special attitude" toward Finland. "It does not mean that we have chosen sides in the war between Germany and Great Britain," said a spokesman. "It means only that we have taken Finland's side in this special instance." More important, Prime Minister Hansson pledged that the movement of the German division had been a "once-and-for-all concession."

Hansson was as good as his word. On July 31, Sweden flatly turned down a German demand that a second division be allowed passage to Finland. Never again would an organized combat unit be granted transit, and although the "leave trains" to and from Norway continued, the balance between troops entering and departing was, at Swedish insistence, gradually restored.

The day was nearing when Sweden would no longer have to truckle to Germany as a requirement for national survival. Like Sweden's Charles XII before him, Hitler found Russia to be an expanse without end. With every mile that he plunged deeper, he became less capable of waging war in Scandinavia—especially against a Sweden increasingly able to put up a stiff fight in its own defense.

In the first three years of the War, Sweden doubled its Army to 250,000, tripled the Army's armored units and greatly strengthened the motorized infantry. The Navy built up its destroyer and submarine forces and added a squadron of fast, light torpedo boats designed for operations in the twisting channels of the Swedish archipelago. The Air Force by 1942 was more than twice the size it had been at the outbreak of war, with most of its new strength concentrated in high-performance fighter planes.

Even as Swedish leaders felt increasingly confident about their own military defenses, their conviction that Germany would win the War steadily eroded. Yet the turn in Swedish policy that followed the Allied victories in Tunisia and at Stalingrad was at first evidenced not so much by positive action in favor of the Allies as by the gradual withdrawal of privileges that once had been conceded to Germany.

In April 1943, a mass citizens' meeting in Stockholm adopted a resolution strongly urging the government to halt the transit trains to Norway, which were odious to a huge majority of Swedes. Significantly, the resolution was supported by the government's mainstay, the Swedish Trade Union Federation. Still, the Swedish leaders hesitated, fearful of taking a step they knew would infuriate the masters of the Third Reich. In July, however, after a German disaster in the great tank battle at Kursk, the Swedes made their decision: Transportation of German war matériel to Norway would cease on August 15; five days later, passage for troops would come to an end. By the time those deadlines arrived, however, Swedish tracks had carried a total of 2,140,000 German troops and enough German freight to fill 100,000 railroad cars.

German displeasure at the cutoff was soon manifest. On August 25, German warships attacked and sank two Swedish trawlers in Danish waters. Several days later, a German fighter shot down a Swedish courier plane returning from England. Such reprisals, however, were a far cry from invasion and were taken as a measure of Hitler's diminishing power to impose his will upon those who offended him.

Transit had been a one-way street, with all benefits accruing to Germany and none to Sweden. Trade with Germany was another matter: The Swedes needed solid fuels from the Reich at least as much as the Germans, who had gained possession of the Lorraine ore fields with the fall of France, required Swedish iron ore. Yet even as they realized that the tides of war were changing, so the Swedes understood that adjustments in their trade policies were necessary.

Pressure from the United States accelerated the change. The Americans had largely replaced the British as the principal Allied trade negotiators with Sweden. And if Winston Churchill professed patience with the Swedish dilemma, the United States did not. The American Ambassador in Stockholm adopted an increasingly threatening tone, suggesting that if Sweden did not curb its exports to Germany, more Swedish products would be put on the blockade blacklist and Swedish assets in the United States would be frozen.

In fact, the increasingly hard-pressed Germans were no longer able to deliver coal and coke to Sweden in scheduled amounts—during 1942 the shortfall had been nearly two million tons. The next year's agreement therefore tied Sweden's strategic exports to the Reich's fulfillment of its own commitments. Sweden contracted to ship Germany some seven million tons of ore, a reduction of three million tons. In return, the Germans pledged to send Sweden four million tons of coal and coke. As it turned out, the Swedes,

A fiery V for Victory signals the pro-Allied sympathies of young Swedes who are gathered outside the Norwegian consulate in Stockholm in 1943. The Swedes were demonstrating to show their support of more than 1,200 students and teachers at Oslo University who had been arrested by the Nazis and interned in concentration camps.

pleading a manpower shortage in the mines, delivered even less ore than they had promised—and late in 1944, with the Nazi regime running out of time, Sweden would order a halt to all trade with Germany.

Meanwhile, in areas other than trade Swedish authorities had been edging toward a policy of assisting the Allies. Ever since the single successful run of their little fleet through the German blockade back in 1941, British agents George Binney and William Waring had been having a discouraging time. Early in 1942, they had chartered 10 more Norwegian vessels caught at Sweden's Goteborg harbor by the Nazi occupation of Norway. After a legal fight in which Germany contested the proprietary rights of Norway's government-in-exile in London, Sweden's Supreme Court upheld the charter and released the ships to the British.

Under intense pressure from Germany, the Swedish government refused permission for the British to base the boats in the secluded fishing port of Lysekil, where their chances of making a successful break would be greatly improved because Lysekil offered more direct access to the North Sea. Instead, said the Swedes, the fleet and its cargo of ball bearings and high-grade steel would have to sail from Goteborg, a port under such heavy surveillance by German agents and trawler crews that the British had almost no hope of achieving surprise. Moreover, the British boats would not be allowed to hug the coast, as they had done in 1941, but would have to move directly into "outer territorial waters"—and from there to the open sea.

At 2 a.m. on March 31, 1942, the 10 ships made their try—with woeful results. Six either were sunk by German air and sea patrols or were scuttled by their crews to prevent them from falling into enemy hands; two others turned back to safety at Goteborg. Only the 17,000-ton tanker *B. P. Newton* and the puny 300-ton *M. T. Lind* reached England.

To compound the debacle, British newspapers, in hailing the arrival of the two successful blockade breakers, said that they had "fired back with good effect" at attacking German aircraft. It turned out that the British had outfitted the ships with machine guns unbeknownst to the Swedes—who reacted sharply, not only in response to German protests but with genuine indignation at the affront to Swedish neutrality. The two ships that had retreated to Goteborg were interned, their captains were fined—and George Binney was ordered to leave Sweden.

But in 1943, as the War turned against the Germans, the Swedish attitude underwent considerable change. Back in England, Binney had persuaded the Ministry of War Transport and the Ministry of Supply that smaller, faster, more maneuverable vessels, equipped with high-powered diesel engines and designed to carry up to 45 tons, had a reasonable chance of evading German patrols off Sweden.

Binney's idea was that the vessels should operate only in winter, when stormy weather would increase their chances of evasion—and that their sailings should coincide with periods of little or no moon. Taking into account this severely limited schedule—and also the likelihood that some crossings would be interrupted by enemy action or crippling storms—Binney computed that the vessels could deliver up to 500 tons of supplies in a winter season.

By autumn 1943, a flotilla of "pocket freighters," as they came to be known, were ready to leave England. There were five of the little craft—the *Master Standfast*, the *Hopewell*, the *Nonsuch*, the *Gay Corsair* and the *Gay Viking*—

British merchant sailors man antiaircraft guns on the afterdeck of the Nonsuch, one of five blockade-runners, capable of 23 knots, that the British used to bring high-precision parts and other vital cargo out of Sweden.

each 117 feet long, built similar to a torpedo boat, manned by a hand-picked British crew of 20 volunteers, flying the Red Ensign of the Merchant Service—and adorned in the captain's cabin by a portrait of Sir Francis Drake.

Waiting in Sweden for the arrival of the pocket freighters was William Waring. He had established an office in Lysekil—where the Swedes had given their permission, previously refused, for the freighters to operate. Conferring regularly with helpful Swedish officials, Waring used Swedish stevedores to assemble cargoes for loading.

Early on an October morning, the *Gay Viking*, first of the tadpole fleet to make the run, dashed through the blockade and safely entered Lysekil's harbor—where she was welcomed by nearly 5,000 Swedish townspeople. Swedish police were detailed to watch over the British seamen (and prevent them from wandering into the port's restricted areas). The sailors were comfortably lodged in the town's best hotel—until, two days after her arrival, the *Gay Viking* was escorted by Swedish warships to the outer limit of neutral waters. From there she darted through the blockade and safely raced 600 miles to her home port of Immingham.

The pocket freighters shuttled between Sweden and Britain in fair weather and foul, mostly without mishap. Only one ship was lost: On the first sailing of the little fleet after *Gay Viking's* initial run, the *Master Standfast* was attacked by a German patrol ship and captured after her captain was killed. The four other craft continued operating for four months, delivering 347 tons of such prized cargo as ball and roller bearings, machine tools and spare parts to England.

Tailoring its neutrality to fit Allied needs was deemed prudent by the Swedish government; making amends to its less fortunate neighbors was an imperative to the Swedish people. From the War's first days, Sweden was a haven for the displaced peoples of northern Europe. Among the first to arrive was the crew of a Polish submarine that escaped to Sweden in the grim autumn of 1939. In pathetic flow came Lithuanians, Latvians, Estonians, Poles and even Germans, seeking asylum from the tyrannies of Nazism and Communism alike. But of an estimated 200,000 refugees, the majority came from Sweden's Scandinavian neighbors—50,000 Norwegians, 108,000 Finns and 18,000 Danes. Sweden received them all, cared for them as best it could, and provided jobs, especially in the fields and forests, for many.

The refugee traffic became almost routine. But in the fall of 1943 came an occasion for Sweden to make a special effort—at the risk of incurring Adolf Hitler's personal displeasure. Early in October, well-founded rumors spread that Hitler had ordered a roundup of all Danish Jews for deportation to Germany. With Sweden's direct help, a rescue fleet of small boats, mostly fishing smacks, was organized to smuggle the threatened Jews out of Denmark. In a matter of weeks, about 7,200 persons were ferried across the 10-mile-wide waterway separating the two nations.

The rescue operation was the genesis of a continuing contraband shuttle between neutral Sweden and occupied Denmark, with security police from the Interior Ministry supervising the Swedish end of the run. Through the shuttle, the Danish underground received from Sweden more than 5,200 machine pistols, 5,000 carbines, nearly 10 million rounds of ammunition and 10,000 hand grenades.

Much more massive was an extraordinary air-transport service that was requested by the Norwegian government-

As Norwegian ski troops guard the drop zone, an American B-24 delivers supplies by parachute in this watercolor by Colonel Bernt Balchen. Flying from bases in northern Sweden, Balchen's irregular air force brought tons of food and medical and military supplies to Norwegian resistance fighters.

in-exile, aided by the Swedes, abetted by the British, and carried out by the U.S. Army Air Forces.

More than 12,500 Norwegian refugees, all men of military age, had volunteered for training in camps established throughout Sweden. Clad in Swedish uniforms with Norwegian shoulder patches and armed with Swedish weapons, they were preparing to act as a police force, bringing order to the chaos that must inevitably result in Norway with the end of the War and Nazi occupation. German envoys in Sweden who asked questions were blandly told that the training bases were "health camps" set up to keep high-spirited young Norwegians out of mischief.

Exiled governments tend to become impatient, and the Norwegians in London, unwilling to wait for the postwar cleanup in their homeland, wanted a part in the shooting war. For the Norwegians in Swedish camps, the British government was willing to arrange advanced training facilities in Canada. Some would receive flight instruction at a base near Toronto while others would go to Nova Scotia for naval training. Though releasing refugees for active military duty was a gross infraction of neutrality, the Swedes permitted the evacuation of 2,000 Norwegians for that purpose. One problem remained: getting them out of Sweden.

That job fell to the Americans, and on January 27, 1944, a Norwegian-born U.S. Army Air Forces colonel named Bernt Balchen received unusual orders: Given five old and battered B-24 Liberators, he was to organize an air-transport service to fly the Norwegians out of Sweden through the German-controlled skies of Norway to London. From there the volunteers would be taken to Canada.

Quartered in a suite in Stockholm's Grand Hotel, Balchen soon had his little outfit—which he later dubbed the "Ve-do-it line"—in operation. The Swedes, even while cooperating in what was at best an illegal venture, were sometimes irksomely legalistic. One Air Ministry official, for example, insisted that Balchen's B-24s meet Swedish regulations by showing registration numbers on their sides. Balchen accommodated them by painting the dark-green planes with black numerals that were barely visible.

The exodus went slowly. The Liberators could carry only 35 passengers each and the Swedes for some reason would allow no more than three flights a night. Yet by May, the 2,000 Norwegians had been moved and the job was done.

Far from folding its wings, however, Balchen's airline remained very much in business. Eventually it expanded to 60 aircraft performing all sorts of odd chores. One assignment came in June of 1944, shortly before the Germans began to launch their self-propelled rockets against England. A prototype V-2 rocket, probably set off at an experimental station in the Baltic island village of Peenemünde, landed in Sweden almost intact. Friendly Swedish scientists gave the bomb to Balchen, who flew it to London. Thus British experts had their first opportunity to examine the devilish new contrivance that soon would bring anguish to London.

During the winter of 1944-1945, Balchen established an advance base at Kalix, on the Gulf of Bothnia in northern Sweden, intending to fly Norwegian volunteers and equipment to Arctic Norway. From there, the Norwegians were to join in the pursuit of Germans retreating from Russia. That the Norwegian role turned out to be minimal was hardly Balchen's fault: Flying in frightful weather—the temperature sometimes fell to –50° F., and engine oil had to be diluted with gasoline to keep it from freezing—the Ve-do-its made run after run. Balchen kept track of the results in his log: "450 tons supplies and 265 military personnel to Bodo," "70 Norwegian engineer troops to Kautokeino," "40 tons hospital equipment from Kirkenes to Banak."

Balchen's transports were still flying on V-E Day. In all, they had moved 1,442 men and 2,456,000 pounds of supplies to the Far North.

By aiding in such enterprises, the Swedes had restored themselves to Allied good graces. And when peace came, Prime Minister Hansson could declare with satisfaction that "a long nightmare finally has lost its hold." Yet for Sweden, the nightmare had been one of the nervous system. Despite many hardships, the Swedes had experienced little of the heartbreak and misery visited upon other peoples. Indeed, there was a widespread notion among Europeans that Sweden had waxed fat on its selective neutrality. An analogy was used to make the point. Two frogs, it seems, had fallen into a pail of cream. One frog, a fatalist, drowned without struggling. But the other—Sweden—was an opportunist: It flailed about so strongly that it not only lived but churned the cream into butter. The truth probably lay somewhere between Hansson's nightmare and the agile frog.

HAVEN IN THE NORTH

Carrying their belongings on their backs, refugees from Roros, Norway, trudge into Sweden in April 1940, during the German invasion of their homeland.

OPEN ARMS FOR NEIGHBORS IN DISTRESS

From all over Europe, refugees made their way to Sweden, and found a warm welcome there. Dozens of Swedish agencies, both private and state-run, rushed to provide the displaced victims of war with shelter, clothing, food, medical care and even job training. In all, Sweden spent an estimated $150 million to help more than 200,000 refugees.

The bulk of the Swedes' generosity was directed to their fellow Scandinavians, chiefly because they had the easiest time reaching Sweden. More than 50,000 Norwegians and 18,000 Danes found refuge there. About 70,000 Finnish children were evacuated to Swedish foster homes for periods ranging from a few months to several years. Many Norwegian freedom fighters took nightly refuge in Sweden, crossing the border to escape German patrols and then returning the next day—buoyed by food and sleep—to continue the fight.

But the Swedes did more than merely accept those who reached their shores. Count Folke Bernadotte, a nephew of the King's and Vice Chairman of the Swedish Red Cross, arranged delicate exchanges in which about 10,000 British, American and German prisoners of war were shipped to Sweden—and then home. Early in 1945, Bernadotte also arranged the transfer to Sweden of 13,000 Scandinavians held in German concentration camps. And as the Reich crumbled, he used that concession as "the thin edge of the wedge" to win further concessions—and freedom for 19,000 more inmates, many of them Jews, from 27 nations.

Finnish refugees from the 1940 Winter War dash through the snow for cover when their Sweden-bound train comes under attack by Russian planes.

Swedish sailors rescue a young refugee from a small boat in the Baltic. By late 1944, nearly 32,000 people from Baltic nations had fled to Sweden.

GRATEFUL GUESTS IN A NEW LAND

The refugees streamed into Sweden from every direction, and by every means. German defectors who jumped from cruise ships passing Danish islands were fished out by partisans in speedboats and later smuggled into Sweden in small fishing vessels. The police in occupied Norway, ordered to help round up Norway's 1,700 Jews, warned them instead; more than half were then spirited to the rugged mountains and forests of eastern Norway, where they hid out until Swedish guides could escort them across the border.

Finns fled from Lapland driving their cattle before them. They wrapped their babies in newspaper to keep them warm; young children—usually barefoot or shod in paper-and-wood shoes—were tied to their mothers lest they become lost. Other youngsters fleeing on crowded trains slept on the luggage racks while their parents stood throughout the trip.

Once they reached a Swedish processing camp, the refugees moved from station to station, registering for Swedish papers, exchanging what money they had, receiving coupons for tobacco and soap. Doctors, who were often refugees themselves, tended the sick and vaccinated the children. Everyone was sent to a "lice sauna" to be disinfected. (One Finn found that "the room was not hot enough to kill the lice—just warm enough to wake them up and get them moving.") Then the newcomers were assigned to temporary billets to await transportation to hospitals, schools and private homes across Sweden.

Most of all, the refugees were made to feel at home. "It felt nice to be treated in a friendly manner," one of them recalled. "Swedish ladies were offering us coffee and cake. We thanked them, and I learned my first Swedish phrase: 'Var sa good'— 'You are welcome.' "

Inside northern Sweden, refugees huddle at a border camp. At such camps, refugees were given hot meals and baths and had their clothes sterilized.

144

Eyes glazed with fatigue and sorrow, a Finnish couple in Tornio awaits entry into Sweden. Adults frequently found it harder to leave home than young people did. "We children thought it was all very exciting," one refugee recalled, "but the grown-ups were crying."

Estonian refugees find temporary haven in a converted gymnasium. As many as five special trains a day distributed the new arrivals throughout Sweden.

Safely removed from the hazards of war in 1944, Finnish children link hands and dance with their Swedish nurse in the playroom of their temporary home.

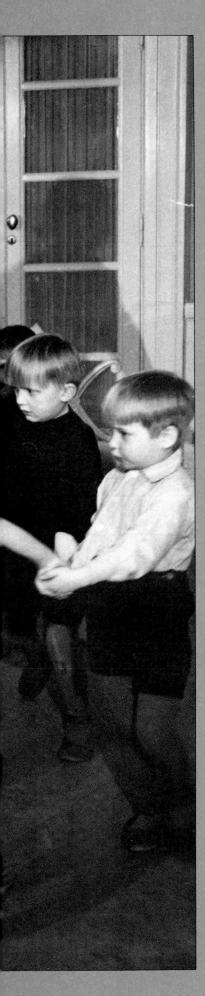

LOVING CARE FOR UPROOTED CHILDREN

The Finns, who were at war most of the time between 1939 and 1945, shipped their children off to Sweden whenever the guns threatened. The sick and the babies went by plane. Many crossed the Gulf of Bothnia in boats, and the rest came on special evacuation trains.

Swedish families took in the children of Finnish relatives, and thousands opened their doors to strangers. Old Swedish manors became foster homes for the healthy and sanatoriums for the tubercular. Hospitals found room for others who were ill.

The children went to school in the villages where they lived and soon became assimilated. Many who spoke no Swedish when they arrived could not speak Finnish when they left years later. Nearly 3,000—most of them war orphans adopted by their foster parents—never left at all.

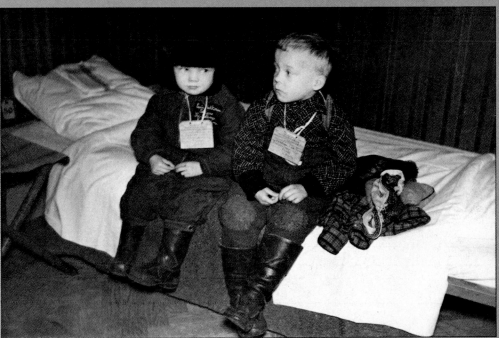

Still apprehensive, two young refugees sit on their double-ended bed in Stockholm's Hotel Anglais.

The supervisor of the Royal Home for Children in Solna, near Stockholm, sets the tables for her 25 Finnish charges.

Norwegian volunteers for paramilitary training muster in front of the Swedish mansion that served as their headquarters in Sörmland, south of Stockholm.

TRAINING SOLDIERS IN EXILE

Thousands of the refugees from Norway were young men who hoped to join Norwegian units fighting with the Allies. In that they were disappointed. Sweden—to protect its neutral status—would let few of them leave. Instead, most were sent to isolated camps to work as lumberjacks.

But by late 1943, Sweden was anticipating an Allied victory. It agreed to train both Norwegian and Danish refugees as "police troops," a euphemism used to fend off German protests. The purpose, the Swedes insisted, was not to evict the Germans but to maintain order once they were gone.

The Swedes grew even less cautious in the War's final months. They formed the "police troops" into infantry battalions, provided ships for a 4,000-man Danforce to support an Allied invasion of Denmark, and set up depots along the border with Norway. The Danish force was not needed, but as the German troops began to withdraw from Norway, 13,000 trained Norwegians moved in.

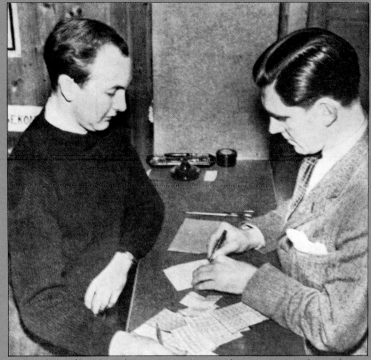

A Swedish official (right) issues ration cards to a Norwegian refugee.

Swedish Prince Gustav Adolf (second from right) inspects Norwegian "police troops" trained to keep order in their homeland once the Germans had fled.

149

COUNT BERNADOTTE'S EVENHANDED MERCY

No individual did more for Europe's wartime prisoners than Count Folke Bernadotte. As the Army official in charge of internment, he provided sustenance, housing and even entertainment for the 12,000 foreign soldiers who for one reason or another found themselves in Sweden. As a Red Cross officer, he arranged in 1943 and 1944 the first successful large exchanges of military prisoners of war, overcoming a deep German distrust of the process.

Bernadotte labored to assure the Germans that his arrangements were fair. He provided the well-cared-for German prisoners who passed through Sweden with the same amenities—chocolate, tobacco, reading matter from home—that Allied POWs got. And, lest the Germans back out at the last minute, he persuaded the British press to mute its outrage at the emaciated condition of the Allied soldiers until the exchange was completed.

In the spring of 1945, Bernadotte and a number of aides embarked on a dramatic mission to Germany. At Bernadotte's urging, Chief of the SS Heinrich Himmler had agreed to release all Scandinavians being held in concentration camps. The Swedes collected them—and as many other inmates as their fleet of buses would hold. They called the prisoners "patients," because most of them weighed less than 100 pounds and many had to be carried. Bernadotte's crew scoured Germany, bribing, tricking and cajoling camp guards to increase their take. They succeeded in liberating "patients" from all over Europe—including 12,000 Jews marked for death.

At his Stockholm family home, Count Folke Bernadotte stands between doors decorated with 18th Century Swedish soldiers.

British soldiers who have spent up to four years in German prisons give the V sign from the ship that carried them home via Sweden in October 1943.

German residents of Sweden salute their arriving compatriots—nearly 2,100 servicemen who were exchanged in 1944 for 2,700 Allied prisoners of war.

Four young women give vent to a broad range of emotions from the window of a railway car carrying them through Sweden after their release from a German

concentration camp. Count Bernadotte's expedition rescued about 4,000 Polish women from a single camp, Ravensbrück, during the final days of the War.

FEISTY LITTLE IRELAND

At a barrier blocking a coastal road in Ireland, shotgun-wielding volunteers of the Local Security Force halt a car to check the identity papers of the driver.

"WHO ARE WE NEUTRAL AGAINST?"

For Ireland to proclaim its neutrality, as it did vigorously on September 3, 1939, was one thing; to protect it was another. The Irish Defense Forces mustered only 6,000 poorly armed officers and enlisted men, a minuscule air force, and no navy at all.

To tighten the island's defenses, the government quickly called up the 5,000 men of its ready reserve and activated the part-time Local Security Forces. Many of these citizen-soldiers were veterans of the Irish Republican Army's 1916-1921 war of independence against Britain, and it was probably one of them who first raised the question: "Who are we neutral against?" Passed from mouth to mouth, the phrase became Ireland's mock war cry.

The question was serious enough. The Army's prewar contingency planning had been directed against a land incursion from British-held Northern Ireland. This threat was now intensified, or so Eire's leaders believed, by Britain's anger over Ireland's stubborn insistence on remaining neutral. At the same time, Eire had to defend its 2,000 miles of coastline against the possibility of a German air-sea-land assault like the ones that overwhelmed several small nations during the first year of the War.

With grudging assistance from Great Britain and the United States, Ireland acquired six motor torpedo boats to build a rudimentary navy, a few fighter planes and antiaircraft guns, and 20,000 American rifles to arm reservists and recruits, who swelled the land forces to the strength of two divisions. The Irish Army's assignment was schizophrenic. The 1st Division was to hold off a German invasion from the south until British reinforcements could be invited to support the Irish defenders. The 2nd Division was deployed on the northern border, and its commander, Major General Hugo McNeill, anxiously sought assurances from the German ambassador that the Axis would help in the event of a British invasion.

For many Irish soldiers, however, the way was clear. More than 4,000 of them deserted and joined Britain's armed forces to fight for the Allied cause.

A priest (top) blesses Ireland's first motor torpedo boat, a British-built craft, while crewmen and the Irish High Commissioner in London look on. At bottom, the newly launched M.1. makes a test run. Intended for more-sheltered waters, the boats proved unsuitable in Ireland's rough seas.

From a distance, sailors on a ship converted for Irish port defense scrutinize an incoming freighter both to confirm its identity and to check it for guns.

Gloster Gladiators fly patrol over Ireland. They were dubbed Faith, Hope, and Charity after a trio of Gladiator fighters that defended Malta against Axis air raids.

AN AIR FORCE ORDERED TO FIGHT ON THE GROUND

Ireland's early air defenses amounted to a few antiaircraft batteries and a modest collection of warplanes, including three obsolete Gloster Gladiators (*left*). It was not until 1943 that Irish fighter pilots got a squadron of modern Hawker Hurricanes, which were also made in Britain. Until then, they augmented their fleet by salvaging planes crash-landed in Ireland by Royal Air Force fliers in distress.

When late in December of 1940 a German airborne invasion seemed possible, cautious senior officers dashed the pilots' hopes of defending their homeland gallantly from the air. They ordered them instead to block airfield runways with their planes and to prepare to fire on German paratroopers with rifles.

Crewmen serve a battery of 3.7-inch antiaircraft guns guarding Dublin. By mistake, guns defending nearby Baldonnel airfield once fired on and nearly shot down a transport carrying Irish pilots to Dublin on leave.

WATCHING THE EDGE OF THE BLITZ

During the blitz, Ireland lay too close to Britain for its own good. With landmarks frequently obscured by fog and clouds, wandering Luftwaffe pilots could mistake its cities and towns for targets in Britain. And Irish urban areas were terribly vulnerable: When the War broke out, even Dublin—300 miles to the west of London—had only a token few antiaircraft guns, and no air-raid shelters.

As a passive defense measure, the Department of Defense laid out 60 markers spelling "EIRE" in letters large enough to be seen from high in the air. Placed at intervals along the coast, the markers were useful but not foolproof. On the night of May 30, 1941, some German planes evidently overshot their British targets and dropped their bombs on two Dublin residential areas. The result was 27 Irish dead, 45 injured and 325 homes destroyed or seriously damaged.

White-painted stones forming letters 30 feet in length proclaim this headland to be neutral Irish territory. The adjacent serial number helped pilots identify the site on their charts.

bombing, explaining that it "may have been caused by high winds" that blew the planes off their course

FROM COAL SCUTTLES TO SOUP PLATES

When Ireland's 6,000-man Army donned its uniforms for mobilization in September 1939, a stranger might have thought that Hitler's Wehrmacht had invaded the British Isles by the back door. "Coal-scuttle" helmets, high-collared, dark green tunics, jodhpurs and black leather puttees gave the Irish Defense Forces a definite made-in-Germany look.

Both Ireland's look and mood changed by June of 1940, when Nazi legions had overrun Western Europe and were poised to cross the Channel. In near-panic, the government of Ireland declared a state of emergency, launched a recruiting drive, and appealed to Britain for additional arms and equipment. While Irish seamstresses sewed uniforms of a lighter green similar to those worn by Britain's Tommies, the War Cabinet in London approved the issue of British "soup-plate" helmets to Irish soldiers in the hope that they would have a "useful psychological effect." But the Cabinet refused to sell Ireland new rifles as long as it remained neutral.

Publicly, Prime Minister Eamon de Valera continued to proclaim that the Army and Cabinet would fight to the last man resisting a British invasion; in secret, the Irish and British Army staffs worked out a plan for repelling a German invasion. Code-named *Plan W,* it called for British troops in Northern Ireland to rush south, where the Irish Defense Forces would be holding a river line against the Germans. To make sure the British came when they were needed—but definitely not before—one of the Irish liaison officers assigned to Belfast was Major Vivion de Valera, the Prime Minister's soldier son.

Looking like British Tommies, Irish infantrymen in

A smiling recruit emerges from a quartermaster depot with his general-issue ration, including uniform, mess kit, brushes and swagger stick. By 1942, Ireland had 30,000 "Emergency Durationists" in uniform.

Defense Force soldiers route-march down a country lane soon after their mobilization in September 1939. Their "coal-scuttle" helmets had been standard issue since 1928.

"PIDDLING PANZERS" AND HOMEMADE ARMOR

With one division posted in the north and the other in the south, half of Ireland's Army would have to move quickly to support the other in the event of invasion. Lacking enough trucks, or the fuel to run them, the infantry trained by making rapid marches across country. In a typical exercise, the soldiers underwent nine hours of daylight drills, marched 13 miles in combat gear, took a one-hour break, then began night operations that involved yet another three-mile hike over rough country, hauling their heavy equipment in two-wheeled "prams."

To create a strike force that was more mobile, the Army formed motorcycle and bicycle squadrons—derisively called Piddling Panzers—and searched for replacements for the 20-year-old Rolls-Royce armored cars used by the motorized cavalry. Solutions were found right at home. A cut-down civilian sedan (below) made a serviceable gun carrier. And the chief engineer of Ireland's Great Southern Railway, using armor plate left behind years before by the British, fashioned a steel turret on a chassis supplied by the Ford automobile works in County Cork. By late 1940, factories in Ireland had produced enough of these unusual vehicles to equip three armored squadrons.

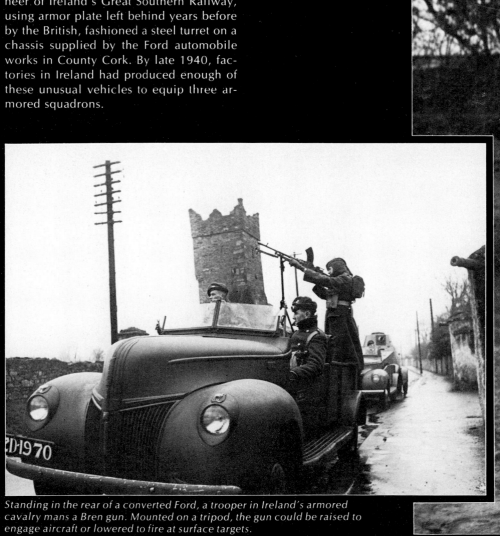

Standing in the rear of a converted Ford, a trooper in Ireland's armored cavalry mans a Bren gun. Mounted on a tripod, the gun could be raised to engage aircraft or lowered to fire at surface targets.

"The enemy of my enemy is my friend." So goes an aphorism whose origins are lost in the mists of time. It is unquestionably among the most basic of human sentiments—the principle that in World War II impelled subject peoples to welcome the German armies, as the Ukrainians did in 1941, or to collaborate with the Japanese, as many colonial Indonesians and some Burmese did in 1942. More than one independent country ignored the larger menace of Axis aggression and adopted, out of long-standing antipathy for one or another of the Allies, a weighted neutrality.

Winston Churchill had little sympathy for neutrals, particularly those that stood in the way of his efforts to grapple with the Nazi foe. His rendering of the ancient adage might well have been "the friend of my enemy is my enemy," and if he could not convert a country to the Allied cause by moral preachments and promises, he would as willingly bend or break its neutrality by blunt threats and pressure.

Neither blandishment nor bluster, however, seemed to affect the Irish or the Turks, two fighting peoples who, out of visceral hatred for their neighbors, defied Churchill's best and worst efforts to compromise their neutrality. Thanks to the leadership of some of the cleverest politicians in Europe, they got away with it.

The neighbor Ireland feared was Great Britain itself. To most of its ardently Catholic citizens, newly independent of British rule after centuries of bitter conflict, "the enemy" in 1939 meant the English and their Protestant Anglo-Irish supporters, who still clung to the Emerald Isle's northernmost counties. Partly to spite Britain for its refusal to cede this last piece of sacred soil, the government of Ireland—or Eire as it is called in Gaelic—refused to join the rest of the British Commonwealth in declaring war on Hitler. Worse still, from Churchill's point of view, the government denied Britain the use of Irish ports traditionally used to guard the entrance to the English Channel and Britain's Atlantic life line.

In Turkey's case, the enemy was the Soviet Union, looming huge and fearsome over the northern border. Turkey had warred intermittently with its gigantic neighbor since the 17th Century. In World War I, the Russophobia of the Turks had driven them into an alliance with Germany against Russia and the Western Allies. Having lost their empire as a consequence of Allied victory in 1918, the impoverished Turks in World War II would choose the safer stance

Neutrality based on fear and hate
A prophetic warning from Atatürk
Churchill's scheme to open the Black Sea
A nimble delaying act in Cairo
Ankara's last-minute declaration of war
The angry island at Britain's back door
A secret emissary to de Valera
German promises of a unified Ireland
The Christmas crisis: awaiting invasion on two fronts
A lunchtime tirade at the White House
A condolence call on the German Embassy
Bitter words in a victory oration

TWO STUBBORN HOLDOUTS

of a neutral republic, seeking to profit from both British and German trade and aid—all the while keeping the hated Russians at arm's length.

Turkey, the rocky remnant of the vast Ottoman Empire, was surrounded by potential invaders. Against its shrunken northern border pressed the Russian colossus; the Balkan States, once Turkish provinces, thrust the weight of Central Europe against its western flank; the eastern Mediterranean, in centuries past a Turkish lake, now bore the fleets of younger powers toward its shoreline and its last strategic asset, the Turkish Straits. This waterway, made up of the Dardanelles, the Sea of Marmara and the Bosporus, linked the Mediterranean and the Black Sea. From bases in Turkey equally telling blows could be struck against the empires of Britain or Germany or Russia.

Other neutrals who in 1940 stood in the path of a belligerent power experienced the pounding of tank treads and hobnailed boots. Turkey's strategic stance astride the crossroads of three continents brought it instead the soft shuffle of patent-leather pumps. To the dusty capital of Ankara came only polished ambassadors, seeking by persuasion and intrigue to subvert the young republic's neutrality and tap its minerals and manpower. There they murmured with cultivated, French-speaking ministers and their wives in a sparkling whirl of parties, fetes and sporting events.

At the center of this diplomatic merry-go-round was a diminutive general-turned-statesman, President Ismet Inönü. During most of the War he was served by Prime Minister Sükrü Saracoglu, an amiable, disarmingly frank expert in the Turkish art of survival politics. The third member of the triumvirate was Foreign Minister Numan Menemencioglu, a lawyer educated at a Jesuit college in Switzerland, who like his friend Saracoglu saw Europe as a chessboard and Allied and Axis officials as opposing chessmen to be manipulated to Turkey's advantage. Like a chess master, he was constantly looking 20 or 30 moves ahead to gauge which pieces would remain on the board for the crucial end game.

Never far from the minds of this threesome were the visions planted there by the founder and first President of the Turkish Republic, Kemal Atatürk. The great Atatürk had decreed that, to survive in a cockpit surrounded by quarreling great powers, his countrymen must remain involved but un-committed in international politics and eschew adventures beyond their borders. Before his death in 1938, he had displayed a prescient appreciation of events to come. As early as 1934, Atatürk had told an American visitor, General Douglas MacArthur, that a war would break out in Europe around the year 1940; that, as a result, Germany would come to dominate the entire continent excepting only Britain and Russia; and that from this war the Soviets would emerge as the principal beneficiaries.

"The Bolsheviks," Atatürk cautioned MacArthur, "have reached a point at which they constitute the greatest threat not only to Europe but to all Asia." This, in infinite variation, was to remain at the core of Turkish thinking throughout World War II. As one Turkish official, who wisely managed to keep his name out of the history books, confided to an Allied diplomat, "What we would really like would be for the Germans to destroy Russia and for the Allies to destroy Germany. Then we would feel safe."

In pursuit of their policy of Turkey first, Europe second, and the Soviet Union last, Inönü, Saracoglu and Menemencioglu would manage to sell, at premium prices, strategic commodities like chromite and copper to both Germany and Britain while receiving from both sides the arms and assistance they needed to defend and develop their country. Little by little the Germans would refurbish Turkey's roads and railroads while the Allies built airfields and port facilities and vied with the Germans in equipping Turkish factories. In return the Turks allowed Axis and Allied agents virtually free rein to play their double games and dirty tricks against each other under the cloak of diplomacy.

The government-dominated press was split fairly equally between pro-German and pro-Allied factions, and Turkish military missions surveyed with equal interest and admiration Germany's Eastern Front in Russia and British defenses in Egypt's Western Desert. Throughout, however, the Turks steadfastly stuck to their rights, conferred by the Montreux Convention of 1936, to control the passage of belligerent ships through the straits. The consummate diplomatic skill with which they pursued their objectives won grudging admiration from the British, respect from the Germans, and tolerance even from the Russians.

Yet it was not merely Turkey's geographical position, its chromite and copper mines, or the guns that commanded the straits that caused the great powers to woo the backward little republic with diplomatic favors and military largesse. Its 50-division Army of 800,000 peasants, toughened by the hard labor and harsher weather of the bleak Anatolian plateau, was, man for man, the equal of any infantry force in Europe. Tireless marchers, masters of trench warfare, and skilled artillerymen, their defense of the Gallipoli Peninsula in World War I had made a lasting impression on their German allies and British foes. Though the Turks in 1939 lacked both armored divisions and air power, theirs was an Army that made Adolf Hitler cautious, Josef Stalin apprehensive, and Winston Churchill bold.

Hitler overwhelmed the rest of Central Europe and the Balkans by blitzkrieg and subversion. Turkey he left alone, halting his panzers 37 miles from the mountainous border; he then assigned Germany's wiliest diplomat, Franz von Papen, the task of assuring that the Turks remained neutral and cooperative. As German Ambassador in Ankara, the suave and unscrupulous Papen maneuvered to keep the Turkish government in a state of anxiety about the belligerents' intentions. From one hand he sprinkled hints of future German generosity toward Turkey by ceding captured Russian provinces, mixed with subtle threats of what the Luftwaffe's

bombers could do to Turkey's wooden cities and flimsy factories. With the other hand Papen sowed seeds of suspicion about Allied plots against Turkish neutrality and independence, and in particular the fear that the British would sacrifice Turkey in order to strike a blow at Germany or to propitiate the Russians. There were numerous kernels of truth in his whispered stories, for Papen had direct access to dispatches summarizing Allied planning conferences, thanks to a German-recruited Albanian spy on the British Ambassador's household staff.

Indeed, making Turkey a sacrificial instrument of Allied strategy was precisely what Winston Churchill had in mind. "Every new enemy helps Hitler's ruin," was his motto, and he badgered his staff with proposals to use Turkish troops, along with British forces in the Middle East, in a grandiose scheme for opening the Black Sea to Allied warships, supplies and military forces. Then the Turks and the British could drive westward with the Russians and "ultimately give them our right hand along the Danube." It was a cherished, chimerical vision shared by no other Allied leader, though by his own account Churchill pressed it on his colleagues "on every occasion, not hesitating to repeat the arguments remorselessly."

The Turkish leaders had quite a different vision from Churchill's. Despite all dangers and temptations, they must preserve the hard-pressed republic and its fragile economy from invasion or blockade. They must avoid such commitments as might draw Turkey's foot soldiers into foreign campaigns yet induce potential allies to provide the modern arms needed to strengthen the country's defenses.

Like field marshals in a war of wits, İnönü and his ministers maneuvered among the British, American, German and Russian statesmen, playing off one belligerent against the other, diverting ally against ally, driving a wedge here, laying a diplomatic ambush there, and occasionally digging in to rebuff a determined ambassadorial démarché. Evenhandedly, they offered congratulations to one side for a victory won, to the other condolences for a battle lost, and assurances of fidelity to both. From 1940 until the very eve of Allied victory, Turkey's outward policy would remain what Prime Minister Saracoglu frequently termed "alliance with Britain and friendship with Germany." It was a neat phrase for a neat trick, which only the Turks could have pulled off.

In October 1939, Turkey had felt it necessary to sign a much-negotiated treaty of mutual assistance with Britain and France as a precaution against Axis designs on the neighboring Balkan States. In return the Allies promised to provide the tanks, guns and aircraft Turkey would need to fulfill its obligations. But when the Wehrmacht swept westward through France in 1940 and then eastward to within 100 miles of Istanbul, Turkey excused itself from joining Britain's heroic but hopeless defense of Greece. As the British themselves conceded, without the modern arms promised but not delivered, Turkey would be at a grave disadvantage in a war of movement on foreign soil. But the treaty with Britain remained in force, and when Turkish diplomats negotiated a mutually protective treaty of friendship with Germany, they made sure that it contained a paragraph acknowledging their separate and prior pact with Britain.

Signed June 18, 1941, the treaty provided Hitler with all he needed from the Turks—at least for the moment. It gave him a neutrally secure southern flank for his armies' eastward plunge into Russia, the right to buy Turkish chromite, copper and other strategic materials, and insurance against any air threat from the south to his vital oil supplies in Ru-

mania. To keep the Turks honest, Hitler installed some fighter and bomber bases on captured Greek islands off Turkey's coastline as a permanent threat to its undefended cities. Then he absorbed himself in the direction of his advancing forces in Russia and North Africa.

Britain, meanwhile, had acquired a new ally in Soviet Russia, and Churchill was determined that the Turks should help him help the Russians. To achieve this, he assigned two of his most skilled diplomatists, Foreign Minister Anthony Eden and Ambassador Sir Hughe Knatchbull-Hugessen.

It was quite a team. Sir Hughe, though 53 years of age, cut a youthfully trim and elegant figure in Ankara society. He had served in Constantinople as far back as 1908 and for many years in Persia. As Ambassador to China in 1937 he had been a witness to Japanese aggression there and had taken a bullet through the middle from a strafing Japanese warplane. The wound might have killed or permanently invalided a weaker man, but Sir Hughe remained as nimble and indefatigable on the dance floor as he was in diplomatic debate. For his frequent tête-à-tête conversations with high Turkish officials, he carried an outsized hip flask of Scotch which he wielded with such effectiveness that one of his regular guests referred to it as "Sir Hughe's revolver."

The Ambassador's role of cajoling confidant was complemented by dapper Anthony Eden's frequent dramatic turns as the stern enforcer of the Anglo-Turkish mutual-assistance treaty. The Turks grew to regard him as the devil's agent, for on his flying visits to the East he always seemed to bring demands for Turkish action that, it seemed to them, had clearly originated in Moscow. As Foreign Minister Menemencioglu afterward asserted, "It was at the instigation of the Russians that Mr. Eden insisted on the precipitous entry of Turkey into the War." In reply, Eden, his guardsman's mustache aquiver, would warn his Turkish peer to "face facts" and recognize that Russia, too, was Britain's ally.

Menemencioglu was not averse to repeating his conversations with Allied diplomats to Franz von Papen, who quoted the Foreign Minister, in a cable to Berlin, as saying that he was "knocking himself out" trying to show the British "that Germany's military potential is the only thing that can resist the Russian avalanche." The Germans exploited Menemencioglu's confidences and his fears with a brief campaign of intense diplomatic and psychological pressure

Combat-ready Turkish troops wind past a battery of 150mm howitzers guarding the 17-mile-long Bosporus strait. Defenses such as these made the Bosporus and its sister strait to the southwest, the Dardanelles, a virtually impregnable barrier between the Mediterranean and Black Seas.

designed to draw Turkey into their increasingly difficult struggle against the Soviets. Menemencioglu strung Papen along with polite expressions of interest until, late in 1942, with the Nazi armies everywhere in retreat, Papen too went on the defensive.

The turn of the tide in the Allies' favor was now about to bring Winston Churchill himself surging eastward, brimming with promises for the Turks and bubbling with confidence that he could persuade them to put aside their objections and join the crusade to hasten the Nazis' unconditional surrender. As Churchill saw it, Turkey's primary concerns were the 15 German divisions to the north and the German fighter and bomber squadrons poised on the nearby islands of Rhodes and Chios. British and American planes based in Turkey, he believed, could nullify the latter threat, and Stalin had previously agreed to deal with the German divisions if necessary. As for Turkish concern about the "Russian avalanche," Churchill disparaged it—the supposed avalanche had hardly gathered momentum, and, as he would soon tell the Turks himself, "things do not always turn out as bad as expected."

Over the objections of Anthony Eden, who had had personal experience with Turkish obduracy, and the doubts of

his military aides, who questioned the Turks' readiness to fight, Churchill arranged to meet with President Inönü at Adana, near the Turkish-Syrian border, and flew there from Casablanca on January 30, 1943. Surrounded by British generals and air marshals, he waited at the airport for the President's train, which looked to him like "a very long enameled caterpillar, crawling out of the mountain defiles."

Inönü had brought the entire Cabinet and General Staff with him, and for two days and nights they plied the Britishers with food and drink aboard the luxurious train. Churchill spread before his hosts a glittering verbal display of the gifts and guarantees the Allies were prepared to offer, "prior and subsequent to any political move by Turkey." In addition to renewing British promises to modernize the Turkish Army "with the greatest speed," Churchill pledged 25 Allied air squadrons, new airfields to be built and equipped by British engineers, unlimited numbers of British antitank and antiaircraft regiments, two battle-hardened British armored divisions, a reserve drawn from the British Ninth and Tenth Armies and a Big Three guarantee of Turkey's postwar borders. It was a lavish offer the Turks could hardly refuse, particularly when all they had to do in return was to "consider" entering the War when they were sufficiently armed.

While their staffs worked out a written agreement by which the British formally offered and Turkey accepted these inducements, the politicians dealt with the question the Turks now brought to the surface—the effect on Turkey if an all-conquering Red Army dominated Eastern and Central Europe. A new flow of Churchillian rhetoric described the nascent United Nations organization and the 20-year alliance between Britain, the Soviet Union and the United States that would guarantee the peace of Europe after the War. When Premier Saracoglu dryly remarked that his government was looking for "something more real," Churchill argued that association in battle with the United States and Britain, and the arms to be provided, would be Turkey's best assurance of dealing with any Soviet menace.

The meeting ended as cordially as it had begun, and Churchill flew home convinced that Turkey would come into the War by Christmas. Subsequently, the Allies shipped 350 tanks, 48 self-propelled guns, 300 field guns, nearly 300 antiaircraft guns, about one million antitank mines and nearly 100,000 infantry weapons as a first installment on

An international newsstand in Istanbul displays magazines from many belligerent nations, including such American periodicals as Harpers and Good Housekeeping. The Ankara government banned imported publications printed in Turkish but permitted those in foreign languages.

Sailors and guests assemble at Istanbul's Taskizak shipyard to watch the launching of a Turkish submarine that was built with Germany's assistance. Before the War, Germany had been Turkey's principal source of industrial goods and in 1941 began supplying war matériel as well.

Churchill's promises. But when the Big Three met again at Teheran in November, the Turks were still refusing to break relations with Germany or even to strain their neutrality by allowing British fighter planes to use the air bases rushed to completion by Allied engineers at Izmir and Badrun. To reinforce the Turks' natural reluctance, Papen had told them in no uncertain terms that if they made their airfields available to the Allies, Germany would take offensive action against Turkey "before the first British aircraft touched the soil of Izmir."

When Sir Hughe Knatchbull-Hugessen and American Ambassador Laurence A. Steinhardt delivered invitations to Inönü and Menemencioglu to meet with Churchill and Roosevelt at Cairo immediately after the Teheran Conference, the Turkish leaders recognized an implied summons to account for their behavior. And they knew, from some heatedly undiplomatic conversations with Anthony Eden the previous month, that the Western leaders would be deaf to arguments that Russia posed a greater danger to Turkey than Germany. Eden had even angrily threatened that the Allies might turn the Russians loose on the straits if Turkey "declined to meet British wishes."

In preparing for the Cairo meeting in December 1943, Inönü and Menemencioglu agreed that two objectives must continue to guide their every move and underlie every agreement with the British and the Americans. Turkey must remain as neutral as possible for as long as possible to conserve its military strength. And, for every promise made to the Allies, it must receive in return the maximum of armaments and military assistance as a hedge against the day when the Turks might have to face the Russians alone.

Whether through instinct or secret information about Allied differences supplied by Papen's spies, the Turkish negotiators managed to exploit every weakness in the Allied front. For the facts were that only Churchill retained any interest in enlisting Turkey as a fighting ally. The Russians had lost their former desire for a Turkish declaration of war, preferring to have their own free hand in the Balkans. The Americans had never really favored Churchill's schemes for sideshow operations in the Aegean and the Balkan States and would not allocate troops or landing craft. Lamenting the "gleaming opportunities" that had thus been "cast aside unused," Churchill had begged Roosevelt at least to help him press the Turks for the use of their air bases to bomb German targets in Rumania and the Aegean. Though even this scheme found little favor with American military ex-

perts, the President indulgently let Churchill have his way.

Inönü and Menemencioglu took brilliant advantage of these divisions. Feigning a belated eagerness to join the crusade against Hitler's Fortress Europe, they insisted that they could fight only as equal partners in an integrated battle plan—which, of course, would take months of joint military talks to work out. Unfortunately, they shrugged, they had left their military staffs in Ankara, so no preliminary planning could be done in Cairo. The Turkish statesmen, however, had been sure to bring long lists of new military equipment needed by their armed forces. The deliveries to date were far short of Turkish requirements—and even below the levels promised by Churchill at Adana.

With Roosevelt as a sympathetic audience, Inönü and Menemencioglu nimbly and glibly hopped from one list to another to demonstrate their unreadiness for war because, as Menemencioglu asserted, "the deliveries in fact represented a very small proportion of the promises." In vain, Churchill, Eden and General Sir Henry Maitland Wilson tried to refute the Turkish complaints or offer new guarantees; the indefatigable Turkish negotiators met each rebuttal with a new objection, and in the end they convinced Roosevelt that Turkey could not yet defend itself against the consequences of belligerency. On December 4, the American President told Churchill that if he were a Turk it would take more arms than Britain had so far supplied to draw him into war.

Defeated and disgusted, Churchill agreed to send yet another military mission to Ankara, but when the British officers arrived early in January, they were authorized only to discuss the preparation of Allied air bases. The Turks, however, wanted detailed plans for an Allied campaign in the Balkans and delivery schedules for the 500 Sherman tanks, 300 fighter planes and 180,000 tons of war matériel they insisted on having immediately. In his conversations with the British and American Ambassadors, Menemencioglu endlessly played on the differences in British, American and Russian postwar objectives as the source of Turkish misgivings about the future of Europe.

On February 3 the British military mission abruptly flew home, and the warmth of Ankara's diplomatic and social life froze under the glacial formality assumed by the Allied Ambassadors. Arms deliveries ceased, and in April the British demanded that Ankara cut off its shipments of strategic chromite ore to Germany or suffer an Allied blockade of its ports; a request for severance of diplomatic ties with Germany followed, and then a demand that the straits be barred to German shipping. The Turks yielded to these coldly presented requirements without demur—for by August 1944, Germany had neither the need nor the means to retaliate against a country that had become a backwater in the flood tide of Allied military successes in Europe. But the Turks could not resist asking for new shipments of war matériel, a request the British ignored and the Americans answered with promises of economic aid.

Not until February 23, 1945, five days before the Allies' final deadline, did the Turkish National Assembly finally make the declaration of war on Germany that the Big Three at Yalta had demanded of all countries as the price of admission to the councils of the postwar United Nations. The policy the Turks called "active neutrality" and *Pravda* denounced as "calculated opportunism" had succeeded. When the War ended, not one bomb had fallen on Turkish soil, not one Turkish soldier had died in combat.

Winston Churchill must have forgiven the Turkish leaders the frustrations they had caused him, for in June 1945, Britain would stand firmly by the Turks when the Soviets made their predictable grab for Turkish territory. But Churchill never forgave another leader whose obstinate neutrality during World War II at times seemed to threaten Britain's very survival. Ireland—like Canada, Australia and South Africa—was a dominion of the British Commonwealth and was expected to fight when England went to war.

Unlike the other Commonwealth members, however, in 1939 the passionately anti-British Irish wanted no part of a war for a King and a country that had given them little but centuries of suffering. Their grievances were well known. Generations of Protestant English Kings, Prime Ministers, generals and landlords had treated Catholic Ireland like a conquered province and dyed the sod of the Emerald Isle red with the blood of Irish martyrs. While putting down periodic rebellions with guns and the gallows, the English had imported dour Scottish Calvinists to settle the island's strategic northeastern counties, which came to be called Ulster and to be dominated by Protestants militantly loyal to the

URBANE WAR
OF THE DIPLOMATS

Some combatants in World War II served their countries as ably in diplomats' mufti as others did in khaki or field gray. In neutral Turkey, Britain's Ambassador Sir Hughe Knatchbull-Hugessen and Germany's Ambassador Franz von Papen, aided by agents of their allies and dependent states, vied for the allegiance of the Turkish government over cocktails and canapés, at horse races and tennis matches, and sometimes in alleys and boudoirs.

Britain's Sir Hughe had the advantage of being a friend and neighbor of Turkey's Foreign Minister—later Prime Minister—Sükrü Saracoglu. Often Sir Hughe would amble across the lawn for a cup of Turkish coffee and a report on Germany's latest political designs. But the guileful Papen counterattacked successfully by bribing Sir Hughe's valet, an Albanian named Elyesa Bazna (code-named Cicero), to take photographs of the secret documents that the British Ambassador brought home to read.

In public, the opposing diplomats kept a wary distance, though in the limited arena of Ankara society they might sit at separate tables at the same club or encounter one another at a government reception. On one such occasion the wife of the British naval attaché, approaching the crowded buffet, caught a dress hook in the gown of none other than Frau von Papen. It took 10 minutes to effect a diplomatic disengagement. And Papen himself, an avid duck hunter, once had a decoy blasted out of the water when he floated it too near the blind of a British military attaché.

There were greater hazards. On a morning walk in February 1942, the Papens were nearly killed when a Turkish assassin—probably employed by agents of the Soviet Union—hurled a bomb at them. The device exploded prematurely, killing the bomb thrower and leaving the Papens shaken but intact.

Turkey's crescent banner hangs alongside the flags of Germany, Great Britain and Italy in Istanbul, Turkey's largest city, where the diplomats and agents of the warring nations operated side by side throughout the War.

Future Turkish Prime Minister Sükrü Saracoglu (left) and United States Ambassador Laurence A. Steinhardt toast each other with Champagne in 1942 at a characteristically elegant diplomatic reception in Ankara.

At the fashionable Ankara Tennis Club, German Ambassador Franz von Papen (left center) and Turkish Foreign Minister Numan Menemencioglu engage in private conversation. A wad of cotton protects Papen's ear, injured in an assassination attempt.

British Ambassador Sir Hughe Knatchbull-Hugessen (center) attends a festival with the top-hatted Minister from Afghanistan.

crown. In the larger, poorer south, English landlords and government officials, by callousness and neglect, had allowed millions of peasants to starve or had forced them to flee to America in overcrowded death ships when the potato crop failed in the mid-19th Century. An armed struggle for independence launched midway through World War I by the Irish Republican Army (IRA) brought on another wave of British military repression that lasted until 1921.

Not until the end of that year did the Irish win a grant of home rule under the King of England, and then only for the 26 Catholic counties of the south. The six northern counties remained part of Britain, partitioned from the new Irish Free State at the demand of their loyalist Protestant majority. Half of Ireland's political leaders accepted the English settlement under the threat of renewed warfare, but the other half, led by Eamon de Valera and the IRA, held out for an island-wide Republic of Ireland. The bloody civil war that followed ended in defeat for the IRA a year later and left Irishmen bitterly divided among themselves over partition and the authority of the King. De Valera converted the Republican Army into the Republican Party and in 1927 entered the Dublin Parliament to seek national independence and unity through peaceful politics. A diehard minority, still calling itself the IRA, went underground to oppose by terrorism both the Irish and the British governments' tolerance of partition.

It was de Valera, however, who as the elected Taoiseach, or Prime Minister, in 1937 won a new constitution that made Eire a republic in everything but name, with a president to replace the authority of the King. In a semilegal, semimystical way, the constitution recognized only a tenuous "external association" with the British crown and Commonwealth, and recognized the island's partition as only a temporizing British expedient. And it was de Valera who, playing on pacifist Prime Minister Neville Chamberlain's fears of another Irish rising if Britain should again go to war with Germany, persuaded the British government in 1938 to give up its treaty rights to three fortified ports in Eire.

These Treaty Ports, as they were known, had been used by the Royal Navy's convoy escorts in World War I and were the last vestiges of Britain's 700-year occupation of the south. Chamberlain called his agreement with de Valera an "act of faith" that traded three run-down bases for Irish friendship. Winston Churchill, then a lone voice in Parliament preaching the inevitability of war with Hitler, accused Chamberlain of "casting away real and important means of security and survival for vain shadows and for ease."

Churchill was more nearly right. What de Valera really wanted was Northern Ireland, and soon after the compact with Chamberlain was sealed the Taoiseach made it clear in a newspaper interview that "if war occurred while British forces were in occupation of any part of Ireland"—meaning the partitioned north—"Irish sentiment would definitely be hostile to any cooperation."

Partition remained a fighting word in Ireland as Britain faced a war with Germany in 1939 and it should have come as no surprise to anyone when, on September 3, de Valera announced in a radio broadcast that the Dail, the Irish Parliament in Dublin, had resolved to "keep our people out of a war." Ireland would not join England in declaring war on Germany, de Valera said, but would follow a policy of strict neutrality toward the belligerents. "With our history, with our experience of the last war, and with part of our country still unjustly severed from us," he explained, "we felt that no other decision and no other policy was possible."

Although Chamberlain and his War Cabinet, formed in August, were keenly aware of de Valera's obsession with partition, they thought he might be persuaded to put the issue aside for the duration of the War. Eire had no navy, mounted a mere fledgling of an Air Force, and its undergunned Army numbered fewer than 20,000 men, including reservists and auxiliaries. To provide for the common defense of the British Isles, most of the Cabinet assumed that de Valera would invite the Royal Navy to repossess its Treaty Port bases at Cobh, Berehaven and Lough Swilly. And they expected him to expel or intern German nationals in the south, including the small German Embassy staff.

Winston Churchill, now First Lord of the Admiralty, was not so sure. "Eirish neutrality," he grumbled to his staff, "raises political issues that have not been faced," and he ordered up a series of studies to answer "the questions arising from the so-called neutrality of the so-called Eire."

On September 12 he got his answers—from Eire. Neither warships, submarines, nor military aircraft, read an *aide-mémoire* sent to London from Dublin, would be permitted even to transit Irish territorial waters. Far from expelling

Ireland's Prime Minister Eamon de Valera reviews troops assembled at Dublin's General Post Office in 1941 to celebrate the 25th anniversary of the Easter Rising against British rule. De Valera, whose battalion of Irish volunteers accounted for half of the British casualties in the Rising, wears a medal commemorating his service in the rebellion.

German Ambassador Edouard Hempel, the British learned, de Valera and his Secretary for External Affairs, Joseph Walshe, had been meeting with the diplomat to discuss Irish neutrality since the week before the Nazis invaded Poland.

The fury these actions provoked in Churchill would remain with him throughout the War. By now he felt certain that U-boats, which were already taking a staggering toll of British Naval and merchant ships, "are being succored from West of Ireland ports." He wanted that stopped, and he demanded at least two of the Treaty Ports for Royal Navy use. After a German submarine sank the battleship *Royal Oak* in British waters in mid-October, Churchill called for action. "The time has come," he thundered to the Cabinet, "to make it clear to the Eire government that we must have the use of these harbors and that we intend in any case to use them."

Fortunately, cooler heads prevailed, for what Churchill was suggesting—seizure of the Irish ports by force—would have meant war. Instead, Chamberlain sent to Dublin a se-

cret emissary, traveling under a pseudonym, to negotiate terms for the wartime relations between the two countries.

The emissary was Sir John Maffey, a distinguished colonial civil servant who had made a career of successful negotiations with the Empire's rebellious border tribes, such as the fierce Afridi of the northwest Indian frontier and the fanatic Muslim warriors of the Sudan. Now he would meet his match in the canny and cantankerous leader of what had been Britain's oldest and nearest colony. An Irishman almost by accident, Eamon de Valera had been born in Brooklyn of a Spanish father and an Irish mother in 1882, but had emigrated to County Limerick at the age of three after his father died. As a youth he had honed his mind in the study of mathematics and Gaelic, had strengthened his body in the brutal Irish versions of Rugby football and field hockey, and had immersed his soul in the mysticism of Celtic Catholicism and history. He had been fighting the British with rifle and rhetoric since 1916.

Hawk-visaged, and painfully nearsighted as a result of a

chronic eye ailment, at six feet one inch de Valera had to peer upward to lock eyes with the six-foot-four-inch Sir John. But he did not budge on the matter of the Treaty Ports, the neutrality of Irish waters or German representation in Ireland. And he literally backed the diplomat to the wall at their first long meeting and again at their second as he pointed to a map of partitioned Ireland and declaimed: "There's the real source of all our trouble." The problem, he tirelessly repeated, was the partition of Ireland; so long as Britain retained sovereignty in the north, Eire would not yield any of its sovereignty, no matter how dire England's needs might be.

But de Valera repeated, too, the pledge he had made to Neville Chamberlain on return of the Treaty Ports in 1938: He would never allow Eire to be used as a base for attacks on Britain, whether by Germans or Irishmen. Out of that pledge grew the concessions he was willing to make.

He would accept Sir John openly as the British representative to Ireland, and he would accept secretly a few plain-clothes British staff officers designated to draw up contingency plans for the joint defense of Ireland in case the Germans attacked. He would instruct Irish coast guardsmen to radio in plain language their reports of German ships and submarines spotted off the coasts; the Royal Navy could intercept the transmissions for their own purposes. He refused to discuss Maffey's suggestion that British warships might enter Irish waters in hot pursuit of German submarines, but let the British interpret his silence as assent. Nor was anything said about Royal Air Force flying boats shortcutting across Irish airspace on their way to search for U-boats and distressed merchant ships.

The War Cabinet was convinced by Maffey's detailed accounts of his meetings that Irish neutrality was solid and unbudgeable. Again Churchill disagreed. He continued to charge that U-boats were being serviced and supplied in Irish bays and harbors "by the malignant minority" of the Irish populace—he meant the IRA—"with whom de Valera dare not interfere." To him, Ireland's neutrality was not just immoral, it was illegal. On October 24 he urged the Cabinet to document publicly Britain's legal claims to the Treaty Ports and then "insist on the use of the ports." But his colleagues felt that Britain still could not afford the fighting that would ensue if it tried to take the Irish ports by force.

Fuming with frustration, Churchill ordered a watch put on the Irish coast by armed trawlers. The fishing craft never turned up a submarine in Irish waters to prove Churchill's assertions, but the Treaty Ports would remain an emotional issue between Ireland and Britain—and would bring them to the brink of war.

In May 1940 anxieties raised in both countries by the dispute over the ports were heightened by the fearful prospect of a German invasion of the British Isles. By now, Churchill had been propelled into the Prime Minister's chair, though Chamberlain remained in the Cabinet. As German panzers swept through France, Chamberlain sent his friend de Valera an urgent warning to beware of "enemy landings from troop-carrying planes." The Germans, the letter read, "do not respect neutrality, and the rapidity and efficiency of their methods are terrifying."

Then at 10:20 p.m. on May 22 the Dublin police raided the Germanically named Villa Konstanz in the capital's suburbs, the home of one Stephen Carroll Held, the Irish stepson of a German citizen. After breaking into a locked room that Held refused to open, detectives found evidence that an air-dropped German spy had recently lodged there—a parachute, parts of a military uniform with German medals and insignia, a typewriter that had been used to compile details of Ireland's military defenses, a radio transmitter and code book, and $19,700 in U.S. currency.

At this point Sir John Maffey begged de Valera to abandon neutrality and join with Britain "in the cause of freedom." Could not an Irish Army brigade be sent to France to help the Allied armies stem the Nazi advance? And should not the German Embassy in Dublin be closed lest it become a fifth column for a German invasion?

But de Valera was the leader of a party, a parliament and a people nursed on enmity for the English and wedded to neutrality. All he gave Maffey in reply was a lecture on the evils of partition and an obsessive tirade on the violent reaction of the IRA and anti-British elements in the Dail if the government deviated even slightly from its policy. The Taoiseach, Maffey reported despairingly to London, "lives too much under the threat of the extremist."

For a while de Valera and his chief assistants, Joe Walshe and Frank Aiken, hardly knew where to turn, so they turned in every direction at once. But it was clear that they still feared the British most. From Ambassador Hempel they demanded unequivocal assurances that Germany would not violate Irish soil, a pledge Maffey had been unable to get from the British government, owing to Churchill's ascendancy in the War Cabinet. Walshe then went secretly to London to plead, perversely, that the British rush troops to southern Ireland if the Germans landed there, but not a mo-

ment earlier. Back in Dublin, he repeatedly sought out Hempel to discuss the Germans' intentions toward Ireland after their victory over Britain, which he seemed to expect. Walshe hoped, Hempel reported in his daily cable to Berlin on July 31, "that in a future peace settlement we will not sacrifice Ireland to England" and that Germany would support "an entirely independent United Irish State."

De Valera and his aides got all the reassurances they

THE IRA'S WAR ON BRITAIN

Even after the Irish won home rule in 1921, the diehards in the Irish Republican Army continued an erratic campaign of terror against the hated British, who remained in six northern counties and three so-called Treaty Ports in the south. When Prime Minister de Valera in 1938 negotiated the return of the Treaty Ports to Irish control, it seemed that diplomacy had triumphed over violence. But the IRA would

not leave well enough alone, warning the British to get out of Northern Ireland as well, or suffer the consequences.

The consequences were a spate of IRA bombings in England, culminating in an explosion in Coventry (below) that killed five bystanders and injured 70. De Valera, recognizing the threat to his own government as well as to Anglo-Irish peace, reacted early in 1940 by jailing hundreds of activists and confiscating their weapons. As a result, the bombings stopped and the IRA's terrorist acts were sharply curtailed for the duration of the Emergency.

Citizens of Coventry stand in shock at the scene of an IRA bombing in August 1939. The bomb was delivered by a bicyclist who walked away.

wished from Hempel and, through him, from Nazi Foreign Minister Joachim von Ribbentrop. The German parachutist, they confided, had been a Luftwaffe officer seeking to infiltrate England through Northern Ireland; he had landed by mistake in the south. He would cause no further trouble if de Valera would agree to give the matter no more publicity. Hempel—unlike Maffey—was able to give his government's guarantee that its forces would not invade Ireland. And, at Berlin's instruction, he hinted broadly that a German victory would result in the unification of Ireland.

Both hopes and fears that Germany might prevail receded in September 1940 when the Royal Air Force triumphed in the Battle of Britain. But de Valera knew better than to relax, for Churchill was now free to unleash his long-repressed fury on Ireland. The Taoiseach was particularly concerned about his isolated position, because American official and public opinion, which often had supported Ireland against England, had clearly been turned against him. Ambassador David Gray, an old friend and relative by marriage of President Roosevelt, was leading the attack. He told everyone, particularly de Valera's pro-Allied political opponents, that the Irish ports must be surrendered to help protect the convoys of food and arms coming from America; Gray even suggested that the United States. would welcome the seizure of the ports by the British.

On November 5, Churchill rose in the House of Commons to complain bitterly about "the most heavy and grievous burden placed upon us" by Ireland's refusal even to "refuel our flotillas and aircraft," which protected both countries' vital supply lines. In response, de Valera fiercely proclaimed that his Army, tiny though it might be, would resist any effort to occupy Irish territory, and that he and his ministers would die fighting at the head of their troops. To back up his words, just before Christmas he ordered half the Army north to guard the border.

With Anglo-Irish relations at a crisis point, Germany decided to press home its advantage. Foreign Minister von Ribbentrop instructed Ambassador Hempel to offer de Valera 46 field guns, 550 machine guns, 10,000 rifles, 1,000 antitank rifles and a huge store of ammunition to bolster the Irish defenses. Hempel was also told to inform de Valera that a Luftwaffe plane bearing new staff officers for the German Embassy—including some meteorologists and "an of-ficer experienced in military reconnaissance"—would be landing at Dublin's Rineanna airport on Christmas Eve.

Ribbentrop's message was as unsettling and unwelcome as Churchill's threats and abuse. The arms offered by the Germans were those abandoned by the British on Dunkirk's beaches in June; the English would regard their appearance in Ireland as both a threat and a mortal insult. Moreover, the uninvited augmentation of the Embassy staff by a military plane looked ominously like the kind of trick that had preceded Germany's take-over of other neutral nations.

From the hospital where he was undergoing treatment to improve his fading vision, de Valera rejected both German initiatives. Hempel replied that his instructions had not been changed. The plane would arrive on December 24. De Valera's orders to his aides were curt, sweeping and explicit: Deploy the rest of the Army to defend Dublin, block the airport runways, and arrest any German who landed.

For Lieut. General Dan McKenna, the Army's Chief of Staff, it was the scariest moment of the Emergency, as the Irish termed the period of World War II. No sooner had he begun an inspection tour of the units manning Eire's northern defenses on December 17 than he was summoned to Dublin before dawn by the Minister for Defense, Oscar Traynor. "It's happened," Traynor informed him excitedly. "Which side is it?" McKenna asked. "The Germans," Traynor replied. Now the whole of Ireland's underequipped defenses were placed on full alert.

A Luftwaffe plane did in fact fly low over Rineanna airport on Christmas Eve, but it made no attempt to land. Nor did any British soldiers try to force the northern border—not that de Valera expected them to. For he had deliberately exaggerated and stage-managed the crisis to show what Ireland would do if faced with a real ultimatum. Churchill and Hitler got the message, but both would make Ireland pay for its leader's histrionics.

Three days after Christmas, Ambassador Hempel, under strong pressure from Berlin, had his stiffest-ever meeting with de Valera, now on the mend from his eye operation. The Taoiseach was calm and precise as he again went over the strict limits of Irish neutrality. Hempel was coldly formal as he remonstrated over the rude rejection of the only request ever made by the German government; he said he would not speak of "the possible concrete consequences" of Ireland's rebuff. They were not long in coming.

On the first and second of January, German bombers dropped bombs on four Irish counties and hit the capital twice. The bombs killed three people and wounded 24. This was not Hempel's doing, for he had long counseled Berlin against any actions that might drive the Irish into belligerency against Germany. Berlin offered no apologies for the bombings, but Ribbentrop finally took Hempel's advice and quit pressing the unwelcome offers of captured British arms and German Embassy officers. De Valera, incredibly, appeared satisfied to let matters rest there. And Adolf Hitler, too—who only a few months earlier had mused about the possibility of occupying Ireland and making it a base for bombing England into submission—turned his back on the troublesome little island and its prickly Prime Minister.

Not so Winston Churchill. While the Irish government and its minuscule Army were passing the greatest test of their neutral policy during the Christmas crisis of 1940, Churchill was preparing a sterner and more protracted test of the Irish people's will with the tacit support of President Roosevelt—a campaign of economic and psychological warfare that would last until the end of the Emergency. To get more supplies through what he called the "de Valera-aided German blockade," Churchill proposed to revise the prewar trade arrangements by which Britain had promised to share with Ireland its shipments of wheat, fuel and fertilizer in return for the Irish beef and beer on which British servicemen thrived. In a private message to Roosevelt, Churchill explained his intentions:

"We are so hard pressed at sea that we cannot undertake to carry any longer the 400,000 tons of feeding-stuffs and fertilizers which we have hitherto convoyed to Eire through all the attacks of the enemy. We need this tonnage for our own supply, and we do not need the food which Eire has been sending us. You will realize also that our merchant seamen, as well as public opinion generally, take it much amiss that we should have to carry Irish supplies through air and U-boat attacks and subsidize them handsomely when de Valera is quite content to sit happy and see us strangle."

Churchill was already holding back shipments of arms promised Eire's Defense Force, and he intended to go much further. The Chancellor of the Exchequer had drawn up a plan for secret economic warfare against de Valera's government that would, by various subterfuges, cut Ireland's fuel supplies to a trickle, reduce the tea ration far below England's and end wheat shipments altogether. Shipments of other goods would be decreased gradually until they ceased. Shipping lines obligated to Britain would be asked not to charter any ships to Ireland, and Irish captains would find their ships assigned to the dangerous outside positions in convoys. With such measures in mind, Churchill assured Roosevelt that the squeeze on Irish supplies would make de Valera "more ready to consider common interests."

It had no such effect, for Churchill still did not appreciate the depth of de Valera's commitment to neutrality or the strength of his popular support. And since the British were careful to attribute the cuts to the exigencies of U-boat warfare, few Irishmen outside the government even suspected that they were being actively punished. De Valera understood Churchill's campaign perfectly, of course. But since the British were in no way claiming credit for the troubles, de Valera was happy to play along and allow his countrymen to regard it all as part of the woes of a world at war.

Irishmen complained bitterly when their tea was rationed and when whole-wheat flour replaced white, and there was real hardship when coal supplies dwindled toward zero. The Dublin government meanwhile ordered farmers to plow one million more acres of land and increase their out-

Workers stack slabs of wet peat turf, cut from bogs near Dublin, after Britain suspended coal shipments to Ireland in 1942. Unused to the staple peasant fuel, Irish city dwellers often did not dry it properly. As a result it was hard to ignite and burned with a smoky, feeble flame.

put of wheat and vegetables. It set up a government corporation to buy and charter ships to haul commodities from the Americas, West Africa, and neutral Spain and Portugal. It urged Dubliners to cut peat from nearby bogs to be dried in huge ricks along the city streets and burned in household fireplaces. Nevertheless, throughout the Emergency the Irish would live far better than their British and Ulster cousins, enjoying their own fresh meat, bacon, butter and eggs, which were rarities in the rest of the British Isles.

This was not quite what Churchill had in mind when he told his Cabinet that they would let the Irish "stew in their own juice." Nor did Ireland become the "howling wilderness" that U.S. Ambassador Gray had predicted when the British curtailed fuel supplies. So Gray took it on himself to teach the Irish another kind of lesson. Responding to a government inquiry about rifles, guns and vehicles to equip its Army—which, thanks to the Christmas crisis, had swelled to 40,000 active-duty soldiers and 200,000 auxiliaries—Gray slyly suggested that a cabinet minister be sent to the United States to seek the necessary arms. Gray, of course, had no interest in Irish neutrality. As he had previously made clear, he was determined to draw Ireland into the conflict on the British side. He saw a mission to Washington as an opportunity to put heavy outside pressure on the Irish.

De Valera's emissary to the U.S. was Frank Aiken, his Minister for the Coordination of Defensive Measures. As matters turned out, the choice could scarcely have been worse. Aiken had fought bravely at de Valera's side during the civil strife as IRA Chief of Staff, but he was a liability as a cabinet minister and diplomat; even the gentlemanly Sir John Maffey privately described him as "rather stupid." Aiken's main contribution to Eire's defensive measures was as chief censor of the press and radio. He and de Valera shared a fanatic belief that Irish citizens should be mentally as well as physically neutral, and Aiken tried to make sure that they would hear, see and speak neither evil nor good of any belligerent.

Many of Aiken's censorship strictures were absurd, like the ban on publishing jokes about the weather, and some were spitefully anti-British. He permitted no references to Irishmen serving in the British forces; obituary notices of men killed in action could give neither their ranks nor the circumstances of their deaths. Some people, Aiken explained tendentiously, cared nothing about the men who died but wanted to use the obituary notices to make propaganda for "the belligerent they desired to favor."

Ambassador Gray believed Aiken was pro-German, and reported as much to Washington when he made the arrangements for the Minister's interview with President Roosevelt on April 7, 1941. He hoped that Aiken would be told the facts of life about American foreign policy, which was to support the British by every means short of war. As Maffey, who was in on Gray's plot, explained in a cable to the British Ambassador in Washington, "it is important that he should return in a chastened mood."

Aiken was squeezed into the President's schedule just before lunchtime. Roosevelt had been briefed on Aiken by David Gray's cables and by Lord Halifax, the British ambassador. F.D.R. immediately took the Irish Minister to task for having stated that "the Irish have nothing to fear from a German victory," a charge Aiken hotly denied. From that moment on, what Aiken had expected to be a discussion of Irish defense needs turned into a nonstop Presidential lecture on Ireland's duty to support England against Germany.

The monologue went on until the time allotted for the interview was up, and an aide entered to usher Aiken out. Stubbornly, the Irishman refused to budge, even after a steward came in and laid a cloth and dinner service on the Chief Executive's desk. Aiken was finally able to explain that Ireland needed arms to repel aggression and asked for the President's pledge of support.

Irish beachgoers cluster around a curiosity of war: a mine, long since defused, that washed ashore at Brittas Bay in County Wicklow. The Irish mined the approaches to three deep bays to discourage the entry of belligerent ships, but the mines sometimes broke free from their moorings.

"Yes," Roosevelt responded curtly, anxious to begin his lunch, "against German aggression."

"British aggression," Aiken insisted.

This set Roosevelt off again, and he retorted that it was "preposterous" to suspect the British of any such intentions.

"Then why can't they say so?" demanded Aiken. "We have asked them often enough."

"What you have to fear is *German* aggression." The President was shouting now.

"Or British aggression," the stubborn Aiken said again.

This time the President's roar was accompanied by a tug on the tablecloth that sent cutlery and dishes flying. Aiken still refused to depart until Roosevelt grudgingly promised to secure a guarantee from Churchill that Britain would not invade Ireland—a guarantee he never got.

Eire's official relations with the United States never quite recovered from the interview or from Aiken's speaking tour of Irish-American fraternal organizations, during which his attacks on British treatment of Ireland sounded to many like pro-German propaganda. And in Dublin, Ambassador Gray was only beginning to play out his repertory of political stratagems, for he had become as obsessed with undermining Ireland's neutrality as de Valera was with bolstering it.

After the Japanese attack on Pearl Harbor brought the United States fully into the War on December 8, 1941, Gray pulled out all the stops. Early in 1942, he proposed to Washington a plan for offering de Valera a tainted gift: In return for leasing its ports to the United States, Eire would be given all the arms, food and industrial goods it needed, plus the promise of American support for ending partition. De Valera's expected refusal could be publicized, and a majority of the Irish people and Parliament would line up against their stiff-necked Taoiseach and force him out of office.

The plan was swiftly pigeonholed. For one thing, the British had no wish to revive the partition issue. For another, the British and American chiefs of staff had by now concluded that Ireland was no longer important to the Allied war effort; the cost of defending and supplying the island would far outweigh its value as an ally.

Yet nothing could stop Ambassador Gray in his single-minded hostility to de Valera, and he had made a convert of his British colleague, Sir John Maffey. Throughout 1943 they bombarded their governments with schemes to embarrass de Valera, while in Ireland they encouraged his political opponents to try to defeat his party in the mid-year elections. Their efforts failed. The grumbling over wartime restrictions cost the Taoiseach some votes, but at the end of the year the country remained solidly behind his policy of neutrality.

Gray now decided to attack de Valera directly, having gone over the heads of the State Department and Foreign Office minions who had quashed his earlier ideas. In a 5,000-word memorandum to President Roosevelt in which he dredged up every negative argument he could think of, including a gross exaggeration of the subversive threat posed by Axis diplomats in Dublin, Gray persuaded the President to authorize a *démarché* to de Valera demanding "as an absolute minimum, the removal of these Axis representatives." De Valera's refusal would put him on record as being hostile to Allied interests.

Gray knew that American, Irish and British counterintelligence agents had been working harmoniously and effectively to negate the espionage potential of the eight diplomats who constituted the entire Axis presence in Eire. Thus, when Gray triumphantly presented the American note to the Taoiseach on February 21, 1944, de Valera grimly reminded him of that fact—and pointed out that expelling the Axis representatives would be interpreted as the prelude to a declaration of war. De Valera then demanded: "Is this an ultimatum?" Gray denied that it was, but the phrase "absolute minimum" sounded like a threat to de Valera, and when Maffey followed Gray with a parallel British note, de Valera exploded: "This is an ultimatum. This is an outrage!" He heatedly told Maffey, and later his Commonwealth colleague, the Canadian High Commissioner, that the Anglo-American notes were a direct threat to Eire's sovereignty. Eire, de Valera thundered, "would fight invasion from any quarter and, even though the outcome was hopeless, would resist to the last man." Again he alerted the Army and sat up all night planning a last-ditch defense.

Soon rumors of an imminent Anglo-American invasion from the north began to flood Dublin. On Sunday, February 27, de Valera seemed to confirm them in a speech: "At any moment the War may come upon us," he declared emotionally, "and we may be called to defend our rights and

our freedom with our lives." The next day Maffey ruefully reported to London that "thousands spent the weekend convinced that an American ultimatum had been delivered, that fighting had begun on the northern border, and that battleships were assembled off Howth."

The Gray-Maffey ploy had misfired badly, and de Valera's counterblast was reverberating around the world as newspapers amplified the rumors. But while the State Department and the Foreign Office hurriedly backtracked and assured de Valera that their notes had been only a friendly reminder about a common threat, Winston Churchill added his own thunder to the teapot tempest. "The time has now come," he told the House of Commons portentously, "to isolate southern Ireland from the outer world during the critical period which is now approaching."

The isolation measures, it was hinted in the press, would prevent anyone from entering or leaving Eire and might include a ban on the shipment of vital necessities as well while the Allies gathered their forces for the long-awaited assault on the Continent. Piled on top of the American "ultimatum," the British restrictions looked like unnecessary harassment of a tiny neutral, many of whose citizens were voluntarily serving with the invasion forces. (In fact, some 60,000 Irishmen served in the British armed forces during the War, and another 100,000 labored in British factories.) Again the Allies had to backtrack and assure de Valera of the temporary and limited nature of their intentions.

The Irish weathered it all quite nicely, though they spent a cold and immobile winter that last year of the War as a result of a further curtailment of British fuel shipments. De Valera, enormously popular at home because, with the whole world watching, he had stood up to Allied bullying, called a special election and won an overwhelming victory.

The V-E Day edition of Dublin's Irish Times (top) flaunts the paper's pro-Allied sentiments with a V-for-Victory arrangement of Allied leaders' portraits. At the microphone of Radio Eireann on May 17, 1945, Prime Minister de Valera (bottom) prepares to deliver the broadcast in which he firmly upheld Ireland's neutral position throughout the War, while Great Britain was fighting for its life.

Then, having brought Ireland safely through the Emergency, and with Allied victory at hand, de Valera coolly committed the most unpopular balancing act of his career. On May 2, 1945, he went with Joe Walshe to the German Embassy—just as he had gone to the American Embassy a few weeks earlier when Franklin Roosevelt died—and expressed the condolences of the people of Ireland to Ambassador Hempel on the death of his chief, Adolf Hitler.

The world and Ireland reacted with shock and disgust to the Taoiseach's ill-timed display of neutral punctilio—though Portugal's two-day mourning period for the Führer went unremarked. By now Frank Aiken's cocoon of censorship had been stripped from the press and the Irish could at last see and recoil from the full horror of Hitler's regime in the pictures of blitzed London and the Nazi death camps. They were still in shock on May 13 when Winston Churchill paused in the midst of a victory tribute to the many Allies who had contributed to Hitler's downfall to level a sneering personal attack on de Valera. "At a deadly moment in our life," Churchill declaimed, referring to the Battle of the Atlantic, Britain had almost been forced "to come to close quarters with Mr. de Valera" and his Cabinet. However, he continued, "His Majesty's Government never laid a violent hand upon them," despite great provocation, "and we left the Dublin Government to frolic with the Germans and later with the Japanese representatives to their hearts' content."

In a radio broadcast of equal eloquence made four days later, de Valera again managed to have the last word, and his rhetoric was as smooth as Churchill's had been savage. He excused the British Prime Minister for being carried away by the passions of a deservedly triumphant moment and praised him for having resisted the temptation, during England's darkest hours, to add "another horrid chapter to the already bloodstained record of the relations between England and this country." However, said de Valera, "Mr. Churchill makes it clear that in certain circumstances he would have violated our neutrality and that he would justify his action by Britain's necessity." That kind of moral attitude, he went on, was what made small nations fear big ones. De Valera concluded his speech by comparing England's standing alone against Germany with the centuries-long stand by Ireland, "a small nation that could never be got to accept defeat and has never surrendered her soul."

The speech won back all the Irish hearts that de Valera's gesture to Ambassador Hempel had lost him—and made Churchill look a little churlish by comparison.

There was, in fact, much to be said for the Taoiseach's peculiarly personal policy of neutrality. Certainly, barring the few "accidents," he saved southern Irish cities from the destructive bombings the Germans visited on Belfast in the north. He had scrupulously honored his pledge not to let Eire become a base for attacks on England, condemning IRA terrorists to death and letting others die in hunger strikes. He had bent neutrality in favor of the Allies in many quiet ways, returning hundreds of crashed Allied fliers with the excuse that they had been flying only training missions. He had allowed a British rescue tug to operate out of Cobh on humanitarian grounds and sent the Dublin fire brigades across the border to save burning Belfast.

Though neither the British nor the Irish secret services ever admitted it, their cooperation against Axis subversion had been close, pervasive and successful. An officer of the U.S. Office of Strategic Services, deriding the many American press reports that claimed Axis agents had the run of Ireland, asserted that "the Irish worked with us on intelligence matters almost as if they were allies."

Neutral Ireland's unfortunate position astride the Atlantic sea-lanes cost it much sympathy, particularly among seamen who lost ships and friends that Irish naval bases might have protected. As a Royal Navy reserve officer, Nicholas Monsarrat, put it in his autobiographical novel *The Cruel Sea*, "In the list of people you were prepared to like when the war was over, the man who stood by and watched while you were getting your throat cut could not figure very high."

But those who condemned Ireland for not joining in the moral crusade against Nazi Germany were answered by a Captain Henry Harrison in a letter that de Valera quoted in a Dail debate on this issue. Other countries, Harrison pointed out, had remained neutral "when Denmark and Norway, Holland and Belgium, Yugoslavia and Greece were in turn ravaged and enslaved." These countries—the Soviet Union and the United States—"fought because they had to, because they were attacked." And he concluded: "Little Ireland was not attacked. That is the difference. That is the sole difference. For there is nothing more certain than that Ireland would have fought back if she had been attacked."

THE RED CROSS OF MERCY

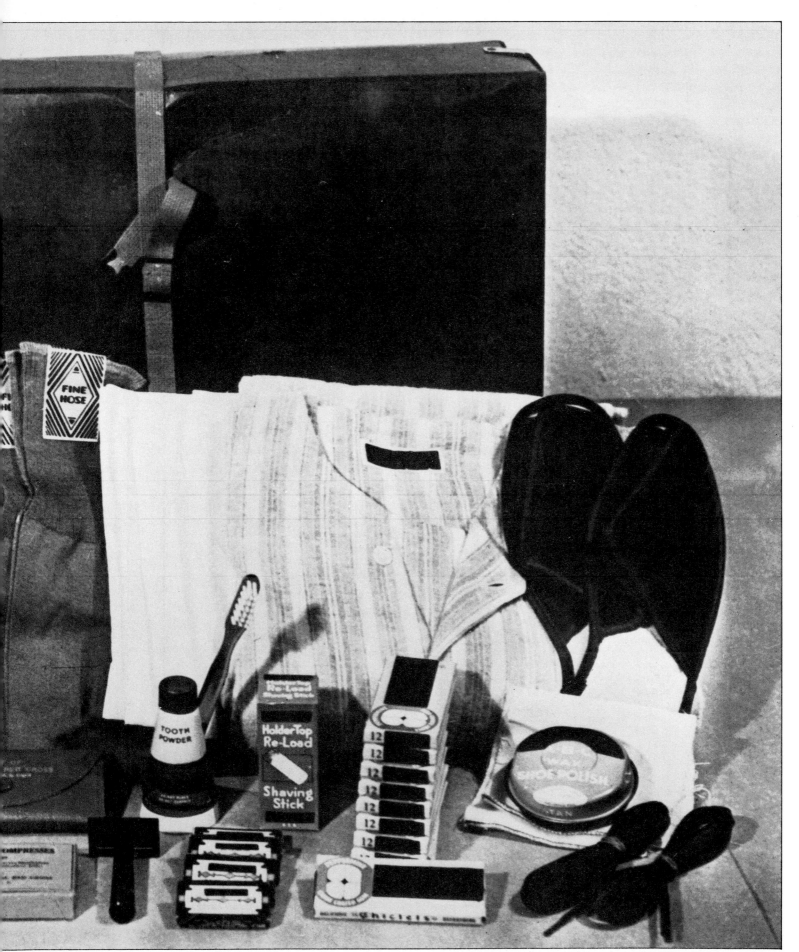

A "capture parcel," sent by the American Red Cross to newly taken prisoners of war, contained 31 items, from pajamas and a toothbrush to vitamins and gum.

GUARDIAN ANGEL TO THE WAR'S VICTIMS

It could be argued that the most important neutral in World War II was the International Committee of the Red Cross. Already renowned for decades of aid to the helpless and suffering, the International Committee between 1939 and 1945 pushed the concept of neutrality to new limits, projecting its moral authority deep into belligerent nations to protect and aid prisoners of war and other noncombatants.

The Red Cross had come into being as a result of one man's experience with the barbarity of war. In 1859, Jean Henri Dunant, a Swiss businessman, witnessed the Battle of Solferino, a ferocious engagement in the Austro-Sardinian War; in eight hours, almost 40,000 men were killed or wounded, and vast numbers of the injured perished for lack of medical care. Deeply affected, Dunant returned home determined to improve the lot of wounded soldiers.

The organization he helped found in 1863 took its name and its symbol by reversing the colors of the Swiss flag. In 1864, an international convention was called in Geneva at which 12 nations agreed to ensure the safety of wounded soldiers and medical personnel. At a later conference these protections were extended to war at sea. The Geneva Convention of 1929, signed by 47 nations, guaranteed the right of POWs to humane treatment.

The committee also promoted the creation of independent Red Cross societies in almost every country. Originally formed to bolster the military medical services of their respective nations, the national societies in World War II contributed most of the vast amounts of food and other relief supplies distributed through the International Committee to POWs and stricken civilian populations.

To implement its work, the International Committee dispatched 528 delegates to nations around the world—courageous Swiss men and women who risked, and on occasion lost, their lives looking after the welfare of POWs, internees and refugees. Where these delegates could impose the Red Cross's tenets, soldiers and civilians who fell into enemy hands were relatively safe. Where they could not, millions died needlessly from brutality and neglect.

A multilingual Red Cross employee monitors the world's airwaves for bits of information about prisoners of war, displaced persons and internees.

A vast chamber in a former Geneva palace is a repository for cards noting the identity, status and next of kin of 36 million POWs, internees and refugees.

A chartered ship disgorges parcels for prisoners of war at Toulon, France. Cargoes delivered by such ships sometimes suffered massive losses from pilfering.

In Philadelphia in August of 1944, mothers and grandmothers of American POWs pack holiday treats into special parcels they hope will reach prison camps overseas in time for Christmas.

AN OUTPOURING OF PARCELS FROM HOME

The American Red Cross parcel, treasured by Allied POWs in every theater, was a marvel of efficient packaging. Volunteers, working on an assembly line that turned out a parcel every four seconds, placed the same item in exactly the same space in each carton. To satisfy European parcel-post limits, they crammed precisely 11 pounds of staples and delicacies into a space 10 by 10 by 4½ inches.

A total of 13,500 volunteers—many of them relatives of prisoners—packed more than 600,000 parcels per month. By War's end the U.S. society had sent 28 million packages to Allied POWs, most through international headquarters in Geneva.

Every shipment of parcels to a European port of entry required another round of delicate diplomacy. The transports that carried them had to be of neutral registry and prominently marked, with their routes and timetables agreed upon in advance by both sides. To avoid nighttime attack, they ran brightly lighted after dark.

As the number of Allied prisoners increased, the demand for cargo space exceeded the capacities of neutral freighters. The International Committee established its own fleet of white ships that were allowed to pierce British and German blockades. And to keep parcels from piling up at U.S. ports, the American Red Cross turned on occasion to sailing ships. In 1943 a four-masted Portuguese bark, *Foz do Douro,* carried 330,000 parcels from Philadelphia to Lisbon in 21 days.

In a huge warehouse, Swiss volunteers unload parcels from the United States. Only after officially passing into the possession of the International Committee

MOVING MOUNTAINS OF PRECIOUS GOODS

International Committee headquarters in Geneva became a world junction, receiving a vast flow of packages from national Red Cross societies and private donors that then had to be transshipped to belligerent nations. Although parcels for prisoners moved in both directions, the amounts sent from the Axis nations to their men in captivity were a mere trickle compared with the deluge of goods shipped the other way by the U.S., British, Commonwealth and other Allied Red Cross societies.

At the height of the War, an average of 50 boxcars a day loaded with Red Cross goods was dispatched to Germany alone. Every car was sealed before it left Switzerland, to guarantee that nothing illicit was added to the shipment—and that nothing was stolen from it.

In addition to food, the International Committee handled an immense range of ordinary items that men in confinement could obtain in no other way. Books, eyeglasses, chewing tobacco, baseball bats and a multitude of other useful or morale-building articles moved through Geneva to prisoners of war and others in need. To some, the most highly valued commodity the Red Cross shipped was mail—millions of letters to and from anxious relatives who were desperate for contact with their missing loved ones.

in Geneva were the parcels allowed into Germany.

To ward off air attack, a supply train bound for Germany shows both Swiss and Red Cross insignia.

At Stalag 3B in Germany, camp officers and a Red Cross delegate (second from right) authenticate the arrival of a horse cart loaded with packages and mail.

PERSONAL DELIVERY BY THE "GENEVA MAN"

The treatment of Allied prisoners by Axis governments varied greatly, but the potential for abuse was never far away. The only institution that could curb such maltreatment was the Red Cross.

Visits by a delegate of the International Committee to German, Italian and, occasionally, Japanese prison camps became the key to ensuring adherence to the 1929 Geneva Convention. The delegate—often called the "Geneva Man"—accompanied parcels to the camps and tried to see that supplies were given to prisoners, not confiscated, held back as punishment or diverted to the black market. The delegate also received private reports from POW leaders on how their men were treated.

The Red Cross had no direct power to enforce compliance with the Convention. But it did make the point—particularly in the European theater—that any mistreatment of a POW might lead to retaliation against men from the offending country held in Allied camps.

After receiving a Red Cross shipment in 1943, Allied POWs tote 55 pounds of parcels apiece into their barracks at Germany's Stalag 20A.

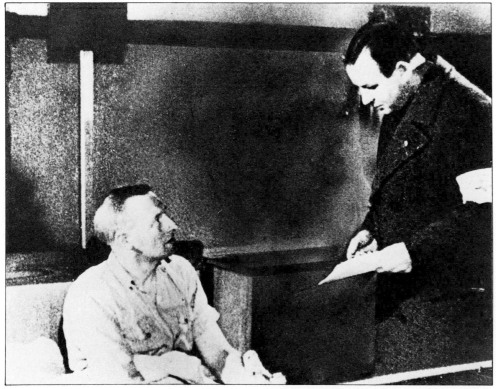

A delegate from Geneva visits a hospitalized prisoner in Germany to see if he is getting proper medical care. All committee delegates had to be citizens of neutral Switzerland.

This weekly American Red Cross shipment supplemented the diet of a POW.

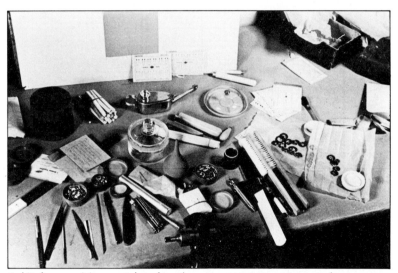

A kit for repairing watches found many uses in a prisoner-of-war camp.

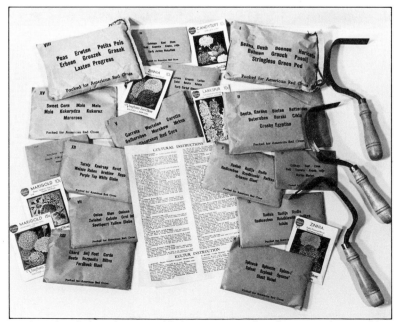

Seeds and tools from home enabled prisoners to plant flowers and vegetables.

At Stalag 8B in German-occupied Poland, the Rhythm Boys—a band of

captured soldiers—show off the instruments that were sent to them in 1942 by the American YMCA through the International Committee of the Red Cross.

COPING WITH JAPANESE DISDAIN

In Asia, the Red Cross faced its most vexing problem—the deep cultural gap between Japan and the Western Allies. To the Japanese, surrender was anathema—a battle must end in victory, retreat or death. Japan had signed the Geneva Convention but its government never ratified it; when the War came, very few Japanese soldiers ever surrendered. Relatives of those who did often felt dishonored and refused to accept letters from their captive husbands or sons; mail delivered by the International Committee lay unclaimed for years in the Tokyo post office.

Such an attitude deprived the Red Cross of its two main weapons—moral suasion and the implicit risk of retaliation—and engendered contempt from the Japanese for the Allied personnel they held captive. Japanese resistance to the work of the International Committee reached an extreme in Borneo in December 1943 when a delegate, Dr. Mattheus Vischer, and his wife were shot as spies because of their efforts to help Allied POWs.

Tragically, enormous numbers of prisoners in the European theater also were beyond the reach of the Red Cross. For a variety of reasons—mutual ethnic hatred, Stalin's animosity toward any troops who surrendered, Hitler's racial policies—Russians and Germans in each other's hands were cruelly treated. They enjoyed few of the protections of the Geneva rules, and millions of prisoners on each side died from starvation, illness and overwork—or were murdered in cold blood.

A rare Red Cross shipment accepted by Japan awaits transfer from a Swedish to a Japanese ship in Portuguese India in 1943.

Delegates from Geneva meet in 1944 with military-prison officials in Tokyo. Japan never granted safe

passage to neutral ships carrying Red Cross parcels, and the vast majority of those sent to Allied POWs in Japanese hands never got through.

Inmates of Buchenwald receive relief supplies from a Red Cross convoy. Not until spring 1945, when the German collapse was in sight, were delegates allowed

Red Cross vehicles await the signal to cross the Swiss border into Germany in March of 1945. The trucks were called "white saviors" by the POWs and displaced civilians to whom they brought badly needed aid.

into the concentration camps; then they were not allowed to leave until the camps were liberated.

CONVOYS OF LIFE IN THE DYING REICH

The closer the Allies came to victory over Germany, the harder it was for the International Committee to assist Allied POWs in German hands. As American and British strategic bombing brought German rail transport almost to a standstill, the massive flow of relief supplies was seriously disrupted. And as the Allied armies rolled up German fronts, the stalag guards put their prisoners on the road toward the interior—hastily and under harsh conditions.

To get supplies moving again, the International Committee dispatched into Germany convoys of trucks, many of which had been donated by the American, Canadian and British Red Cross societies. The convoys filled the void left by the disabled railroads, sometimes dropping off parcels directly to Allied prisoners as they passed them on the road.

The chaos of Germany's collapse enabled the International Committee, for the first time, to provide direct help to the surviving inmates of concentration camps. Committee delegates were allowed to enter a few camps to distribute supplies, and in some instances they were able to browbeat camp commanders out of massacring inmates by warning of the postwar reckoning to come.

SMOOTHING THE RETURN TO FREEDOM

Once prisoners were freed, they frequently needed more than the limited attention a liberating army could give them. Indeed, the prisoners at some remote camps did not even have a friendly army to turn to. They suddenly found themselves free simply because the nation holding them prisoner had surrendered and most of their guards had quietly decamped.

At this point, representatives of the International Committee stepped in to help the POWs, many of them broken in body and spirit, begin the transition to civilized life. In the Far East especially, the "Geneva Man," accompanied by a team of medical personnel, became the first compassionate outsider the prisoners had seen since they had been captured.

Entering Japanese camps in the summer of 1945, often days ahead of any Allied military contingent, such teams imposed the authority of both the Red Cross and the Allied armed forces on ruthless but wavering camp commanders. In many cases, their immediate assistance saved the lives of POWs who were near death from disease and starvation.

As an additional service, the International Committee collected the names and addresses of freed prisoners and gave their families the first notice that they would be coming home.

Emaciated Dutch POWs, being flown to Rangoon after liberation from a Japanese camp in Thailand, eagerly rummage through "release kits" supplied by the American Red Cross. The parcels reintroduced prisoners to such everyday items as cigarettes, hair combs, stationery, playing cards and paperback novels.

BIBLIOGRAPHY

Acheson, Dean, *Present at the Creation*. W. W. Norton, 1969.

Adams, Thomas A., *Irish Naval Service*. World Ship Society, Monograph No. 4, 1982.

Adleman, Robert H., and George Walton, *Rome Fell Today*. Little, Brown, 1968.

American Red Cross, *Prisoners of War Bulletin*, June 1943 through June 1945.

Andenaes, Johs., O. Riste and M. Skodvin, *Norway and the Second World War*. Oslo: John Grundt, 1966.

Andersson, Ingvar, *A History of Sweden*. Praeger, 1955.

Ash, Bernard, *Norway 1940*. London: Cassell, 1964.

Balchen, Bernt, *Come North with Me*. E. P. Dutton, 1958.

Barker, Ralph, *Blockade Busters*. W. W. Norton, 1976.

Béguin, Pierre, *Le Balcon sur L'Europe*. Neuchâtel: Les Éditions de la Baconnière, 1951.

Bell, J. Bowyer, *The Secret Army: The IRA, 1916-1970*. John Day, 1970.

Bernadotte, Folke, *The Curtain Falls*. Alfred A. Knopf, 1945.

Bisbee, Eleanor, *The New Turks*. University of Pennsylvania Press, 1951.

Bolinder, Jean, *40-Tal*. Malmo: LiberLäromedel, 1978.

Bonjour, Edgar:
    Geschichte der Schweizerischen Neutralität, Vol. 5. Basel: Helbing & Lichtenhahn, 1970.
    Swiss Neutrality. George Allen & Unwin, 1946.

Burdick, Charles B., *Germany's Military Strategy and Spain in World War II*. Syracuse University Press, 1968.

Carlgren, Wilhelm M., *Swedish Foreign Policy During the Second World War*. Transl. by Arthur Spencer. St. Martin's, 1977.

Carr, Raymond, *The Spanish Tragedy*. London: Weidenfeld and Nicolson, 1977.

Carroll, Joseph T., *Ireland in the War Years*. Crane, Russak, 1975.

Chamot, André, *Le Temps de la Mob en Suisse Romande, 1939-1945*. Lausanne: Éditions Payot, 1979.

Churchill, Winston S., *The Second World War*:
    Vol. 1, *The Gathering Storm*. Houghton Mifflin, 1948.
    Vol. 2, *Their Finest Hour*. Houghton Mifflin, 1949.
    Vol. 4, *The Hinge of Fate*. Houghton Mifflin, 1950.
    Vol. 5, *Closing the Ring*. Houghton Mifflin, 1951.

Collins, Larry, and Dominique Lapierre, *Or I'll Dress You in Mourning*. Simon and Schuster, 1968.

Colvin, Ian:
    Flight 777. London: Evans Brothers, 1957.
    Master Spy. McGraw-Hill, 1951.

Congressional Record, Vol. 95, Part 5. May 5, 1949, to May 31, 1949.

Coogan, Timothy Patrick, *Ireland Since the Rising*. Praeger, 1966.

Cortada, James W., *United States-Spanish Relations: Wolfram and World War II*. Barcelona: Manuel Pareja, 1971.

Curtis, Monica, ed., *Norway and the War: September 1939-December 1940*. London: Oxford University Press, 1941.

Derry, T. K., *A History of Scandinavia*. University of Minnesota Press, 1979.

Dürrenmatt, Peter, *Kleine Geschichte der Schweiz Während des Zweiten Weltkrieges*. Zurich: Schweizer Spiegel Verlag, 1949.

Dwyer, T. Ryle, *Irish Neutrality and the U.S.A.: 1939-1947*. Dublin: Gill and Macmillan, 1977.

Eden, Anthony, *The Memoirs of Anthony Eden: The Reckoning*. Houghton Mifflin, 1965.

Feis, Herbert, *The Spanish Story*. W. W. Norton, 1966.

Fox, Annette Baker, *The Power of Small States*. The University of Chicago Press, 1959.

Frischauer, Willi, *Goering*. London: Odhams Press, 1950.

Gallagher, J. P., *Scarlet Pimpernel of the Vatican*. Coward-McCann, 1967.

Gallo, Max, *Spain under Franco*. Transl. by Jean Stewart. E. P. Dutton, 1973.

Garliński, Józef, *Hitler's Last Weapons: The Underground War against the V-1 and V-2*. London: Julian Friedmann, 1978.

General Guisan un der Zweite Weltkrieg: 1939-1945. Lausanne: Éditions Marguerat, 1974.

Gordon, David, and Royden Dangerfield, *The Hidden Weapon: The Story of Economic Warfare*. Da Capo Press, 1976.

Gudme, Sten, *Denmark: Hitler's "Model Protectorate."* Bungay, Suffolk: Richard Clay, 1942.

Gullers, K. W., and C. A. Nycop, *Då: Våra Beredskapsår 1939-1945*. No date.

Hambro, C. J., *I Saw It Happen in Norway*. Appleton-Century, 1943.

Harper, Glenn T., *German Economic Policy in Spain During the Spanish Civil War, 1936-1939*. The Hague: Mouton, 1967.

Hartmann, Frederick H., *The Swiss Press and Foreign Affairs in World War II*. University of Florida Press, 1960.

Hayes, Carlton J. H., *Wartime Mission in Spain: 1942-1945*. Macmillan, 1945.

Hediger, Ernest S., *Foreign Policy Reports*:
    Geneva Institutions in Wartime. Foreign Policy Association, Inc., May 1, 1943.
    Switzerland in Wartime. Foreign Policy Association, Inc., January 1, 1943.

Hills, George, *Franco: The Man and His Nation*. Macmillan, 1967.

Hinshaw, David, *Sweden: Champion of Peace*. G. P. Putnam's, 1949.

Hull, Cordell, *The Memoirs of Cordell Hull*. 2. Macmillan, 1948.

Joesten, Joachim, *Stalwart Sweden*. Doubleday, Doran, 1943.

Johansson, Alf, *Finlands Sak*. Stockholm: Almänna Förlaget, 1973.

Junod, Marcel, *Warrior without Weapons*. Transl. by Edward Fitzgerald. Geneva: International Committee of the Red Cross, 1982.

Kahn, David, *Hitler's Spies: German Military Intelligence in World War II*. Macmillan, 1978.

Kimche, Jon, *Spying for Peace: General Guisan and Swiss Neutrality*. London: Weidenfeld and Nicolson, 1961.

Kleffens, Eelco Nicholas van, *Juggernaut over Holland*. Columbia University Press, 1941.

Kleinfeld, Gerald R., and Lewis A. Tambs, *Hitler's Spanish Legion: The Blue Division in Russia*. Southern Illinois University Press, 1979.

Knatchbull-Hugessen, Hughe, *Diplomat in Peace and War*. London: John Murray, 1949.

Koht, Halvdan, *Norway, Neutral and Invaded*. Macmillan, 1941.

Langer, William L., and S. Everett Gleason:
    The Challenge to Isolation, 1937-1940. Harper & Brothers, 1952.
    The Undeclared War, 1940-1941. Peter Smith, 1968.

Lapica, R. L., ed., *Facts on File Yearbook: 1942*, Vol. 2. Facts on File, Inc., 1943.

Lewis, Bernard, *The Emergence of Modern Turkey*. Oxford University Press, 1975.

Lindberg, Hans, *Svensk Flyktingpolitik under Internationellt Tryck, 1936-1941*. Stockholm: Almänna Förlaget, 1973.

The Earl of Longford and Thomas P. O'Neill, *Eamon de Valera*. Dublin: Gill and Macmillan, 1970.

Marton, Kati, *Wallenberg*. Random House, 1982.

Meier, Heinz K., *Friendship under Stress: U.S.-Swiss Relations, 1900-1950*. Bern: Herbert Lang, 1970.

Monsarrat, Nicholas, *The Cruel Sea*. Alfred A. Knopf, 1951.

Moulton, J. L., *The Norwegian Campaign of 1940*. London: Eyre & Spottiswoode, 1966.

Muir, Hugh, *European Junction*. London: George G. Harrap, 1942.

"Neutral Eire Returns One Supporter of the Allied Nations." *Picture Post*, July 10, 1943.

"Neutral Switzerland." *Newsweek*, December 30, 1940.

Neutral War Aims. London: Burns Oates, 1940.

Ogley, Roderick, *The Theory and Practice of Neutrality in the Twentieth Century*. Barnes & Noble, 1970.

Orvik, Nils, *The Decline of Neutrality, 1914-1941*. Humanities Press, 1971.

Papen, Franz von, *Memoirs*. Transl. by Brian Connell. E. P. Dutton, 1953.

Payne, Stanley G., *Falange: A History of Spanish Fascism*. Stanford University Press, 1961.

Paz, Alberto Conil, and Gustavo Ferrari, *Argentina's Foreign Policy, 1930-1962*. Transl. by John J. Kennedy. University of Notre Dame Press, 1966.

Peers, E. Allison, *The Spanish Dilemma*. London: Methuen, 1940.

Petrow, Richard, *The Bitter Years: The Invasion and Occupation of Denmark and Norway, April 1940-May 1945*. Morrow Quill, 1979.

Piekalkiewicz, Janusz, *Schweiz 39-45: Krieg in einem Neutralen Land*. Stuttgart: Motorbuch Verlag, 1979.

"Pope Greets Americans in Vatican." *Life*, June 26, 1944.

"Pope's Fears for Rome Take New Turn as City Becomes a German Target." *Newsweek*, June 12, 1944.

Proctor, Raymond L., *Agony of a Neutral: Spanish-German Wartime Relations and the Blue Division*. Idaho Research Foundation, 1974.

Rappard, William E., "Switzerland in a Changing Europe." *Foreign Affairs*, July 1938.

Reist, Werner, *Switzerland: Life and Activity*. Zurich: Werner Reist, 1952.

Report of the International Committee of the Red Cross on Its Activities During the Second World War (September 1, 1939-June 30, 1947):
    Vol. 2, *The Central Agency for Prisoners of War*. Geneva, 1948.
    Vol. 3, *Relief Activities*. Geneva, 1948.

Rich, Norman, *Hitler's War Aims: The Establishment of the New Order*. W. W. Norton, 1974.

Rings, Werner, *La Suisse et la Guerre, 1939-1945*. Lausanne: Éditions Ex Libris, 1975.

Schwarz, Urs, *The Eye of the Hurricane: Switzerland in World War II*. Westview Press, 1980.

Scott, Franklin D., *Scandinavia*. Harvard University Press, 1975.

Share, Bernard, *The Emergency: Neutral Ireland, 1939-1945*. Dublin: Gill and Macmillan, 1978.

Siegfried, André, *Switzerland: A Democratic Way of Life*. London: Jonathan Cape, 1950.

Spaak, Paul-Henri, *The Continuing Battle: Memoirs of a European, 1936-1966*. Transl. by Henry Fox. Little, Brown, 1971.

Steffan, Jack, *The Long Fellow: The Story of the Great Irish Patriot, Eamon de Valera*. Macmillan, 1966.

Sweden: A Wartime Survey. Stratford Press, 1943.

Tevnan, James, and Terence Horsley, *Norway Invaded*. London: Withy Grove Press, 1940.

Thomas, Hugh, *The Spanish Civil War*. Harper & Row, 1977.

Torell, Ulf, *Hjälp till Danmark: Militära och Politiska Förbindelser, 1943-1945*. Stockholm: Allmänna Förlaget, 1973.

Toynbee, Arnold, and Veronica M. Toynbee, eds. *Survey of International Affairs, 1939-1946*:
    The Eve of War, 1939. Oxford University Press, 1958.
    The Initial Triumph of the Axis. Oxford University Press, 1958.
    The War and the Neutrals. Oxford University Press, 1956.

Trythall, J. W. D., *El Caudillo: A Political Biography of Franco*. McGraw-Hill, 1970.

"Turkey: It Stands Firm between Armies." *Life*, September 14, 1942.

Udgaard, Nils Morten, *Great Power Politics and Norwegian Foreign Policy*. Oslo: Universitetsforlaget, 1973.

Weber, Frank G., *The Evasive Neutral*. University of Missouri Press, 1979.

Weibull, Jörgen, Carl-Fredrik Palmstierna and Björn Tarras-Wahlberg, *The Monarchy in Sweden.* Stockholm: The Swedish Institute, 1981.

Weisband, Edward, *Turkish Foreign Policy, 1943-1945.* Princeton University Press, 1973.

Wilson, Hugh R., *Switzerland: Neutrality as a Foreign Policy.* Dorrance, 1974.

The Work of the ICRC for Civilian Detainees in German Concentration Camps

from 1939 to 1945. Geneva: International Committee of the Red Cross, 1975.

Young, Gordon, *Outposts of Peace.* London: Hodder and Stoughton, 1945.

Younger, Calton, *A State of Disunion.* London: Frederick Muller, 1972.

Ziemke, Earl F., *The German Northern Theater of Operations, 1940-1945.* Department of the Army Pamphlet No. 20-271. U.S. Government Printing Office, 1959.

Zuylen, Pierre van, *Les Mains Libres.* Paris: Desclée de Brouwer, 1950.

PICTURE CREDITS

Credits from left to right are separated by semicolons, from top to bottom by dashes.

COVER and page 1: UPI. 6, 7: Map by Bill Hezlep.

A VISION DIMMED—11: AB Text & Bilder, Malmo. 13: Norsk Telegrambyrå, Oslo. 14: Wide World. 16: Norsk Telegrambyrå, Oslo. 18: The Museum of Denmark's Fight for Freedom 1940-1945, Copenhagen. 20, 21: Giordani, courtesy Sotto Segreteria di Stato, Vatican City; Felici from Black Star. 22: Dutch State Institute for War Documentation. 23: UPI. 24: Schimmelpenningh, The Hague. 26: Hans Bredewold Collection, Leyden.

SWITZERLAND IN ARMS—28, 29: Ringier Bilderdienst, Zurich. 30: Eidgenössisches Militärdepärtment, Bern. 31: Armee Archiv, Bern. 32, 33: Monika Graf, Langenthal, Switzerland—A.T.P. from Black Star; Monika Graf, Langenthal, Switzerland. 34, 35: UPI. 36: Éditions Marguerat, Lausanne. 37: Roland Schlaefli, Lausanne; Éditions Payot, Lausanne—William Vandivert for *Life*. 38: E.M.D., Bern—Emmen Flugzeugwerke, Emmen, Switzerland. 39: Bundesamt für Militärflugplätze, Dübendorf, Switzerland. 40, 41: Courtesy Janusz Piekalkiewicz, Rösrath-Hoffnungsthal (2); Photopress, Zurich. 42: Ringier Bilderdienst, Zurich. 43: André Roch, Geneva. 44, 45: Division de Montagne 10, Saint-Maurice, Switzerland.

THE PERPETUAL NEUTRAL—48: RIA Photo, Zurich. 49: UPI. 50: Map by Bill Hezlep. 51: Courtesy Janusz Piekalkiewicz, Rösrath-Hoffnungsthal—From *Der General: Die Schweiz im Krieg 1939-45*, © 1974 by Ringier & Co. AG, Zofingen, Switzerland. 52: Bundesamt für Militärflugplätze, Dübendorf, Switzerland. 54: Photo Steiner/Monika Graf, Langenthal, Switzerland. 55: René Graber, Le Locle, Switzerland. 56, 57: Ringier Bilderdienst, Zurich. 58: Hoffmann Photokino, Basel. 59: Emil Luthard, Zurich. 60, 61: Éditions Payot, Lausanne; Janusz Piekalkiewicz, Rösrath-Hoffnungsthal—UPI. 62: Ringier Bilderdienst, Zurich.

SPAIN'S BITTER LEGACY— 64, 65: © S.P.A.D.E.M., Paris/V.A.G.A., New York, 1982, copied by Henry Groskinsky. 66: Robert Capa from the John Hillelson Agency Ltd., London. 67: Metcalf from Black Star. 68: Marcel Rebiere for *Life*—UPI. 69: Wide World. 70, 71: © Time Inc. 1943. 72, 73: Metcalf from Black Star. 74, 75: Wide World; Metcalf from Black Star.

DICTATORS ON A HIGH WIRE—78: Wide World. 79: Pictures Inc. 80: Wide World. 81: Vicesecretaria de Educación Popular, Madrid—Photoworld. 82: EFE Atlantic, Berlin. 85: UPI. 87: Pan Am. 89: UPI. 90: Courtesy Nino Arena, Rome.

A RUSH TO FIGHT COMMUNISM—92, 93: Photoworld. 94: Denver from Black Star. 95: Bildarchiv Preussicher Kulturbesitz, Berlin (West). 96, 97: Photoworld, courtesy Gerald R. Kleinfeld and Lewis A. Tambs, from *Hitler's Spanish Legion: The Blue Division in Russia*, by Gerald R. Kleinfeld and Lewis A. Tambs, published by Southern Illinois University Press and Feffer & Simon, Inc., London & Amster-

dam. 98, 99: Courtesy Gerald R. Kleinfeld and Lewis A. Tambs. 100, 101: Lapi-Violett, Paris; courtesy Gerald R. Kleinfeld and Lewis A. Tambs (2)—Ullstein Bilderdienst, Berlin (West). 102: Courtesy Gerald R. Kleinfeld and Lewis A. Tambs. 103: U.S. Army, courtesy Gerald R. Kleinfeld and Lewis A. Tambs—ADN Zentralbild, Berlin (DDR). 104: Courtesy Gerald R. Kleinfeld and Lewis A. Tambs—Photoworld. 105: Photoworld.

THE PRICE OF NEUTRALITY—106, 107: Carl Mydans for *Life*. 108, 109: © Karl W. Gullers, Stockholm. 110, 111: James Sawders; © Karl W. Gullers, Stockholm. 112, 113: AB Text & Bilder, Malmo. 114, 115: © Karl W. Gullers, Stockholm; AB Text & Bilder, Malmo (2). 116: © Karl W. Gullers, Stockholm. 117: AB Text & Bilder, Malmo—© Karl W. Gullers, Stockholm. 118, 119: © Karl W. Gullers, Stockholm; AB Text & Bilder, Malmo.

SWEDEN: A BAROMETER OF WAR—122: Walter Sanders. 123: AB Text & Bilder, Malmo (2); © Karl W. Gullers, Stockholm. 125-130: AB Text & Bilder, Malmo. 131: UPI. 132: © Karl W. Gullers, Stockholm. 133: © Pressens Bild AB, Stockholm. 134: Thomas Veres. 136: UPI. 137: Imperial War Museum, London. 138: National Archives.

HAVEN IN THE NORTH—140, 141: AB Text & Bilder, Malmo. 142: From *Viisi Sodan Vuotta*, W. Soy, Helsinki, 1975. 143, 144: AB Text & Bilder, Malmo. 145: © Karl W. Gullers, Stockholm—from *Estland i Sverige*, Oversikt i ord och bild av Bernard Kangro; © Eesti Kirjanike Kooperatiiv AB, Lund, Sweden. 146, 147: Eliot Elisofon for *Life*; AB Text & Bilder, Malmo (2). 148: © Karl W. Gullers, Stockholm. 149: From *Et Flyktningesamfunn Vokser Fram, Nordmenn i Sverige 1940-1945*, by Ole Kristian Grimnes, published by H. Aschehoug & Co. (W. Nygaard), Oslo, 1969—AB Text & Bilder, Malmo. 150: © Karl W. Gullers, Stockholm. 151: From *Folke Bernadotte af Wisborg*, published by Lendfors Bokförlag, AB, Stockholm—AB Text & Bilder, Malmo. 152, 153: AB Text & Bilder, Malmo.

FEISTY LITTLE IRELAND—154, 155: Keystone Press Agency Ltd., London. 156: Central Press Photos Ltd., London—Department of Defence, Dublin. 157: BBC Hulton Picture Library, London. 158, 159: Department of Defence, Dublin. 160, 161: Department of Defence, Dublin. 162, 163: Keystone Press Agency Ltd., London. 164, 165: BBC Hulton Picture Library, London.

TWO STUBBORN HOLDOUTS—168: Salahattin Giz, Istanbul. 170: Hart Preston for *Life*. 171: Salahattin Giz, Istanbul. 173: Hart Preston for *Life*. 174, 175: Hart Preston for *Life* (2)—Bosshard from Black Star. 177: Keystone Press Agency Ltd., London. 179: Central Press Photos Ltd., London. 181: Bord Na Móna, Dublin. 182: C. Kavanagh, Ireland. 184: The British Library, London—Irish Press Ltd., Dublin.

THE RED CROSS OF MERCY—186-203: Courtesy American Red Cross.

ACKNOWLEDGMENTS

For help given in the preparation of this book, the editors wish to express their gratitude to Thomas A. Adams, London; Lars Arnö, A. M. Brisbois, The Royal Embassy of Sweden, Washington, D.C.; Drago Arsenijevic, *Tribune de Genève*, Paris; Dieter Bausinger, M. V. Lang, Renate Tietze, Wild Heerbrugg, S. A., Heerbrugg, Switzerland; Alain Berlincourt, Colonel Daniel Reichel, Chef de la Bibliothèque Militaire Fédérale et du Service Historique, Bern; Walther Binder, Stiftung für Photographie und Video, Zurich; Jan Birgersson, Press Information Chief, Swedish Red Cross, Stockholm; Klaus-Richard Böhme, Associate Professor, Royal Staff College of the Armed Forces, Stockholm; Barbara Bornhauser, Bild Documentation, Ringier Pressehaus, Zurich; Hans Brattesta, The Royal Embassy of Norway, Washington, D.C.; Colonel Ole Buch, Assistant Armed Forces Attaché, Embassy of Denmark, Washington, D.C.; Balthazar Burckhardt, Bern; Jeannette Chalufour, Archives Tallandier, Paris; Philippe Chapatte, Section des Réfugiés, Division de l'Assistance et du Droit de Cité des Réfugiés en Suisse, Bern; T. C. Charman, M. J. Willis, The Imperial War Museum, London; Rudy Clemen, American Red Cross, Washington, D.C.; Gaston Corthésy, Éditions Payot, Lausanne; Paolo Cresci, Florence; Isabelle Desarzens, *L'Illustré*, Lausanne; Colonel Donnet, Commandement de la Division de Montagne 10, Saint-Maurice, Switzerland; Nevil Duport, Lausanne, Switzerland; Comm. Francesco Giordani, Rome; René Giorgis, Chef de la Division des Douanes Suisses, Bern; The Government Institute for War Documentation, Amsterdam; Ewald Graber, Éditions Benteli, Bern; René Graber, Le Locle, Switzerland; Hans-Peter and Monika Graf, Graf Documentation Center, Langenthal, Switzerland; the Reverend Robert Graham, S.J., Rome; Harald Schmid de Gruneck, Delegate to International Organizations, International Committee of the Red Cross, New York; Felix Hoffmann, Basel; Elizabeth Hooks, American Red Cross, Washington, D.C.; Dr. Lou de Jong, Amsterdam; Oscar Kersenbaum, Buenos Aires; Heidi Klein, Dr. Roland Klemig, Bildarchiv Preussicher Kulturbesitz, Berlin (West); Hans-Jörg Klossner, Hans-Rudi

Stadler, Kurt Waldmeyer, Bundesamt fur Militärflugplätze, Dübendorf, Switzerland; Jürg Lampertius, Ullstein Bilderdienst, Berlin (West); Alf Lidman, Pressens Bild, Stockholm; Jean Lorette, Chief Curator, Royal Army Museum, Brussels; Karl Lüond, Glattbrugg, Switzerland; Emil Lüthard, Lausanne; Tuula Markkanen, Embassy of Finland, Washington, D.C.; Margaret Markstaller, Public Relations Officer, Swiss Embassy, Washington, D.C.; Lucien Matthey, Karl Steiner, Donat Stuppann, Fabrique Fédérale d'Avions, Emmen, Switzerland; Françoise Mercier, Institut d'Histoire du Temps Présent, Paris; Robert Munteanu, World Health Organization, Geneva; Meinrad Nilges, Bundesarchiv, Koblenz; Herbert Ortstein, Zentralbibliothek der Bundeswehr, Düsseldorf; the Reverend Romeo Panciroli, Pontificia Commissione Comunicazioni Sociali, Vatican City; Walter Pforzheimer, Washington, D.C.; The Photo Center of the Finnish Defense Forces, Helsinki; Janusz Piekalkiewicz, Rösrath-Hoffnungsthal, Germany; Hannes Quaschinsky, ADN-Zentralbild, Berlin (DDR); M. Raggenbass, Kreuzlingen, Switzerland; Gerhart M. Riegen, Secretary-General, World Jewish Congress, Geneva; Professor André Roch, Geneva; Dieter Rohde, Langenhagen, Germany; Colonel Hans Roschmann (Ret.), Überlingen-Bodensee, Germany; Bertil Rubin, AB Text & Bilder, Malmo, Sweden; Marianne Rygdkvist, Gullers International, Stockholm; R. J. Scott, Limerick; W. Soy, Helsinki; H. C. Spong, Clevedon, Avon, England; Enno Stephan, Cologne; Wolfgang Streubel, Ullstein Bilderdienst, Berlin (West); Eugen Suter, RIA Photos, Zurich; Colonel Michel Terlinden, Air Museum, Brussels; Toponomic Branch, Defense Mapping Agency, Washington, D.C.; Jean Vanwelkenjuyzen, Second World War Study Center, Brussels; the Reverend Manuel Vaz Leal, Chaplain, Panasqueira Mines, Portugal; Monsignor Carlo Maria Viganò, Sotto Segreteria di Stato, Vatican City; Colonel Jean-Jacques Willi, Service Central de Documentation du D.M.F., Bern; Marjorie Willis, BBC Hulton Picture Library, London; Commandant Peter Young, Army Press Office, Dublin; Jacob Zwaan, Amsterdam.

The index for this book was prepared by Nicholas J. Anthony.

INDEX

Numerals in italics indicate an illustration of the subject mentioned.

A

Acheson, Dean, 58
Adana conference, 170, 172
Adelboden, *61*
Aiken, Frank, 178-179, 182, 185
Aircraft types: Amerika bomber, 90; B-17 Flying Fortress, *60-61;* B-24 Liberator, *60-61, 138,* 139; Dakota, 127; Gloster Gladiator, *158-159;* Hawker Hurricane, 159; Heinkel-111, 38; Junkers-88, 89; Lancaster, 52; Messerschmitt-109, *30,* 38, *39,* 51-52; Messerschmitt-110, 51, *52;* Morane-Saulnier, *38;* Saab B-17, 125; Stuka, 125
Algeciras, 82
Alliance of Nationalist Youth, *14*
Altmark incident, 15, *16*
Ankara, *174-175*
Atatürk, Kemal, 167
Augustus II, King of Poland, 121
Austria annexation by Germany, 125
Azores, 76, 78, 86, *90,* 91

B

B. P. Newton, 137
Badajoz conference, 84
Balchen, Bernt, 138-139
Baltic Sea, 125
Barcelona, 56, 66, 71, 83
Barrón y Ortiz, Fernando, 79
Basel, *36,* 47, 56, 57, *58*
Bazna, Elyesa (Cicero), 168, 173
Bech, Premier of Luxembourg, 88
Béguin, Pierre, 47
Belgium: defense plans, 25-27; German invasions, 6, 10, 19, 23, 25-27, 49, 79; neutrality tradition, 25
Bern, 47, *49,* 51
Bernadotte, Folke, 142, *150,* 153
Bernadotte, Jean Baptiste, 124
Bertil, Prince of Sweden, 122, *123*
Binney, George, 127-128, 137
Bismarck, Otto von, 53
Björnson, Björnstjerne, 11
Blockade rules, 12
Bosporus, control of, 167-168, 171-172
Bothnia, Gulf of, 129
Bräuer, Curt, 13-15
Brittas Bay, *182*
Buchenwald, *200-201*
Burgerdijk, 22

C

Cádiz, 56, 79
Campbell, Ronald, 91
Canaris, Wilhelm, 79-83, 88-89
Canary Islands, 79, 82
Cape Verde Islands, 78
Carmona, Oscar, *90*
Carol, King of Rumania, 88
Castro, Augusto de, 91
Chamberlain, Neville, 176-178
Chappuis, Friedrich von, *103*
Charles XII, King of Sweden, 121-124, 135
Chautemps, Camille, 88
Chenhalls, Alfred, 89
Christian X, King of Denmark, *11, 18*
Churchill, Winston: and Azores, 91; conference with Inönü, 170; de Valera attacked by, 185; and Denmark invasion, 17; and German attack on airliner, 89; on German naval power, 124-125; and invasion

of Ireland, 183; and Irish neutrality, 172, 176, 178, 180, 184; and military aid to Ireland, 181; and military aid to Turkey, 170-172; on neutral nations, 166; and Norway invasion, 13-15; relations with Turkey, 168; sanctions against Ireland, 181-182; on Spanish neutrality, 77; on Swedish defense, 120; on Swedish trade with Germany, 136; on Swiss neutrality, 46; and Treaty Ports, 176-178; and Turkey as belligerent, 169-172. *See also* United Kingdom
Ciano, Galeazzo, 82
Collaboration, motives in, 166
Concentration camps. *See* Prisoners, welfare and repatriation
Condor Legion, 77
Coventry, 127, *179*

D

Dahlerus, Birger, 130
De Valera, Eamon, *177, 184;* and Axis diplomats, 183; and British invasion, 162, 183-185; and British military aid, 178; Churchill attack on, 185; condolences on Hitler's death, 185; and German military aid, 180; neutrality policy, 176-178, 180-181, 183-185; terrorist jailed by, 179; and Treaty Ports, 176-180; and unification, 176, 178
De Valera, Vivion, 162
Denmark: German invasion, 6, 15, 17, *18,* 19, 22-24, 108, 126, 128; military aid by Sweden, 138; neutrality policy, 16-17; refugees from, 138, 142
Dübendorf Air Base, 52, *60-61*
Dublin, *159-163, 177, 181*
Dulles, Allen W., 9, 54
Dunant, Jean Henri, 188
Dyxhoorn, Adriaan Q. H., 23-24

E

Eden, Anthony, 58, 91, 169, 171-172
Eire. *See* Ireland
Estonian refugees, 138, *145*
Estoril, 88, *89*
Ethiopia, invasion by Italy, 10, 125

F

Felix, Operation. *See* Gibraltar, seizure of
Finland: defense plans, 42; German campaign in, 135; medical services, *13;* military and economic aid from Sweden, 126; refugees from, 138, *142,* 144-147; Soviet invasion, 6, 11, 13, 126, 128, 135; Swedish volunteers in, 126
Foz do Douro, 191
France: alliance with Turkey, 168; German and Italian invasions, 79; Jews expelled, 59; and Low Countries defense, 23, 25, 27; military aid to Turkey, 168; in Norway campaign, 129, 132-135; prisoners interned, *54;* and Scandinavian neutrality, 13; trade with Spain, 79; trade with Turkey, 169
Franco, Nicolás, 86
Franco y Bahamonde, Francisco, 66, *69;* alliance with Portugal, 78, 86; and Allied invasion, 84; on character of war, 84; conference with Hitler, 82-83, *85;* conference with Salazar, 84; and Gibraltar seizure, 79-83; military and economic aid to Germany, 85-86; neutrality policy, 76-79, 85-86; and North Africa landings, 85; plot against, 84-85; and political prisoners, 71; relations with Hitler, 77, 79, 82, 84-85, 91; relations with Mussolini, 91; relations with Salazar, 77-78; and Spain as belligerent, 82-85; and Tangier occupation, 79; trade policies, 77, 79, 82-83; victory celebration, *78;* and volunteers against Soviet Union, 84-

85, 104. *See also* Spain
Frederick IV, King of Denmark, 121
Furstner, Johannes T., 24

G

Gay Corsair, 137
Gay Viking, 137-138
Geer, Dirk Jan de, 19, 23
Gellhorn, Martha, 132
Geneva Conventions, 62, 188, 194
George VI, King of England, 12
Gerhard, Karl, *133*
Germany: aircraft development, 90; aircraft interned, 52; aircraft losses, 51; airliner attacked by, 88-89; alliance with Soviet Union, 19, 126; alliance with Spain, 77, 83; alliance with Turkey, 168-169; Austria annexed by, 125; and Azores occupation, 90-91; Belgium invaded by, 6, 10, 19, 23, 25-27, 49, 79; blockade by, 106-108, 118, 126-127, 129, 133; code book loss, 52; demands on Switzerland, 46-48, 51-53; Denmark invaded by, 6, 15, 17, *18,* 19, 22-24, 108, 126, 128; Finland campaign, 135; France invaded by, 79; and Gibraltar seizure, 79-83; gold assets distributed, 63; intelligence operations, 14, 54, 88-89, 178, 180-181, 183, 185; Ireland neutrality violations, 159, *160-161,* 180-181; and Jewish refugees, *134,* 150; Luxembourg invasion, 6, 27, 79; military aid to Ireland, 180-181; military aid to Turkey, 170; military and economic aid from Spain, 79, 83-86; military and economic aid to Spain, 76, 83; naval treaty with Britain, 124-125; Netherlands invasion, 6, 19, 22-23, 25, *26,* 49, 79; neutrality, views on, 10, 22, 128; Norway campaign, 6, 11, 15-17, 23-24, 108, 126, 128-130, 135; and Norway neutrality, 12-16; operations in Ireland, 178, 180-181, 183, 185; prisoners, treatment of, 52, 198, *200-201;* propaganda by, 23, 47-48, 53, 90, *109,* 133; Red Cross shipments to, *193-195;* refugees from, 138, 144; relations with Ireland, 179-181; relations with Sweden, 124; relations with Switzerland, 47, 50, 57-58; relations with Turkey, 168, 171; reprisals against Sweden, 136; shipping sunk by, 91, 126, 136-138; smuggling by, 88, 130; Soviet invasion, 84, 135, 169; and Spanish volunteers against Soviet Union, 85; and Swedish neutrality, 128-131; Swiss airspace violation, 51; and Swiss press, 53; Switzerland invasion plans, 49, 53-54; trade with Sweden, 129, 136-137; transit rights in Sweden, 130-131, *132,* 133, 135-136; Turkey declares war on, 172; V-2 rocket, 139. *See also* Hitler, Adolf
Gibraltar seizure planned, 76, 79-83, 86
Goebbels, Joseph, 91
Göring, Hermann, 38, 52, 79, 130-131
Goteborg, *106-107,* 126-127, *130,* 137
Grafenwöhr, 97
Gray, David, 180, 182-183
Guernica, *64-65,* 66
Guisan, Henri, *30-31,* 49, *50,* 51
Gustav Adolf, Crown Prince of Sweden, 122, *123, 149*
Gustav V, King of Sweden, *11, 122,* 124, 126, 128, 131, 135
Gustloff, Wilhelm, 48

H

Haakon VII, King of Norway, *11,* 12
Hägg, Gunder, 133
Hägglöf, Gunnar, 130-131
Hague, The, *24,* 25
Hague Conventions, 9-10

Halifax, Lord, 182
Hambro, Carl, 15
Hansson, Per Albin, 126, 135, 139
Harrison, Henry, 185
Hausamann, Hans, 54
Hayes, Carlton, 85-86, 91
Held, Stephen Carroll, 178
Hempel, Edouard, 177, 179-181, 185
Hendaye conference, 82-83, 85
Himmler, Heinrich, 52, 150
Hitler, Adolf: and aircraft interned, 52; assassination plot against, 48; and Azores occupation, 90; conference with Franco, 82-83, 85; and Denmark invasion, 128; and Finland campaign, 135; and German Navy power, 124-125; and Gibraltar seizure, 82-83, 90; and Ireland as belligerent, 181; Jews mistreated by, 138; and Norway invasion, 13-15, 128; and Portuguese neutrality, 78; prisoners, treatment of, 198; relations with Franco, 77, 79, 82, 84-85, 91; relations with Swiss, 53; relations with Turkey, 168-169; Rhineland remilitarization, 10; and Soviet invasion, 135, 169; and Spain as belligerent, 82-85; on Spanish volunteers, 94, 103; and Swedish neutrality, 128-129, 131; and Swedish trade with Britain, 127-128; and Swiss air defenses, 51; and transit rights in Sweden, 132. See also Germany
Hoare, Samuel, 79, 84
Hoiningen-Heune, Oswald von, 88
Hopewell, 137
Howard, Leslie, 89
Hull, Cordell, 11
Huxley, Julian, 10

I

Ilmen, Lake, 100-101
Inönü, Ismet, 167-168, 170-172
International Committee of the Red Cross, 62, 87, 186-203
Ireland: air defenses, 158-159, 161; and Axis diplomats, 183-184; and British invasion, 166, 172, 179-180, 182-185; British sanctions against, 181-182, 184; casualties, 161, 181; censorship, 182, 184; defense plans, 156, 159, 162-165, 182; food and fuel production, 181, 182, 184; German bombings, 160-161, 181; German operations in, 178, 180-181, 183, 185; German threat to, 159, 162, 164; IRA terrorism, 179; military aid from Britain, 162, 178-179, 181; military aid from Germany, 180-181; military aid from United States, 182-183; mining of harbors by, 182; naval forces, 156-157; neutrality policy, 6, 9, 166, 172, 176-178, 180-181, 183-185; partitioning protests, 172-176, 178-179; reaction to Nazi conduct, 185; relations with Britain, 172-176, 180, 185; relations with Germany, 179-180; security measures, 154-159, 161; and Treaty Ports, 176-180; volunteers for Britain, 156, 184. See also De Valera, Eamon
Irish Republican Army, 176, 179
Irish Times, 184
Istanbul, 170, 173
Italy, 10, 62, 76, 79, 125. See also Mussolini, Benito

J

Japan, 55, 84, 198-199, 202-203
Jews: French policy on, 59; German mistreatment, 134, 138, 150; Sweden as refuge, 134, 138-139, 142, 144, 150; Switzerland as refuge, 59

Johnen, Wilhelm, 52
Jordana, Francisco, 84-85
Jossing Fjord, 16

K

Kamprath, Joachim, 52
Karlsruhe, 97
Kattegat, 17
Keitel, Wilhelm, 88
Kent, Duke of, 90
Kiruna, 110-111, 129
Kjolsen, Frits Hammer, 17
Knatchbull-Hugessen, Hughe, 169, 171, 173, 175
Koht, Halvdan, 13-16

L

La Coruña, 79
La Línea, 82
Lanz, Huertz, 82
Latin American nations, 14
Latvian refugees, 138
Lausanne, 33
Le Locle, 55
League of Nations, 10, 125
Lend-Lease Act, 90
Leopold III, King of the Belgians, 8-9, 23, 24, 25
Lippmann, Walter, 91
Lisbon, 1, 56, 86-89
Lithuanian refugees, 138
Lomax, John, 57
Louise, Crown Princess of Sweden, 122, 123
Lunding, Hans, 18
Luxembourg invasion, 6, 27, 79

M

M. T. Lind, 137
Maastricht, 26
MacArthur, Douglas, 167
McKenna, Dan, 180
McNeill, Hugo, 156
Madrid, 66, 68, 71, 74-75, 77
Maffey, John, 177-179, 182-184
Mahle, Paul, 52
Malmo, 118-119
Mann, Erika, 47
Master Standfast, 137-138
Meier, Heinz K., 63
Menemencioglu, Numan, 167, 169-172, 175
Mikosch, Hans, 79-82
Molotov, Vyacheslav, 11, 128
Monsarrat, Nicholas, 185
Monte Gorbea, 85
Montreux Convention (1936), 167
Muir, Hugh, 88
Munch, Peter, 17-18
Muñoz Grandes, Agustín, 84-85, 102-103
Mussolini, Benito, 10, 77, 83, 91, 125. See also Italy

N

Narvik campaign, 12, 128-131, 133-135
Netherlands: defense plans, 19, 22-23, 24, 27; German campaign in, 6, 19, 22-23, 25, 26, 49, 79, 135; neutrality policy, 19, 23
Neutral nations: demands on, 6, 11, 19; involvement in war, 9
Neutrality rules, 8-10, 27
New York Herald Tribune, 91
Nonsuch, 137
North Africa campaign, 58, 85, 120, 136
Norway: Allied campaign in, 12, 128-135; annexed by Sweden, 124; defense plans, 15-16; German campaign in, 6, 11, 15-17, 23-24, 108, 126, 128-130, 135; military aid from Sweden, 138, 139; militia in Sweden, 148-149; refugees from, 138-139, 140-141, 142, 144, 149; shipping immobilized, 137;

and Swedish transit rights, 135; training by Britain, 139
Novgorod, 98-99, 101, 121
Nygaardsvold, Johan, 13

O

Office of Strategic Services, 54, 185
Oslo, 13
Oslo States, map 6-7, 8, 10
Oster, Hans, 17

P

Paderewski, Ignace, 88
Papen, Franz von, 168-171, 173, 175
Pappenheim, Rabe von, 27
Pearl Harbor, attack on, 84
Peenemünde, 139
Pepper, Claude, 91
Peter the Great, 120-121, 124
Petsamo, 127
Picasso, Pablo, 64-65
Pierlot, Hubert, 8, 88
Pilet-Golaz, Marcel, 49-50, 59
Pius XII, Pope, 20-21
Poland: German-Soviet invasion, 11, 15, 32; refugees from, 138, 152-153
Portugal: alliance with Britain, 78, 90-91; alliance with Spain, 78, 86, 90; economic aid to Spain, 86; economic conditions in, 76, 78; Hitler mourned by, 185; intelligence operations in, 86-89; neutrality policy, 6, 9, 76, 78-79, 86, 90; political crises in, 78; refugees in, 1, 86, 87, 88, 89; relations with Britain, 86; relations with Spain, 77-78; strategic importance, 86; trade with Britain, 90. See also Salazar, António de Oliveira
Pravda, 172
Prisoners, welfare and repatriation, 142, 150, 151, 186-203

Q

Quisling, Vidkun, 15

R

Raeder, Erich, 13-15, 90, 128
Ramsen, 62
Refugees: from Baltic States, 138, 143, 145; from Germany, 138, 144; from Norway, 138-139, 140-141, 142, 144, 148-149; in Portugal, 1, 86, 88, 89; in Sweden, 138-139, 140-149, 152-153; in Switzerland, 49, 59-61, 62
Reich and the Sickness of European Culture, The (Steding), 10
Reijnders, Izaak H., 19, 22-24
Renthe-Fink, Cecil von, 18
Ribbentrop, Joachim von, 84, 128, 131, 180-181
Richardson, Donovan, 16
Richert, Arvid, 131
Rogley, Roderick, 9
Rome, 20-21
Roosevelt, Franklin D.: and Azores occupation, 90-91; and Irish invasion fears, 182-183; and Lend-Lease to Britain, 90; on neutrality, 10-11; and North Africa landings, 85; and Turkey as belligerent, 171-172. See also United States
Rössler, Rudolf (Lucy), 55
Rougemont, Denis de, 50
Rütli Meadow, 31, 50

S

Saint Gotthard Tunnel, 50
St. Servaas Bridge, 26
Salazar, António de Oliveira, 79; and alliance with Spain, 78, 86; and Allied invasion, 84; and Azores occupation, 91; conference with

Franco, 84; economic aid to Germany and Spain, 86; economic policies, 78; and gold reserves safety, 86; and invasion by Spain, 86; neutrality policy, 76, 78-79, 86; and North Africa landings, 91; relations with Britain, 86, 90; relations with Italy, 91; relations with Spain, 77. *See also* Portugal
Sandler, Rickard, 125
Saracoglu, Sükrü, 167-168, 170, 173, *174*
Sas, Gijsbertus, 17, 22-24
Schaffhausen, 58, *59*
Scheer, Maximilian, 90
Schellenberg, Walter, 84
Schmidt, Paul, 83
Schwarz, Urs, 49
Segerstedt, Torgny, 135
Serrano Súñer, Ramón, 84
Sevareid, Eric, 87, 88
Seville, *68*, 71, 83
Simon Bolivar, 22
Simplon Tunnel, 50
Skagerrak, 17, 108, 126-127, 129
Skorzeny, Otto, 52
Solna, *147*
Sörmland, *148*
Soviet Union: alliance with Germany, 19, 126; Finland invaded by, 6, 11, 13, 126, 128, 135; German invasion, 84, 135, 169; intelligence operations, 55; military aid to Spain, 77; neutrality policy, 10-11; and Norway neutrality, 13; prisoners, treatment of, 198; relations with Turkey, 168; Spanish volunteers against, 84-85, *92-105*; Swedish hostility toward, 120-124, 126; and Swedish neutrality, 128; and Swedish transit rights, 135; and Turkey as belligerent, 171; as Turkey's main enemy, 166-167, 170-171; Viking ventures in, 121, 124. *See also* Stalin, Josef
Spaak, Paul-Henri, 27
Spain: alliance with Germany, 77, 83-84; alliance with Portugal, 78, 86; as belligerent, 82-85; casualties, 77, 94, 100, *104-105*; children, indoctrination of, *80-81;* economic aid from Britain, 83-84; economic aid from Portugal, 86; economic conditions, in, 66, 68, 73, 77; executions in, 71; food production and shortages, 66, *68-69*, 77; and Gibraltar seizure, 79-83, 86; housing construction and shortages, 66, *72-74;* military and economic aid from Germany, 77, 83; military and economic aid to Germany, 79, 83-86; Nationalist forces, *67*, 76; neutrality policy, 6, 9, 76-79, 85-86; and North Africa landings, 85; police repression, 66; political prisoners, *70-71;* propaganda by, 84; relations with Portugal, 77-78; Republican forces, *66*, 76; Tangier occupied by, 79, 82; trade with France, 79; volunteers against Soviet Union, 84-85, *92-105*. *See also* Franco y Bahamonde, Francisco
Stalin, Josef, 128, 168, 198. *See also* Soviet Union
Stalingrad, 120, 136
Stauning, Thorvald, 17
Steding, Christoph, 10
Steinhardt, Laurence A., 171, *174-175*
Stockholm, *109, 116, 118, 131,* 132, *136, 147, 150*
Sweden: aircraft strength, 125, 136; arms supply to Norwegian resistance forces, *138, 139;* blockade effect on, *106-107,* 116, 126-127, 133; and British transit rights, 137-138; casualties, 126; censorship and security measures in, 133; civil defense, *131;* defense plans, 111, 120, 125, *129,* 132, 136; as ethnic and geographic entity, 124; export trade, 126; food production and shortages,

108, *112-113, 116-117;* fuel production and shortages, 112, 114-115, *118-119,* 133, 136; German smuggling in, 130; German threats and reprisals, 128, 130-131, 136; and German transit rights, 130-131, *132,* 133, 135-136; hostility toward Soviet Union, 120-124, 126; housing shortage, 133; industrial progress, 124; Jewish refugees in, *134,* 138, 142, 144, 150, 152-153; labor force and wages, 112-113, 133, 137; lumber industry adaptations, *114-115,* 133; military and economic aid to Finland, 126; naval forces, 125, *130,* 136; neutrality policy, 6, 9, 120, 124, 126, 128-131; Norway annexed by, 124; Norwegian forces training in Norway, *148-149;* ore and metals industry, *108, 110-111,* 124, 128-129; in prisoner repatriation, 142, 150, *151;* recycling program, 114, *115;* refugees in, 138-139, *140-149, 152-153;* relations with Britain, 124; relations with Germany, 124; Royal Family, *122-123;* shipping losses, *106-107,* 126, 136; smuggling control, *125;* social life in, 132-133; trade with Britain, 126-129, 137; trade with Germany, 129, 136-139; transportation facilities, *118-119,* 133; and V-2 rocket, 139; Viking heritage, 120-121; volunteers in Finland, 126, *127*
Switzerland: air defenses, *30, 38-39,* 50-53, 60; aircraft interned by, *52, 59, 60-61;* airspace and border violations, 51, *58-59,* 60; assets frozen, 63; casualties, 59; censorship in, 53; defense plans, *28-45,* 47-49, *map 50,* 51, *57;* demands on, 46-47, 53, 57-58, 63; executions by, 53; financial services in, 62-63; food production and shortages, 55, *56;* fortifications, *40-41,* 48, 50, *map 50;* German assets in, 63; German invasion plans, 49, 53-54; German pressures on, 46-48, 51-53; import-export trade, 56-58; intelligence operations in, 54-55; Jews, policy on, 59-62; morale, 34, 51; mountain training, *42-45;* Nazi movement in, *47, 48,* 53; neutrality policy, 6, 9-10, 30, 46; prisoners interned, *52, 54,* 60, *61,* 62; and prisoner welfare, 62; as protecting power, 62; railway demolition plans, 50, *51;* refugees in, 49, 59-61, *62;* relations with Germany, 47, 50, 57-58; sabotage in, 53; security measures, 49, 53-54; smuggling in, 57-58; transportation system, 56-57; weapons strength, 48-49

T
Tagus River, *87,* 88
Tamm, Fabian, 128, 130-131
Tandberg, Olle, 133
Tangier, 79, *82*
Tannenbaum, Operation, 49
Teheran Conference, 171
Terceira, 91
Thalia, 79
Thurnheer, Hans, 51
Toledo, 67
Tornio, *145*
Toulon, *190-191*
Traynor, Oscar, 180
Tubang Pass, *44-45*
Tunnel of the Virgin, 55
Turkey: alliance with Britain and France, 168; alliance with Germany, 168-169; and Bosporus control, 167-168, 171-172; censorship in, 167, *170;* defense plans, 167, *168,* 171; and entry into War, 169-172; German threats to, 168, 171; and Greek defense, 168; intelligence and intrigue in, 167-168, 173; military aid to, 167-168, 170, *171,* 172; neutrality policy, 6, 9, 166, 167,

171; relations with belligerents, 168, 171; and Soviet threat, 166-167, 170-171; strategic position, 167; trade with belligerents, 167, 169, 172

U
United Kingdom: airliner attacked, 89; alliance with Portugal, 78, 90-91; alliance with Turkey, 168; and Axis diplomats in Ireland, 183-184; and Azores occupation, 90-91; blockade by, 133; contraband policy, 12, 25; economic aid to Spain, 83-84; IRA bombing in, 179; as Irish enemy, 166; Irish volunteers in service of, 156, 184; Lend-Lease to, 90; and Low Countries defense, 23, 25, 27; military aid to Ireland, 162, 178-179, 181; military aid to Turkey, 168; naval treaty with Germany, 124-125; neutrality, views on, 13-15, 22; Norwegian campaign, 129, 132-133, 135; and Norwegian neutrality, 12-15; and Norwegian shipping, *137;* and Portuguese neutrality, 78; refugee training, 139; relations with Ireland, 172-176, 180; relations with Portugal, 86; relations with Sweden, 124; relations with Turkey, 168; sanctions against Ireland, 181-182, 184; shipping losses, 137-138; and Spanish neutrality, 84; and Swedish neutrality, 13; and Swedish transit rights, 135, 137-138; Swiss airspace violations, 51, 58; trade with Portugal, 90; trade with Spain, 79; trade with Sweden, 126-129, 137; trade with Turkey, 167, 172; and Treaty Ports, 176-180. *See also* Churchill, Winston
United States: aircraft and airmen interned, *60-61;* arms supply to resistance forces, *138,* 139; and Axis diplomats in Ireland, 183-184; and Azores occupation, 90-91; intelligence operations, 54; Lend-Lease by, 90; and military aid to Ireland, 182-183; neutrality policy, 10-11; refugee training, 139; and Swedish trade with Germany, 136; Swiss airspace violations by, *59,* 60; Swiss assets frozen by, 63; and Treaty Ports, 180. *See also* Roosevelt, Franklin D.

V
Valencia, *70-71,* 83
Van Kleffens, Eelco, 19, 24-25
Van Overstraeten, Raoul, 27
Van Zuylen, Pierre, 25-27
Vatican City, 20
Vischer, Mattheus, 198

W
Walker, George Platt, 27
Wallenberg, Raoul, *134*
Walshe, Joe, 177-179, 185
Waring, William, 127-128, 137-138
Weizsäcker, Ernst von, 131
Welles, Sumner, 14
Weserubung, Operation, 15-17
Wilhelmina, Queen of the Netherlands, 19, 23, *24*
Wilson, Henry Maitland, 172
Wilson, Woodrow, 10
Wingqvist, Sven, *111*
Winkelman, Henri, 24, 27
Witzig, Rudolf, 79-82

Y
Yalta Conference, 172
Young, Stephen M., 46

Z
Zeeland, 22
Zurich, *28-29,* 47, *48, 56,* 58
Zurich, Lake, 47